Cyber Warfare

This book is a multidisciplinary analysis of cyber warfare, featuring contributions by leading experts from a mixture of academic and professional backgrounds.

Cyber warfare, meaning interstate cyber aggression, is an increasingly important emerging phenomenon in international relations, with state-orchestrated (or apparently state-orchestrated) computer network attacks occurring in Estonia (2007), Georgia (2008) and Iran (2010). This method of waging warfare – given its potential to, for example, make planes fall from the sky or cause nuclear power plants to melt down – has the capacity to be as devastating as any conventional means of conducting armed conflict. Every state in the world now has a cyber-defence programme and over 120 states also have a cyber-attack programme.

While the amount of literature on cyber warfare is growing within disciplines, our understanding of the subject has been limited by a lack of cross-disciplinary engagement. In response, this book, drawn from the fields of computer science, military strategy, international law, political science and military ethics, provides a critical overview of cyber warfare for those approaching the topic from whatever angle. Chapters consider the emergence of the phenomena of cyber warfare in international affairs; what cyber-attacks are from a technological standpoint; the extent to which cyber-attacks can be attributed to state actors; the strategic value and danger posed by cyber conflict; the legal regulation of cyber-attacks, both as international uses of force and as part of an ongoing armed conflict, and the ethical implications of cyber warfare.

This book will be of great interest to students of cyber warfare, cyber security, military ethics, international law, security studies and IR in general.

James A. Green is Associate Professor of Public International Law at the University of Reading. He is author of *The International Court of Justice and self-defence in international law* (2009), and co-editor of *Conflict in the Caucasus: Implications for international order* (with C.P.M. Waters, 2010) and *Adjudicating international human rights: Essays in honour of Sandy Ghandhi* (with C.P.M. Waters, 2015).

Routledge Studies in Conflict, Security and Technology
Series Editors: Mark Lacy, Dan Prince, Sylvia Walby and Corinne May-Chalal
Lancaster University

The *Routledge Studies in Conflict, Technology and Security* series aims to publish challenging studies that map the terrain of technology and security from a range of disciplinary perspectives, offering critical perspectives on the issues that concern publics, business and policymakers in a time of rapid and disruptive technological change.

Nonlinear Science and Warfare
Chaos, complexity and the U.S. military in the information age
Sean T. Lawson

Terrorism Online
Politics, law, technology
Edited by Lee Jarvis, Stuart Macdonald and Thomas M. Chen

Cyber Warfare
A multidisciplinary analysis
Edited by James A. Green

Cyber Warfare
A multidisciplinary analysis

Edited by James A. Green

LONDON AND NEW YORK

First published 2015
by Routledge
2 Park Square, Milton Park, Abingdon, Oxon OX14 4RN

and by Routledge
711 Third Avenue, New York, NY 10017

Routledge is an imprint of the Taylor & Francis Group, an informa business

© 2015 selection and editorial matter James A. Green; individual chapters, the contributors

The right of the editor to be identified as the author of the editorial matter, and of the authors for their individual chapters, has been asserted in accordance with sections 77 and 78 of the Copyright, Designs and Patents Act 1988.

All rights reserved. No part of this book may be reprinted or reproduced or utilised in any form or by any electronic, mechanical, or other means, now known or hereafter invented, including photocopying and recording, or in any information storage or retrieval system, without permission in writing from the publishers.

Trademark notice: Product or corporate names may be trademarks or registered trademarks, and are used only for identification and explanation without intent to infringe.

British Library Cataloguing-in-Publication Data
A catalogue record for this book is available from the British Library

Library of Congress Cataloging-in-Publication Data
Cyber warfare : a multidisciplinary analysis / edited by James A. Green.
  pages cm. – (Routledge studies in conflict, security and technology)
  Includes bibliographical references and index.
  1. Cyberspace operations (Military science) 2. Just war doctrine.
  I. Green, James A., 1981- editor of compilation.
  U163.C936 2015
  355.4–dc23   2014043880

ISBN: 978-1-138-79307-1 (hbk)
ISBN: 978-1-315-76156-5 (ebk)

Typeset in Times New Roman
by Wearset Ltd, Boldon, Tyne and Wear

For my Dad, David Green, whom I love dearly (even if I rarely tell him), on the occasion of his sixtieth birthday.

I vividly remember him helping me with a school project on bears by us looking them up together on a Microsoft *Encarta* CD-ROM, using the family's first, brand new home computer. We marvelled together – father and son – at how far technology had come; he said something about the future having 'arrived'…

Contents

List of illustrations	viii
Notes on contributors	ix
Acknowledgements	xii
List of abbreviations	xiii

	Introduction JAMES A. GREEN	1
1	**A short history of cyber warfare** RICHARD STIENNON	7
2	**Understanding cyber-attacks** DUNCAN HODGES AND SADIE CREESE	33
3	**The attribution of cyber warfare** NEIL C. ROWE	61
4	**The strategic implications of cyber warfare** DANNY STEED	73
5	**The regulation of cyber warfare under the *jus ad bellum*** JAMES A. GREEN	96
6	**The regulation of cyber warfare under the *jus in bello*** HEATHER A. HARRISON DINNISS	125
7	**The relevance of the Just War Tradition to cyber warfare** DAVID WHETHAM AND GEORGE R. LUCAS, JR	160

Index	174

Illustrations

Figures

2.1	A request for a website broken down into the four layers of the Internet Protocol suite (TCP/IP)	37
2.2	A simplified model of attack steps	39
3.1	An example network	66
5.1	The relationship between the concepts of armed attack, force and intervention	111

Tables

2.1	The targetability characteristic	45
2.2	The controllability characteristic	46
2.3	The persistence characteristic	47
2.4	The effect characteristic	49
2.5	The covertness characteristic	50
2.6	The mitigatable characteristic	51

Contributors

Sadie Creese is Professor of Cybersecurity in the Department of Computer Science at the University of Oxford. She is Director of Oxford's Cyber Security Centre, Director of the Global Centre for Cyber Security Capacity Building and co-Director of the Institute for the Future of Computing at the Oxford Martin School. Her research experience spans time in academia, industry and government. She is engaged in a broad portfolio of cyber security research spanning situational awareness, visual analytics, risk propagation and communication, threat modelling and detection, network defence, dependability and resilience, and formal analysis. She has numerous research collaborations with other disciplines and has been leading interdisciplinary research projects since 2003. Prior to joining Oxford in October 2011 she was Professor and Director of e-Security at the University of Warwick's International Digital Laboratory. Professor Creese joined Warwick in 2007 from QinetiQ, where she most recently served as Director of Strategic Programmes for QinetiQ's Trusted Information Management Division.

Heather A. Harrison Dinniss is a Senior Lecturer at the International Law Centre of the Swedish National Defence College. She is the author of *Cyber war and the laws of war* (Cambridge University Press, 2012). Her research focuses on the impact of modern warfare on international humanitarian law; in particular on cyber warfare, advanced and autonomous weapons systems and the legal aspects of enhancement techniques on members of the armed forces. She has previously taught at the London School of Economics and Political Science (LSE), the School of Oriental and African Studies (SOAS) at the University of London, and Victoria University of Wellington (NZ). She was awarded her PhD from the LSE in 2009, and is also a graduate of Victoria University of Wellington (NZ), with a Masters of Law (Hons), an LLB, and a BA in Psychology. Heather is also a barrister and solicitor of New Zealand.

James A. Green is Associate Professor of Public International Law at the University of Reading, where he has been a member of staff since 2006. Previously, he studied for his doctorate at the University of Nottingham and, in 2005, was a visiting research scholar at the University of Michigan. He is the author of *The International Court of Justice and Self-defence in International*

Law (Hart Publishing, 2009), which was the winner of the Francis Lieber Prize, awarded by the American Society of International Law's Lieber Society, as well as the co-editor of *Conflict in the Caucasus: Implications for international order* (with C.P.M. Waters, Palgrave, 2010). He has published numerous articles on international law in leading journals. Dr Green is co-editor-in-chief of the *Journal on the Use of Force and International Law* and is a member of the International Law Association Committee on the Use of Force. His next monograph, *The Persistent Objector Rule in International Law* will be published in 2015 by Oxford University Press.

Duncan Hodges is a lecturer in the Centre for Cyber Security and Information Systems at Cranfield University. He was awarded his PhD from the University of Bath in 2005. After completing his PhD he continued to work as a researcher within the Centre for Space, Atmospheric and Oceanic Science at the University of Bath. Leaving Bath in 2008 he went to work for the UK government as a civil servant. In early 2012 he left the civil service to join the Department of Computer Science at the University of Oxford as a Researcher where he worked in the interdisciplinary Cyber Security Centre upon its instigation. In late 2014 he left the University of Oxford to join the Defence and Security theme at Cranfield University.

George R. Lucas, Jr recently retired as the Distinguished Chair in Ethics in the Vice Admiral James B. Stockdale Center for Ethical Leadership at the US Naval Academy (Annapolis), and is currently Professor of Ethics and Public Policy (tenured) at the Graduate School of Public Policy at the Naval Postgraduate School (Monterey, California). He has taught at Georgetown University, Emory University, Randolph-Macon College, the French Military Academy (Saint-Cyr), the Catholic University of Louvain (Belgium), and served as Philosophy Department Chairman at the University of Santa Clara in California. He has received research fellowships from the Fulbright Commission and the American Council of Learned Societies, and will be a visiting guest professor at Notre Dame University during the academic year 2014–2015. Professor Lucas is the author of five books, more than 60 journal articles, translations and book reviews, and has also edited eight book-length collections of articles in philosophy and ethics. His next book, *Military ethics: What everyone needs to know*, will be published by Oxford University Press in 2015, while an edited collection, *The Routledge Handbook of Military Ethics* is also forthcoming in 2015.

Neil C. Rowe, PhD, is Professor of Computer Science at the US Naval Postgraduate School where he has been since 1983. His main research interests are the modelling of deception, information security, surveillance systems, image processing, and data mining. Recent work has focused on cyber warfare, digital forensics, and the problems of large-scale data analysis. He is the author of *Artificial Intelligence through PROLOG* (Prentice Hall, 2nd edition, 1987) and 160 technical papers.

Richard Stiennon is an industry analyst who has written extensively about threat-driven changes to the IT security space. He is the author of *Surviving Cyberwar* (Rowman & Littlefield, 2010) which is a history of cyber conflict prior to the Google Aurora incident. He writes the Cyber Domain column for Forbes.com and provides running commentary on developments on Twitter @cyberwar. He was a manager of Technical Risk Services at PricewaterhouseCoopers before becoming VP Research at Gartner. He was VP Threat Research at Webroot Software and then Chief Marketing Officer for Fortinet, the largest vendor of Unified Threat Management devices. Stiennon has a BS in aerospace engineering from the University of Michigan and an MA in War in the Modern World, King's College London.

Danny Steed is Lecturer in Strategy and Defence at the University of Exeter's newly established Strategy and Security Institute. He is involved in the design and delivery of the MA in Applied Security Strategy, and has research interests in strategic theory, strategic history, intelligence, and cyber warfare.

David Whetham is a Senior Lecturer in the Defence Studies Department of King's College London, based at the Joint Services Command and Staff College at the UK Defence Academy where he coordinates or delivers the military ethics component of courses for between two and three thousand British and international officers a year. In Spring 2011, Dr Whetham was a Visiting Fellow at the Stockdale Center for Ethical Leadership, Annapolis, and in 2009, was a Visiting Fellow with the Centre for Defence Leadership and Ethics at the Australian Defence College in Canberra. He is also a regular visiting lecturer in military ethics at the Baltic Defence College, and the Royal Brunei Armed Forces Command and Staff Course. Dr Whetham's publications include *Ethics, Law and Military Operations* (Palgrave, 2010) and *Just Wars and Moral Victories: Surprise, deception and the normative framework of European war in the later Middle Ages* (Brill, 2009). Dr Whetham is the Vice President of the European Chapter of the International Society for Military Ethics (Euro ISME) which holds an annual conference for military practitioners, academics and defence policymakers.

Acknowledgements

The image used in Figure 5.1 in this book originally appeared in James A. Green, *The International Court of Justice and Self-defence in International Law* (2009, Hart Publishing), at p. 33, and is reprinted by permission of Bloomsbury Publishing plc.

Abbreviations

ANO	Advance Networks Operations
APT	Advanced Persistent Threats
AS	Autonomous Systems
ASN	AS Number
AV	Anti-virus
BGP	Border Gateway Protocol
CCW	Certain Conventional Weapons
CERT	Computer Emergency Response Team
DDoS	Distributed Denial of Service
DIB	Defence Industrial Base
DNS	Domain Name System
DoD	Department of Defense
FBI	Federal Bureau of Investigations
GCHQ	Government Communications Headquarters
GIG	Global Information Grid
GOSCC	Global Operations and Security Control Centre
GREAT	Global Research and Analysis Team
ICJ	International Court of Justice
ICRC	International Committee of the Red Cross
ICTY	International Criminal Tribunal for the former Yugoslavia
IHL	International Humanitarian Law
IoC	Indicator of compromise
IP	Internet protocol
ISP	Internet Service Provider
ISR	Intelligence, surveillance and reconnaissance
IT	Information Technology
IW	Information warfare
MTR	Military–Technical Revolution
NCW	Network-centric Warfare
NGO	Non-governmental Organisation
NPR	National Public Radio
NSA	National Security Agency
OWASP	Open Web Application Security Project

PLA	People's Liberation Army (China)
PLC	Programmable Logic Controllers
RBN	Russian Business Network
RMA	Revolution in Military Affairs
SEA	Syrian Electronic Army
TCP	Transmission Control Protocol
UNCIO	United Nations Conference on International Organisation
USB	Universal Serial Bus
VPN	Virtual Private Network

Introduction

James A. Green

This book is about cyber warfare. Its core aim is to present examinations of cyber warfare from a variety of disciplinary perspectives. This presents a problem, however. Even within disciplines, there is no agreed definition as to exactly what 'cyber warfare' *is* (Carr, 2011: 1–2). The terminological contours of what constitutes cyber warfare – as distinct from related (but equally hazily defined) concepts such as 'cyber-terrorism', 'cyber espionage' or 'cybercrime' – cannot be set out with any degree of certainty.

Indeed, some argue that the very term 'cyber warfare' is something of a misnomer. This is on the basis that the large-scale cyber-attacks that have thus far occurred in the context of international relations – such as those in Estonia (2007), Georgia (2008) and Iran (2010) – have been relatively 'isolated' and 'low-level' in nature and have rarely resulted in physical damage, meaning that these actions do not fit the notion of 'war' as commonly understood (Rid, 2013). Indeed, for some, the threat of cyber aggression at the international level has been exaggerated by both governments and commentators, meaning that the term 'cyber war' can be viewed as being inherently hyperbolic (Farivar, 2009). To some extent, such assertions are understandable: 'war' is a loaded word that has different meanings within and without disciplines (as well as in the general consciousness), and one can certainly make a good case that there has yet to occur an act of cyber aggression that comfortably meets all understandings of 'a war'.

It is, therefore, worth being clear at the outset that the term 'cyber warfare' as adopted in this book is not necessarily used to denote *scale* or *protraction*, or even '*violence*' per se, in the sense of a 'war' as it is perhaps generally understood. Isolated or smaller scale acts of cyber aggression – including those that damage infrastructure without having direct kinetic effects – may well still qualify. It is for this reason that the term 'war*fare*' is adopted, rather than 'cyber war'. Warfare is used to denote 'warlike' acts, even if one can debate whether all actions falling within our concept are truly acts of 'war'. Cyber warfare 'is a more open-ended term, more useful in exploring an environment that is not only virtual but also largely unchartered' (Cornish *et al.*, 2010: 2).

Thus, the term 'cyber warfare' (which is at times used synonymously in this book with 'cyber-attacks' and 'cyber aggression') is employed broadly to convey an *interstate* element in the use of technological force in cyberspace: that is, 'the realm of computer networks (and the users behind them) in which information is stored, shared and communicated online' (Singer and Friedman, 2014: 13). In other words, this book is focused on acts of cyber aggression as between *countries*, rather than as instigated by individuals or (solely by) non-state groups. The definition of cyber warfare adopted in this book is therefore a slightly adapted version of that used by Shakarian *et al.* (2013: 2) – which itself is custom-built from various sources, including Clausewitz's paradigmatic definition of 'war':

> Cyber warfare is an extension of policy by actions taken in cyberspace by state actors (or by non-state actors with significant state direction or support) that constitute a serious threat to another state's security, or an action of the same nature taken in response to a serious threat to a state's security (actual or perceived).

This definition presents its own problems of attribution and causation, as will be considered in subsequent chapters. However, it is important to be clear that, while this book focuses on 'serious' threats (and thus excludes from its analysis comparatively 'minor' disruptive acts conducted in cyberspace, such as pure information retrieval or 'cyber espionage'), the analysis herein is not limited to situations involving vast armies of cyber warriors clashing on the virtual battlefield. Equally, it should always be kept in mind that just because the existing examples of what this book is terming 'cyber warfare' have been relatively isolated and small-scale does not necessarily mean that future attacks of this sort will be. Indeed, the examples of cyber aggression that have occurred in practice show a notable progression of scale, with at least one recent instance leading to actual physical damage, as opposed to purely economic consequences (the 'Stuxnet' attack against Iran in 2010).

Contrary to the views of a minority of commentators who have downplayed the threat posed by interstate cyber-attacks (e.g. Rid, 2013; Ranum, 2004), this book argues that cyber warfare is an emerging phenomenon in international relations, with state-orchestrated (or apparently state-orchestrated) computer network attacks against other states occurring with increasing frequency and scale. This method of waging warfare – given its potential to make planes fall from the sky or cause nuclear power plants to melt down, for example, – has the capacity to be as devastating as any conventional means of conducting armed conflict (Garrie, 2012: 5). However, cyber warfare is comparatively inexpensive (Schreier, 2012: 31), difficult to trace (Rosenzweig, 2012: 75–84), can be instigated almost instantaneously (Clarke and Knake, 2010: 31) and can be launched across great distances (Roscini, 2014: 2). Cyber warfare can also 'invert' the power dynamics of modern international relations, at least in some cases. This is in the sense that the more technologically dependent that a state is, the more vulnerable it is to cyber-attack and, broadly speaking, the more powerful and developed the state, the more 'wired' it will be (Olivier, 2012: 24–25).

Every state in the world now has at least some form of cyber-defence programme, and over 120 states are working on cyber-*attack* programmes too (Carr, 2011: 1). The current US 'cyber budget' under the Obama administration is estimated at 4.7 billion USD, and in 2010, it spent 358 million USD simply on the headquarters in which to house its new 'Cyber Command' (Strobel and Charles, 2013). At the time of writing, the US National Security Agency (NSA) has recently confirmed that significant cyber-attacks have been launched against Ukraine in the context of the de facto annexation of Crimea (Sasso, 2014), and it is highly likely (if far from entirely established) that these emanated directly from Russia. Cyber warfare – or whatever term one prefers to use – is here to stay.

Yet a crucial impediment to our understanding of cyber warfare and its actual and potential implications is that there is a general lack of understanding of what the phenomenon entails in practice. As General Michael Hayden, former Director of the Central Intelligence Agency, has stated, 'rarely has something been so important and so talked about with less and less clarity and less and less understanding' (quoted in Singer and Friedman, 2014: 4). More specifically, there is very little in the way of cross-pollination between disciplines (as well as engagement from academia as a whole with governmental decision-makers and security experts, and *vice versa*). There is now a considerable body of literature on the subject *within* disciplines, but relatively little between or across them. As Dunn Cavelty (2010: 125) has noted, the literature on cyber warfare 'is fragmented and rather disjointed [because]... [t]he topic is situated at the crossroads of various issues'. Thus lawyers have little idea of the technology that they seek to regulate; strategists do not pay enough heed to the wider ethical and legal implications of acts of interstate cyber aggression; and computer scientists delineate the intricacies of the technology with relatively little focus on its political and strategic implications. With this concern in mind, the present volume draws together a number of key commentaries on cyber warfare: its contributors come from the disparate fields of computer science, military strategy, international law, political science and military ethics. By collecting these various perspectives, this book seeks to act as a multidisciplinary reference point for anyone (academics, professional actors and decision-makers) engaging with the subject of interstate cyber warfare.

In Chapter 1 of the volume, Richard Stiennon sets out a short history of cyber warfare. He traces its development by examining a number of key touchstones, including the growth of cyber espionage, the influence of strategic thinking in China and the development in the United States of the 'Revolution in Military Affairs'. Beyond this, Stiennon analyses more recent cyber operations that fit the definition of cyber warfare given above, and charts the modern rise of cyber commands within states. Duncan Hodges and Sadie Creese then, in Chapter 2, provide a computer science analysis of what cyber-attacks *are* as a technical matter. More specifically, Hodges and Creese set out a taxonomy of the characteristics of cyber-attacks to identify a context in which it is possible to understand them. This taxonomy helps us to explore, manage and understand the consequences of each action: Hodges and Creese illustrate this with number of examples of different cyber-attacks, to give an indication of the breadth of attack that a state could launch to achieve a particular mission.

In Chapter 3, Neil C. Rowe considers the crucial issue of *attributing* cyber-attacks to states (or, indeed, any actor) from a computer science perspective. Cyber warfare presents specific problems for attribution for various reasons, each of which Rowe examines. However, he ultimately argues that the scale and novelty of effective cyber warfare, as opposed, say, to cyber espionage, often makes it possible to find the computers and devices responsible. Clues can come from the examination of files and network data, and investigators can take advantage of knowledge of prior similar attacks. Chapter 4 turns to a strategic analysis of the cyber warfare phenomenon. Danny Steed reviews the current state of strategic thinking on cyber warfare, and identifies why there is a lack of strategic understanding on the subject. He then analyses specific case studies to draw out the strategic implications substantiated by the practical application of cyber warfare. Steed's core contention is that claims in the literature that not enough is yet known about cyber warfare to subject it to robust strategic analysis are incorrect. There is, Steed argues, now enough evidence to begin making strategic sense of cyber warfare.

Chapter 5 is the present writer's own contribution to the volume, and it begins the legal analysis of cyber warfare by considering the regulation of the phenomenon under the *jus ad bellum* (that is, the law on the use of force: i.e. when force can lawfully be employed by a state). As there are no specific rules of international law regulating cyber warfare, there is a longstanding debate as to whether cyber-attacks rightly fall under the scope of Article 2(4) of the UN Charter 1945, which prohibits the use of 'force' between states. Chapter 5 explores the debate as to whether cyber operations can correctly be considered 'force' under this provision, but then ultimately suggests that an alternative approach – focusing on a legal duty of 'cyber due diligence' – may in fact better restrain aggressive cyber operations. Complimenting this analysis, Heather A. Harrison Dinniss examines, in Chapter 6, the application of the *jus in bello* (that is, the law governing the conduct of hostilities once an armed conflict is underway) to cyber warfare. Harrison Dinniss assesses the general applicability of the *jus in bello* to cyber operations, but then provides more detailed analysis of various key provisions of the *jus in bello*. She turns, first, to the crucial principle of distinction, and assesses how this is to be applied in the cyber context. Chapter 6 also considers the various ways in which the principle of precaution may be relevant to cyber-attacks, provides an examination of a number of *jus in bello* requirements for measures of special protection and shows how these rules are relevant to cyber warfare. The law's restrictions on the 'means and methods' of warfare are also analysed in the cyber context.

Chapter 7 concludes this collection by moving away from the legal analysis of Chapters 5 and 6 to an ethical analysis. David Whetham and George R. Lucas, Jr explore whether the Just War Tradition – which has provided a useful framework for balancing ethical considerations in times of conflict for over two millennia –

can continue to respond to the new phenomenon of cyber warfare and whether the current Just War principles themselves are appropriate as they are, or whether some may need adapting, interpreting differently or replacing entirely for the Tradition to remain relevant. Whetham and Lucas conclude that various negative and dismissive judgements concerning the relevance of the Just War Tradition for the moral evaluation of cyber warfare that have appeared in the literature are based on a fundamental misconception of the nature of the Tradition itself.

Ultimately, if cyber warfare is to be properly understood and its injurious consequences limited, there is a need for deep *inter*disciplinary analysis. This book has a rather more modest, *multi*disciplinary aim: it is designed to set out in an analytical manner the fundamental issues and debates concerning cyber warfare from different viewpoints, rather than necessarily integrating them. The goal is to provide a critical overview of cyber warfare for those approaching the topic from whatever angle, in part to act as a starting point for future (and what will need to be increasingly intertwined) collaboration on the subject.

References

Carr, J. (2011) *Inside cyber warfare: Mapping the cyber underworld*, 2nd edition, Sebastopol: O'Reilly.

Clarke, R.A. and Knake, R.K. (2010) *Cyber war: The next threat to national security and what to do about it*, New York: Harper Collins.

Cornish, P., Livingstone, D., Clemente, D. and York, C. (2010) 'One cyber warfare', November, *Chatham House Report* [online], available: https://www.chathamhouse.org/sites/default/files/public/Research/International%20Security/r1110_cyberwarfare.pdf [9 May 2014].

Dunn Cavelty, M. (2010) 'Cyberwar', in Kassimeris, G. and Buckley, J.D. (eds) *Ashgate research companion to modern warfare*, Farnham: Ashgate.

Farivar, C. (2009) 'A brief examination of media coverage of cyber-attacks (2007–present)', in Czosseck, C. and Kenneth Geers, K. (eds) *The virtual battlefield: Perspectives on cyber warfare*, Amsterdam: IOS Press.

Garrie, D.B. (2012) 'Cyber warfare, what are the rules?', *Journal of Law and Cyber Warfare*, vol. 1, no. 1, pp. 1–7.

Olivier, M. (2012) 'Cyber warfare: the frontline of 21st century conflict', *LBJ Journal of Public Affairs*, vol. 20, pp. 23–42.

Ranum, M.J. (2004) *The myth of homeland security*, Indianapolis: Wiley Publishing.

Rid, T. (2013) *Cyber war will not take place*, London: Hurst.

Roscini, M. (2014) *Cyber operations and the use of force in international law*, Oxford: Oxford University Press.

Rosenzweig, P. (2012) *Cyber warfare: how conflicts in cyberspace are challenging America and changing the world*, Santa Barbara, ABC-CLIO.

Sasso, B. (2014) 'NSA nominee confirms Ukraine is under cyberattack', 11 March, *National Journal* [online], available: www.nationaljournal.com/tech/nsa-nominee-confirms-ukraine-is-under-cyberattack-20140311 [9 May 2014].

Schreier, F. (2012) 'On cyberwarfare', *Geneva Centre for the Democratic Control of Armed Forces (DCAF) Horizon 2015 Working Paper Series*, no. 7 [online], available: www.dcaf.ch/Publications/On-Cyberwarfare [9 May 2014].

Shakarian, P., Shakarian, J. and Ruef, A. (2013) *Introduction to cyber-warfare: A multi-disciplinary approach*, Waltham: Syngress.

Singer, P.W. and Friedman, A. (2014) *Cybersecurity and cyberwar: What everyone needs to know*, Oxford: Oxford University Press.

Strobel, W. and Charles, D. (2013) 'With troops and techies, US prepares for cyber warfare', 7 June, *Reuters* [online], available: www.reuters.com/article/2013/06/07/us-usa-cyberwar-idUSBRE95608D20130607 [9 May 2014].

1 A short history of cyber warfare

Richard Stiennon

Introduction

This chapter weaves together two strands of history that provide an understanding of the rapid rise in cyber preparedness on the part of the military and government organisations of the developed world. The first of these strands relates to the fact that networked forces hold the promise of being able to pierce the fog of war in combat, an understanding that inspired the concept of a Revolution in Military Affairs (RMA) based on Network-centric Warfare (NCW). The roots of cyber warfare can be traced back to the development of radar and radio communication and the body of technology that became known as Electronic Warfare (EW), a category that has now been subsumed by cyber warfare. In the 1990s, states became increasingly aware of the potential value of cyber operations to the furtherance of the national interest in the military sphere. Equally, as the power of networking began to impact military manoeuvres (as illustrated by the rapid deployment of the US Sixth Fleet to the Straits of Taiwan in 1995) it became apparent that with networking came vulnerabilities that could be targeted to gain military advantage.

The second strand of history, along which the development of cyber warfare can be traced, therefore concerns the rise of cyber *threats*. The rise of global connectivity and the impact of the Internet on commerce, communication and social interaction, have made possible attacks that, even if not directed by states, served their purposes. The increased threat of cyber-attack has been a key driver for organisational change, investment and the development of cyber capabilities by other states.

The Distributed Denial of Service (DDoS) attacks against Estonia's infrastructure (combined with pro-Russia social unrest) in April 2007 and similar attacks against Georgia's networks in August 2008 (during the short war with Russia) are the two most prominent events that sparked the formation of cyber strategies and cyber militarisation around the world in response. The effective, if only short-term, disabling in 2010 of Iran's nuclear refining operations at Natanz by the Stuxnet virus program (which was allegedly a creation of American and Israeli intelligence services, and part of the US Operation 'Olympic Games') further ushered in the era of projection of force by cyber means.

Tracing this history requires a working definition of 'cyber warfare' to avoid confusion and to constrain the discussion to pertinent events and developments, as well as to confine the inevitable thoughts on how cyber warfare is shaping fighting forces, policy development and technology challenges. It is therefore worth here reiterating the definition of the concept set out in the Introduction to this volume:

> Cyber warfare is an extension of policy by actions taken in cyberspace by state actors (or by non-state actors with significant state direction or support) that constitute a serious threat to another state's security, or an action of the same nature taken in response to a serious threat to a state's security (actual or perceived).

Reference to this definition will help to avoid confusion with the other uses of cyber-attacks, namely cybercrime and 'hacktivism', although both of these areas are inevitably intertwined with cyber warfare because the actors involved often support the aims of sovereign states or contribute technology and methodology that are adapted by the growing cyber operations within the military or intelligence operations of states. Indeed, the roots of 'cyber warfare' as defined in this book are inexorably intertwined with the growth of state-directed acts of cyber espionage (or at least, *apparently* state-directed acts – see Chapter 3 in this volume for discussion of the technical problems associated with attributing cyber-attacks conclusively to state actors, and Chapter 5 in relation to the particular problem of so attributing such actions legally). The first section of this chapter therefore necessarily considers the implications of interstate cyber espionage – as this underpins the birth of modern cyber warfare – before turning to 'cyber warfare' proper.

Creating and tracking the history of cyber warfare is complicated by the lack of temporal perspective. The task brings to mind how difficult it would be to write about the evolution of the use of the long bow by a contemporaneous researcher in the decades preceding the battle of Crecy. It can be argued that the impact of cyber operations on war fighting will be felt much more in the future than it has yet been in the past. In other words, cyber warfare is still in its infancy. Having said this, the rapid rise of cyber warfare, tracked over a period of less than two decades, still presents many interesting cases of step function increases in capabilities and impacts derived from computer and network attacks.

This chapter starts with one such step function, which can be seen as a key point in relation to the emergence of interstate cyber espionage and, thus, as a crucial reference point in the history of cyber warfare: the discovery of targeted cyber-attacks against US military laboratories in 2004, which were collectively given the code name 'Titan Rain'. The chapter then considers the importance and impact of military academic thinking in China in the early 1990s, and examines a number of other crucial cyber-attacks (beyond Titan Rain) for which China was (at least said to be) responsible. The Military–Technical Revolution

(MTR) promulgated by writers in Russia following the first Gulf War, and its development and expansion in the United States into the modern RMA, is then discussed. Next the chapter moves to a consideration of three key instances of cyber warfare 'proper' that have occurred in recent years: the attacks on Estonia (2007), Georgia (2008) and Iran (the Stuxnet infection of 2010). Finally, the chapter examines the modern rise of cyber commands – particularly in the United States, but also in various other states – a development that very much suggests that cyber warfare is now here to stay.

The growth of cyber espionage attacks and the role of China

Titan Rain

Shawn Carpenter was a network administrator at Sandia Labs in 2003 when he was called upon to help with a forensic analysis in a breach of another Lockheed Martin facility in Florida. He has attested to being highly influenced by Clifford Stoll's book, *Cuckoo's Egg*, on perhaps the first recorded incident of Soviet-sponsored hacking into a US research lab, that of Lawrence Berkeley National Laboratory, in 1986. It was in Florida that Carpenter got his first experience analysing a network-based attack. He found a file on a server in China that contained a complete network scan report of the US Army post of 'Fort Dix' (Joint Base McGuire–Dix–Lakehurst). By the spring of 2004 Carpenter was back at Sandia and detected signs that the same attackers he had researched in Florida were probing Sandia's networks. Against the direct instructions of his supervisor, he backtracked the attacks to servers in Asia, where he found hundreds of documents belonging to multiple US research and military facilities, including Fort Dix, the Redstone Arsenal, the Defense Contract Management Agency and even the World Bank. Working in his own time Carpenter eventually became a confidential informant for the FBI and was called on to research numerous 'Advanced Persistent Threats' (APTs) that were together given the code name 'Titan Rain'.

Titan Rain can be viewed as a crucial point in the history of cyber warfare, because it had two important impacts. The first of these was a seminal article on Carpenter's experience that appeared in *Time Magazine* (Thornburgh, 2005). That article significantly raised public awareness of Chinese cyber espionage, and therefore the possibilities for, and threat of, cyber warfare 'proper'. Second, the initial discovery of Titan Rain in Florida set Lockheed Martin on the path to developing its theories of the 'Cyber Kill Chain' and how to counter such targeted attacks. Lockheed's methodology, developed in response to continuous APT-style attacks, included the use of network monitoring and malware analysis to derive key indicators of compromise (IoCs) that would then be associated with named 'campaigns'. Similar IoCs, such as domains, IP addresses, exploits and versions of malware, would indicate a high probability of association with the same threat actors. When a new action associated with some of those IoCs occurs, those actions are treated with extreme suspicion and can be investigated further. The Cyber Kill Chain is therefore a combination of methods to detect, degrade and deny, during the phases of an attack including reconnaissance, weaponisation and delivery, and its development has been a crucial step along the path towards better cyber security.

Chinese thinking on cyber warfare

Before exploring the evolution of cyber espionage in relation to other occurrences, beyond Titan Rain, it is necessary to first consider the development of thought on cyber warfare in the early 1990s – called information warfare (IW) at the time – and, particularly, early Chinese thinking on the subject. Most of the important theoretical advances in the potential uses of IW came from Chinese writers, and, as will be discussed below, the vast majority of advanced persistent threat (APT) attacks have seemingly since originated from China: Titan Rain was just the first notable example.

Chinese theoreticians have been considering the implications of IW since at least 1993. They were quick to adopt Soviet writing on technology and modern warfare, which stressed, generally, the desirability of precision-targeting of weapons and better command and control. However, the Chinese thinking on what turned into a large body of Western writing on the RMA particularly stressed the *information warfare* aspects of modern technology (see e.g. Wang, 1993; Zhu *et al.*, 1994; Dai and Shen, 1996; Shen, 1997).

According to China researcher Timothy L. Thomas (author of *Decoding the Virtual Dragon*, 2007, a publication of the US Army's Foreign Military Studies Office), Dr Shen Weiguang is known in China as the father of IW theory. In 1995 Shen wrote an introductory article on IW for the *PLA Daily Newspaper*. In it he stated that the main target of IW is the enemy's cognitive and trust systems and the goal is to exert control over the enemy's actions.

Thomas discovered more interesting thinking in a 2004 article by General Xu Xiaoyan, the former head of the Communications Department of the Chinese General Staff. Xu dissects the realm of IW. At the granular level he pointed out the need for:

> [n]etwork confrontation technology – intercepting, utilizing, corrupting, and damaging the enemy's information and using false information, viruses, and other means to sabotage normal information system functions through computer networks.
>
> (Thomas, 2007: 66)

Thomas noted that '[i]f Xu's suggestions were accepted, then one might expect to see more active reconnaissance and intelligence activities on the part of the PLA [the People's Liberation Army, i.e. China's military] (as seems to be occurring!)'. This observation came hot on the heels of Titan Rain. However, the United States and other targets of Chinese cyber espionage initially did very little to counter these attacks (that is, until recently, as will be examined below).

Other notable instances of Chinese cyber espionage

While incidents of Chinese cyber espionage are numerous, there are several that particularly served to heighten awareness. Espionage is an important aspect of war fighting, especially in terms of intelligence, surveillance and reconnaissance (ISR). This is particularly the case in the context of cyber warfare, as the reconnaissance phase of cyber-attacks is becoming one of the most important. There is a growing body of evidence indicating that reconnaissance has an important role in cyber war fighting (see Chapter 2 of this volume for discussion of the reconnaissance phase of cyber-attacks). Several important attacks have been enumerated by various research firms and writers, and these will be discussed below.

GhostNet (2009)

The report of a botnet that appeared to be targeting diplomatic and NGO offices that are associated with the Dalai Lama's operations in Dharamsala, India was the first that documented a digital espionage network targeting diplomatic offices. Nart Villanueve and Greg Walton of the research group SecDev were called in to investigate suspicious network and computer behaviour. Team members travelled to Dharamsala and discovered malware on multiple machines within the Dalai Lama's offices. That malware was sending information back to a command and control server (a process known as 'beaconing') that was not secure. This allowed the investigators to log in to the server and see the administrative console that identified the IP addresses of all of the machines in the botnet. They documented the machines as belonging to embassies, consulates and NGOs, all with a connection to southeast China and Tibet relations. The SecDev report on this 'GhostNet' operation found that:

> [t]he investigation ultimately uncovered a network of over 1,295 infected hosts in 103 countries. Up to 30% of the infected hosts are considered high-value targets and include computers located at ministries of foreign affairs, embassies, international organizations, news media, and NGOs. The Tibetan computer systems..., from which our investigators began, were conclusively compromised by multiple infections that gave attackers unprecedented access to potentially sensitive information.
>
> (SecDev, 2009)

The SecDev GhostNet report was the first of its kind to enumerate a state-actor espionage network, as opposed to the typical cybercrime botnet, meant to steal user banking credentials. The SecDev researchers published a follow-up report, 'Shadow in the Clouds', which tracked the GhostNet infection further and found a botnet Command and Control server in Chengdu, People's Republic of China (SecDev, 2010).

Operation Aurora (2009–2010)

From 15 December 2009 to 4 January 2010, attackers breached at least 34 high-tech and financial services companies in the United States: a series of APT attacks that has become known as 'Operation Aurora'. Google was the first to announce the breach with a blog post by David Drummond, Senior Vice President, Corporate Development and Chief Legal Officer (Drummond, 2010). He attributed the attack to China. Research published subsequently by McAfee detailed the sophisticated attack methodology of Operation Aurora, which included Adobe, Yahoo! and Morgan Stanley among its targets. McAfee claimed that the attackers sought source code from the tech companies (Varma, 2012).

In November 2010, the *New York Times* reported that the trove of State Department cables included evidence that the Operation Aurora attacks were directed by the Chinese Politboro:

> The Google hacking was part of a coordinated campaign of computer sabotage carried out by government operatives, private security experts and Internet outlaws recruited by the Chinese government. They have broken into American government computers and those of Western allies, the Dalai Lama and American businesses since 2002.
>
> (Shane and Lehren, 2010)

The final and most impactful research report was the 'APT1' report published by Mandiant, a cyber forensics firm. That report, published in February 2013, focused attention because, for the first time, attribution evidence was compiled and published that pointed directly to the Chinese government. As the report (Mandiant, 2013) stated:

> APT1 is believed to be the 2nd Bureau of the People's Liberation Army (PLA) General Staff Department's (GSD) 3rd Department, which is most commonly known by its Military Unit Cover Designator (MUCD) as Unit 61398.

Another groundbreaking element of the report was that Mandiant released an addendum that listed 3,000 IoCs that allowed the industry to search immediately for signs of Unit 61398 on their own networks. One reason that cyber research groups and government agencies had been reluctant to do this previously was the worry that they would be 'burning' their intelligence, in the sense that the threat actors would go to ground and change their IP addresses, online personae and methods. This indeed happened (see Fung, 2014). In May 2014, the US Justice Department filed a detailed indictment against the named agents of PLA Unit 61398, which listed six targets of their attacks including Westinghouse Electric, US Steel and Alcoa (Nakashima and Wan, 2014).

The Defence Industrial Base attack (2007)

In 2007, Representatives of the Pentagon revealed that a major exfiltration of 'terabytes of data' from the Defence Industrial Base (DIB) had occurred. The reputed target of the attacks was design information for the US F-35 Joint Strike Fighter. The *Wall Street Journal* (Gorman *et al.*, 2009) reported that, according to officials, 'the intruders were able to copy and siphon off several terabytes of data related to design and electronics systems'.

This exfiltration of critical design data was further corroborated by the Defense Science Board in a portion of its report to Congress that was leaked to the *Washington Post* in May 2013. In addition to the F-35 Joint Strike Fighter, weapons systems such as the Patriot missile 'PAC-3; an Army system for shooting down ballistic missiles, known as the Terminal High Altitude Area Defense, or THAAD; and the Navy's Aegis ballistic-missile defense system' were hacked (Nakashima, 2013). The full implications of the attack on the DIB are perhaps yet to be seen, but the fact that the attack focused directly on military weaponry in itself means that the attack was a particularly concerning one, especially in light of the absence of secure software development processes within most weapons programmes.

The attack on RSA (2011)

RSA, the Security Division of storage giant EMC, was the victim of an overwhelming cyber-attack in 2011. The attackers used techniques very similar to those in other so-called APT attacks, but the repercussions for EMC, and the security community as a whole, were dramatic. The SecurID one-time password, generating tokens for tens of thousands of RSA customers, had to be reissued. Rarely has a cyber breach affected so many organisations. However, the biggest change following the attack on RSA was the realisation on the part of anyone who is responsible for protecting digital assets that attackers are targeting those assets. What was most evident was that the attackers had a particular resource in mind; and they were successful at exfiltrating it.

At the time of the 'event', EMC was a customer of Netwitness: one of the fastest growing security vendors in a crowded marketplace. One of Netwitness' first employees was Shawn Carpenter. Netwitness is a network forensic tool that examines captured packet data for suspicious behaviour. This capability, deployed at EMC, was critical to the investigation that revealed (over a three-to-five-day period) the extent of the breach. Malware analysis of infected machines revealed encryption keys that were then used by EMC to decrypt the exfiltration traffic captured by the Netwitness devices. This traffic revealed that the secret seeds to the SecurID tokens had 'left the building'.

While EMC has not gone on record to identify its antagonists, most of the industry has assumed – as with the vast majority of APTs – that the Chinese government was behind the attack. Yet, because of the national security implications of the attacks and the involvement of multiple US intelligence agencies in the investigation, EMC was obligated not to point the finger at China. It is telling, however, that, on 27 March 2012, General Keith Alexander (head of the US National Security Agency (NSA) and CyberCommand (USCYBERCOM)) testified to the Senate Armed Services Committee on Chinese attacks on the Defense Industrial Base that '[t]here are some very public [attacks].... The most recent one was the RSA exploits' (quoted in Hoover, 2012).

The 2011 attacks on RSA are where the APT story comes full circle. Lockheed Martin, the operator of Sandia Labs, which had deployed Shawn Carpenter to its Florida facility to help clean up after the Titan Rain breaches in 2003, was the actual target of the group that breached RSA. After the 2003 detection of the Titan Rain APTs, Lockheed established its Cyber Intelligence and Response Technology (CIRT). By 2006, Lockhead had devised a custom methodology for APT detection. Using this Cyber Kill Chain methodology, Lockheed Martin has been fending off the threats from nation-state actors (Hutchins et al., 2010). These are actors that have inexhaustible resources, an educated and trained workforce of cyber-attackers, and military and economic motivations for extricating as much confidential data as possible.

Lockheed's threat-based approach can be thanked for its immediate recognition that RSA SecureID tokens were being misused. Only a month after the RSA breach Lockheed detected that a campaign of attack that it had been monitoring and thwarting for months had escalated, with the attackers attempting to log in remotely with a spoofed SecurID credential. Less than 24 hours after the compromised access tokens were first detected, Lockheed had shut down all access and notified all of its employees that remote access had been revoked and they would have to come into the office to work. Apparently the major campaign running against Lockheed, which even included a sophisticated attack against a supplier of security technology (EMC), had been stopped cold. This demonstration of 'best-in-class' security response capability was a measure of the advanced stage of Lockheed's defensive posture – a posture that will have to be mimicked by every organisation that is subject to targeted attacks.

The various acts of cyber espionage emanating from China discussed in this sub-section – which, themselves, are of course only a few examples amongst many – act as crucial reference points for tracing the history of full-blown 'cyber warfare'. They have highlighted the very real possibility of significant harm being inflicted through cyberspace, and therefore have led to an increased awareness of the threat that cyber-attacks pose, and also led to the development of ever more sophisticated security mechanisms to combat such threats.

The revolution in military affairs

The Gulf War origins of the RMA concept

During the final phases of the Cold War, Andrew Marshall, head of the US Department of Defense Office of Assessment and Strategic Planning, pushed for a strategy that relied heavily on sensors and information systems to counter

Russia's superior ability to amass forces in Europe (Liaropolous, 2006). From 1976, the United States had been moving towards an 'offset strategy' (which included stealth bombers and fighters), and an 'assault breaker' strategy (which looked to an 'intelligence grid' of ISR, coupled with communications and precision-guided weapons) to counter the threatened Soviet incursion into Western Europe (Owens, 2000: 80–2). Russian strategists seized upon these concepts, and devised a move towards the use of precision weapons and improvements in sensors and command communications. Russia termed this approach a 'Military–Technical Revolution' (MTR).

The 1991 Gulf War, a coalition military action against Iraqi forces in Kuwait that resulted in the complete withdrawal of Iraq following an astoundingly short engagement, caught the attention of military thinkers in both Russia and China. On the Russian side, the Gulf War served to validate the MTR by underlining a new shift in war fighting that included better communication, better targeting and better coordination of fighting forces. Chinese thinking, as discussed above, focused more specifically on the IW aspects of the military possibilities of new technologies.

Andrew Marshall, a former RAND analyst-turned-military advisor reporting to the Secretary of Defense, used a broader term than Russian scholars to identify the changing nature of modern warfare: the 'Revolution in Military Affairs' (RMA). To Marshall, a much more important revolution than that identified by Russian and Chinese thinkers was occurring. He likened it to the changes that occurred after WWI that led to the inventions of Blitzkrieg, submarine warfare and air warfare. Marshall favoured the term RMA over MTR because changes to organisational structure, hierarchies and force deployments could be included in the 'revolution'.

Marshall defined an RMA as a major change brought about by new technologies combined with a dramatic change in doctrine and organisations (see Gibish, 1996). Krepinevich (1994: 30) extended that definition, with the implications for order of magnitude increases 'in the combat potential and military effectiveness of armed forces'.

The RMA and Network-centric Warfare (NCW), particularly in the United States

The volume of writing on RMA reached a peak in 2001 and has tailed off since the terrorist attacks of 11 September 2001, when coalition forces were faced with the necessity of fighting protracted wars against insurgencies in Afghanistan and Iraq (Rosen, 2010: 470). While the RMA continues to influence ongoing organisational changes in the United States and elsewhere, the most evident impact of the RMA concept has been the aspects of it that concern the technological revolution of the military, and especially those aspects that bear on cyber warfare. The US military has certainly undergone a transformation towards more 'jointness' (House Hearing, 112 Congress, 2011): for example, when leaders are cycled through each branch of the military and the requisition process for new weapons systems, this has been led by joint requirements. Despite this move towards 'jointness', however, the key demonstrable effect of RMA has been the move to a networked fighting force. While one can debate the accuracy and exact impact of the RMA concept, it is possible, with the perspective of 20 years since the first Gulf War, to point to dramatic changes that have occurred in weapons systems, command and control and ISR, particularly in the United States.

With Marshall having set the stage, after being influenced by his reading of Russian academic publications on MTR around the time of the Gulf War, Arthur Cebrowski, who was appointed director of the Office of Force Transformation by Donald Rumsfeld in 2001, became the chief proponent of NCW at the Pentagon. His 1998 paper, 'Network-centric warfare: its origin and future proceedings', written while he was still Director for Space, Information Warfare, and Command and Control, is imbued with the excitement of the halcyon days of the Internet boom. Cebrowski (with Garstka, 1998) stated:

> [w]e are in the midst of a revolution in military affairs (RMA) unlike any seen since the Napoleonic Age, when France transformed warfare with the concept of *levée en masse*. Chief of Naval Operations Admiral Jay Johnson has called it 'a fundamental shift from what we call platform-centric warfare to something we call network-centric warfare', and it will prove to be the most important RMA in the past 200 years.

In 1998, Cebrowski argued for a transformation in the military that would have the same benefits to operations that network-centric computing had on the US economy. In hindsight it is possible to observe that the rapid move to a NCW footing came without the requisite precautions to endure the resiliency of those systems against cyber-attack. As such, the change in thinking towards the RMA (or other versions of this elsewhere, such as the MTR) is a key factor in tracing the history of cyber warfare, in part because it crucially awakened states to the *military possibilities* of cyberspace, but also because it occurred so quickly that it also left states militarily vulnerable to the cyber aggression of others.

Cyber warfare 'proper'

Despite the rapid rise of cyber espionage as a tool of nation states and the impact of the RMA, it was events in Estonia (2007) and Georgia (2008) that most scholars point to as the beginning of the era of cyber warfare (in the sense defined in this volume). These key points along the 'timeline' of cyber warfare will be discussed in this section, as will the Stuxnet attack on Iran (2010). Stuxnet constituted a further development in the short history of cyber warfare, in that it was a (seemingly) state-perpetrated cyber-attack that led to actual *physical damage*.

Estonia (2007)

In April 2007 Russia orchestrated a crisis that challenged Estonia's sovereignty. At the centre of the conflict was 'the Bronze Soldier': a bigger-than-life statue of a Soviet soldier erected in central Tallinn in 1947. Khrushchev had attended the inauguration of this memorial to the soldiers who had 'liberated' Estonia from Nazi Germany. Estonia announced that the statue and the graves of the soldiers buried around it would be moved to a cemetery on the outskirts of the city. While it is difficult to establish who instigated the ensuing riots, the moving of the Bronze Soldier was a polarising event that set ethnic Russians against ethnic Estonians. 'Fascist' became the rallying cry of the pro-Russian crowds as they gathered in candlelight vigils and at flower laying ceremonies and, ultimately, took to looting and burning Tallinn's shopping district.

The next phase of the protests took Estonia by surprise: massive DDoS attacks against Estonia's banking, telecom and government infrastructure that commenced as soon as the Bronze Soldier was relocated. The head of security at Swedbank reported that over 80,000 unique IP addresses were identified as the source of the attacks, which included Get floods and Ping floods (Stiennon, 2010: 87–8). Fax machines and cell phones of members of the Estonian Parliament were deluged with calls. Key web servers of government agencies and the office of the President succumbed to the attacks. The cyber-attacks on Estonia began on the Friday afternoon of 27 April 2007, and lasted several weeks. Russian-language forums carried instructions for downloading DDoS tools and identified targets.

According to Gadi Evron, a security researcher who travelled from Israel to Estonia in the wake of the attacks to provide assistance, there were many posts to Russian language forums prior to the commencement of the attacks:

> In the days leading up to the attack, numerous clues pointed to a large-scale operation that was being planned online. Russian language Internet discussion forums were abuzz with preparations for an online attack. Three days before the expected onslaught, Estonia planned to release the news of the coming strike in hopes that European media attention would oblige the EU to pressure the Kremlin to intervene, whether or not the attacks emanated from the Russian authorities.
>
> (Evron, 2008: 122)

Estonia certainly took the view that the scope of, and organisation behind, the attacks against it pointed to the direct involvement of the Russian state. The Estonian President Toomas Hendrik Ilves, was therefore willing, at least implicitly, to point the finger at Russia: 'I turn to Russia, Estonia's neighbour, with a clear message – try to remain civilized!' (Radio Free Europe, 2007). For Estonia, it was clear that at least some of the cyber-attacks originated from within the Kremlin, and there is certainly a degree of circumstantial evidence supporting this conclusion. Having said this, subsequent investigations were unable to yield conclusive attribution to the Russian government for the attack (Evron, 2008:

122; see also the discussion in Chapter 3 of this volume). Indeed, this is one of the reasons that 'crowd sourced attacks' of the sort seen in Estonia in 2007 have become powerful modern weapons: because of their 'plausible deniability'. The aggressor state can claim that an attack was a private action motivated by social outrage, rather than being centrally instigated and controlled cyber warfare.

Estonia's response and recovery from the cyber-attacks of 2007 is important to understand. This took three phases: communication, network response and server infrastructure hardening. When it was recognised that the DDoS attacks were coming from outside Estonia, the first step was to block ingress. The attackers, recognising this defensive measure, then spun up botnets that resided within Estonia to continue the disruption. As Estonia continued to work to filter the attacks in the network and build a robust series of proxy servers to handle the volume of requests, the attacks eventually subsided.

The occurrence of these cyber-attacks – which Estonia, at least, attributed to its Russian neighbour – led to Estonia calling upon NATO to invoke Article V of the NATO Treaty. Under that provision, an (armed) attack on one NATO state is equated to an attack on all, meaning that other NATO states are obliged to come to the aid of the victim in collective self-defence. In 2007, NATO was not prepared to recognise cyber-attacks as constituting 'armed attacks' triggering Article V. However, it is notable that, seven years later at the NATO meeting in Wales, a resolution recognising just such a possibility was agreed, albeit without the details required to define an Article V triggering cyber-attack or the appropriate responses to it (*Reuters*, 2014).

Georgia (2009)

In 2008 Georgia was in conflict with Russia over the status of two of its northern regions: Abkhazia and South Ossetia. Russia supported these regions in their attempts to become independent, while Georgia was trying to hold on to these breakaway territories. It is notable that much of the legal and political rhetoric on both sides in the Russia–Georgia conflict of 2008 matches that of the Russia–Ukraine conflict of 2014 (see Green, 2014).

Cyber-attacks began against Georgia the month before Russia's use of military force. On 20 July, the ShadowServer Foundation, an independent research organisation, documented a carefully orchestrated attack against President Saakashvili's website. ShadowServer observed that a botnet that it had never seen before (called 'Machbot') was communicating with a command and control server in the United States to obtain instructions for a DDoS attack (Tikk *et al*., 2008: 37). These commands caused the botnet to flood the presidential website with http, tcp and icmp packets, causing it to be unavailable for a 24-hour period. Other websites hosted on the same server were down as well, including that of the Social Assistance and Employment State Agency website (www.saesa.gov.ge).

On 7 August 2008, tensions, over South Ossetia in particular, increased. Georgia claimed that South Ossetian rebels were firing missiles into Georgian settlements in the region (Allison, 2008: 1147-8); while, at the same time, Russia claimed that several of its in-place 'peacekeeping' troops had been killed (Green, 2010: 64-8). It now appears that Georgia was the first to mobilise its military, moving its tanks and troops into South Ossetia (which of course, at least legally, remained part of Georgian territory). Russia was prepared and reacted quickly in the early hours of 8 August 2008, by sending tanks across its border with Georgia (though the Roki Tunnel – linking North Ossetia in Russia with South Ossetia in Georgia – which Russia controlled) and launching air strikes against military targets within Georgia proper (IIFFMCG Report, 2009: 10-11).

Massive cyber-attacks were launched against Georgian websites on the evening of 7 August, before Russia invaded. The effects of the cyber-attacks, regardless of who was responsible for them, were to disable the websites that Georgia used to communicate with its populace and the world, as well as the websites of Georgian banks and other ministries. These cyber-attacks introduced the 'fog of war' into the theatre of operations, at least as far as the Western world was concerned.

A website, StopGeorgia.com, which was attributed to the Russian Business Network (RBN), posted instructions for targeting 36 different servers in Georgia. A Google translation of the page was provided by Jart Armin, who maintains that the RBNExploit.com website (for this translation, see Harley, 2008: 24) made the following statement: '[w]e – the representatives of Russian hako-underground, will not tolerate provocation by the Georgian in all its manifestations. We want to live in a free world, but exist in a free-aggression and Setevom space.'

In addition, traceroutes from the United States showed that access to the websites of the Georgian Ministry of Defence (www.mod.gov.ge), the Georgian Ministry of Foreign Affairs (www.mof.gov.ge) and to the presidential website were blocked at TTnet (AS9121), a service provider in Turkey that according to GerogiaUpdate.gov.ge 'is associated with AbdAllah_Internet which is linked with cybercrime hosting such as thecanadianmeds.com. These are known Russian Business Network routes.' Traffic from the Ukraine to the Ministry of Foreign Affairs was redirected through Bryansk.ru to a forged page as well.

Similarly, analysis of the 2008 attacks on Georgia provided at www.georgiaupdate.gov.ge attributes them to the RBN. The RBN is a cyber-criminal organisation that has been blamed for spyware, massive spam operations, an elaborate web-based attack network based on IFrames vulnerabilities in Internet Explorer, extensive phishing attacks and the operation of a global carding operation connected to Russian organised crime. It is supposedly headquartered in St Petersburg, Russia and some of its members are ex-KGB operatives. Many innovations in creating malware that harvests computers to enlist them in botnets are also attributed to the RBN. As with the 2007 attacks against Estonia, there was strong circumstantial evidence indicating that the RBN was supported and directed by the Kremlin in attacking Georgia in 2008. Again, however, this was never satisfactorily established.

The international reaction to the cyber-attacks on Georgia is worth noting. By 13 August 2008, Estonia deployed two cyber advisors from the Estonian Computer Emergency Response Team to assist with defence and, presumably, to share what Estonia had learned when it was under attack from Russia in 2007. Meanwhile, Poland provided space on its own presidential website for President Saakashvili to post updates on the developing situation.

The successful attacks on Georgia's networks, banks and key government websites was unique in that it was the first time that cyber warfare had been wedded to traditional methods of conducting warfare. The cyber-attacks against Georgia in 2008 occurred in the wider context of an outbreak of physical hostilities. This fact has changed the threat landscape for all states that rely on computing and networks to conduct commerce, communicate with their citizens and interface with their critical infrastructure. States now have to assume that any future armed conflict may well involve coincident elements of cyber warfare.

Stuxnet (2010)

Stuxnet is the name given to malware that researchers believe was used to disrupt Iran's capability to refine weapons-grade uranium. As such, it is the first documented example of a state-sponsored cyber-attack being used to achieve geopolitical effect, that is: slowing the entry of Iran into the nuclear club. Moreover, the Stuxnet attack was the first instance of an act of cyber warfare that caused direct physical damage.

On 1 June 2012, David Sanger exposed the story behind Stuxnet in a front-page story in the *New York Times*. The lead from the story read:

> From his first months in office, President Obama secretly ordered increasingly sophisticated attacks on the computer systems that run Iran's main nuclear enrichment facilities, significantly expanding America's first sustained use of cyberweapons, according to participants in the program.
> (Sanger, 2012)

While the United States has yet to admit to Stuxnet formally, journalists at the *Washington Post* and NPR have confirmed that they too have sources that support Sanger's story (Nakashima, 2012; Gjelten, 2011). Similarly, Edward Snowden, the Booz Allen Hamilton NSA whistle-blower, also claimed in an interview that Stuxnet was co-written by the United States and Israel (JTA, 2013). Stuxnet was part of a secret campaign dubbed Operation 'Olympic Games'. It was preceded by spyware that operatives called 'the bug', which mapped the networks and systems inside Natanz, the Iranian uranium refinement facility that Stuxnet targeted. Stuxnet was then reportedly delivered via a Universal Serial Bus (USB) thumb drive and, over several years, did significant damage to the gas centrifuges used to refine uranium. Stuxnet was successful, according to admissions from Iran. Analysts hypothesise that Stuxnet set back Iran's plans to develop nuclear weapons by as much as two years (*CBSNews*, 2010).

The Stuxnet attack represents a particularly notable development in the history of cyber warfare because its sophistication may well be representative of future attacks deployed against military capabilities, both in terms of mode of attack and effects. As such, it is worth going through the various steps that were involved in the Stuxnet attack in turn: (1) delivery; (2) search and install; (3) compromise; and (4) destruction.

Step 1: Delivery

A secure operation, such as the refining of uranium for nuclear power and, reputedly, at Natanz, nuclear weapons production, would be segmented from the Internet. The best practice for any critical environment is to ensure that there is no connection to any other network. Internet Protocol networks have to be scanned continuously to ensure that this 'air-gap' is not compromised. Network discovery tools are required to ensure that the secure network has not been connected or bridged to the outside world via a rogue WiFi hotspot, satellite link, or trusted third-party connection. When a critical network is completely cut off from the rest of the world, there is a tendency to be lax in traditional security operations, as was demonstrated in the cases of Bradley Manning and Edward Snowden (both of whom used USB devices to steal secret documents).

Every production system needs some way of securely transferring data from the trusted side to the untrusted side, and USB thumb drives are often the means for doing so. The Stuxnet authors recognised that USB tokens were the most viable vector for attacking Iran's nuclear environment. They used a previously unknown vulnerability in Windows software that would automatically execute a program if it was viewed with Windows Explorer (see Microsoft Security Advisory 2934088, 2014). This was close to the type of vulnerability that the Agent.btz worm used to infect the US Secret Internet Protocol Routing Network (SIPRNet).

Step 2: Search and infect

Once an initial infection was accomplished, probably by an insider or a contractor, the Stuxnet worm would spread to adjacent machines on the network. Unlike APTs that usually report back to a command and control server at this point, Stuxnet had to be autonomous because of the air-gap in the network. Its goal was to find and infect machines running Siemens' Step7 Software. Worms have a tendency to get out of control and, if they are not throttled, they can spread to the entire Internet in moments. The 2003 SQL Slammer worm spread to 80,000 machines in less than 12 minutes and caused most of the Internet to screech to a halt (Moore *et al.*, 2003). Even Robert Tappan Morris recognised this when he crafted the first Internet worm in 1988. He attempted to avoid a wildfire by only allowing each infection to spread to a few machines before stopping and it still cascaded out of control. Stuxnet used the same throttling. Each infection would only spread to several machines (Kehoe, 1992).

Step 3: Compromise via root kit installation

Once Stuxnet was lodged on a PC running Step7, it would replace the dll (dynamic link library) used to communicate with the machine controllers on the plant floor. Step7 is the control software used to communicate new instructions to Programmable Logic Controllers (PLCs). Stuxnet would intercept these commands, look for a particular block of data and replace it. If the particular block it was looking for was not detected, it would hand commands off to the original dll, effectively hiding its presence in the many infections that occurred that did not further its mission.

In addition to the '0-day' vulnerability Stuxnet used for initial infection, it took advantage of three other previously unknown vulnerabilities for privilege escalation, which is required to install software on locked-down PCs (Naraine, 2010). The attackers also realised that the operating system would only install software that was digitally signed: they used stolen digital certificates from Realtek Semiconductor and JMicron Technology so that it would appear that the installation was signed by a trusted party (Raiu, 2010).

Step 4: Sabotage

Once Stuxnet found its way onto the machine that controlled the right PLC attached to the right motor control, it modified the instructions sent to that motor, causing it to spin at different rates. Machinery rotating at high rates is very sensitive to changes in rotation rates, and gas centrifuges for refinement of radioactive uranium spin at 6,000 rpm. Reports from Iran indicate that its enrichment operations have suffered continuous setbacks since the Stuxnet infection.

Stuxnet is the high-water mark for targeted attacks so far: it caused direct physical damage to the centrifuges in the Natanz plant, and caused significant geopolitical 'damage' well beyond this. However, the methodologies that were used in the Stuxnet infection were not, themselves, new, even if the result – industrial sabotage – was unprecedented. Nonetheless, with the Stuxnet attack, the era of cyber warfare entered a new phase. Countering a targeted attack on the level of Stuxnet requires a revamping of traditional IT security operations. The examples given in the next section indicate that most military systems have not been designed to counter this level of targeting.

The rise of cyber commands

Attacks against US military

In 2007 the Pentagon revealed that its email servers, particularly those of the Joint Chiefs, had been compromised. It is significant that the Pentagon said that it could not determine how long the email servers had been under the control of the attackers. A later report estimated the cost of recovering from the attack to be over $100 million (Sevastopulo, 2007).

The air-gapped SIPRNet was designed to be completely separate from regular military and civilian networks although it spans the globe and connects many defence contractors, albeit via standalone terminals. Richard Clarke, Former National Coordinator for Security, Infrastructure Protection, and Counter-Terrorism for the United States, said in an interview with author Peter Singer: '[w]hy is it that every time a virus pops up on the regular Internet, it also shows up in SIPRNet?' Clarke's implication was that, like most networks, there were unaccounted-for connections to the Internet (Singer, 2009: 201).

The lack of controls within SIPRNet itself was demonstrated in a dramatic fashion when a USB-born virus was spread throughout the world after it was introduced in a forward active military operation, probably in Afghanistan (Nakashima, 2011). The infection had a dramatic impact on the US Department of Defense (DoD): Lynn (2010) termed it 'a wake-up call'. It is therefore important to look at what was actually a fairly simplistic attack that would have been easily blocked by most organisations.

The malware was identified by the Finnish anti-virus (AV) firm F-Secure on 26 June 2008 as worm_w32_agent_btz, or Agent.btz for short (F-Secure, 2008). It was a variant of a previously seen worm called SillyFDC:

> Four months later, in October 2008, NSA analysts discovered the malware on the Secret Internet Protocol Router Network, which the Defense and State departments use to transmit classified material but not the nation's most sensitive information. Agent.btz also infected the Joint Worldwide Intelligence Communication System, which carries top-secret information to US officials throughout the world.
>
> (Nakashima, 2011)

The NSA's Advance Networks Operations (ANO) was the group that discovered Agent.btz and developed a way to neutralise it. The Joint Task Force–Global Network Operations (JTF–GNO) was responsible for 'Buckshot Yankee', the clean-up effort, while the NSA's Tailored Access Operations (TAO) conducted network surveillance to find variants of Agent.btz. All of these groups were later subsumed into USCYBERCOM.

Buckshot Yankee came with a tremendous cost as 15,000 networks and seven million PCs in the DoD were scrubbed and re-imaged. The attack was 'the most significant breach of US military computers ever' (Lynn, 2010). In a telling 2009 interview, Lieutenant General Jeffrey Sorenson, Chief Information Officer of the Army, revealed that:

> [i]n many cases, as we've learned through the most recent Army 'Rampart Yankee' and [the DoD] 'Buckshot Yankee' exercise – where we had to go off and remediate computer systems because of some infected thumb drives – that was a rather laborious, manually intensive effort to essentially achieve a capability that we would like to have, which would be machine-to-machine.
>
> (Quoted in Rosenberg, 2009)

In other words, in 2009 military systems running Windows did not have a mechanism to push software updates effectively, something that most organisations were doing using Microsoft's System Center Service Manager (SCSM).

The DoD's immediate reaction to Buckshot Yankee was to ban the use of USB devices, including thumb drives and CDs. This ban was not lifted until 2010 and the DoD is still trying to deploy end-point control technology to allow USB thumb drives to be used safely. William Lynn, who was Deputy Secretary of Defense for Cyber in 2007 when the attacks occurred, claimed that this attack, as late as 2008, was the single most important cause of the Pentagon recognising the rising threat from cyber-attacks and they used it to justify setting up the sub-unified Command of USCYBER404COM. Most military systems now in operational use were designed and specified well before 2008, raising the unanswered question of the cyber hardening incorporated into their design (i.e. increasing security through limiting the systems' 'surface of vulnerability') before the military became fully cognisant of the threat.

The rise of US CyberCommand

The US military, in response to the attacks it was experiencing on its networks, consolidated its cyber war-fighting capability in USCYBERCOM, led by the head of the NSA, General Keith Alexander. USCYBERCOM cut off efforts on the part of the Navy and Air Force to create their own cyber branches, in favour of a sub-unified command that includes each branch.

The DoD NetOps Strategic Vision is the 2008 evolution of the Pentagon's NCW vision, from a decade earlier, of a combined sensor and command grid (Owens, 2000: 150). The Global Information Grid (GIG) encompasses all communications, networks, and computers within the purview of the DoD. The NetOps Strategic Vision document uses familiar concepts from the early RMA literature, discussed above. It calls for a 'new unified NetOps capability based on these goals: Share GIG Situational Awareness; Unify GIG Command and Control; Institutionalize NetOps' (Grimes, 2008). In addition, the Strategic Vision calls for centralised policy and distributed decision-making supported by the information available from the GIG.

The 2008 Vision document sets lofty goals that reflect how the concepts of Network-centric Warfare have permeated the thinking of the US military to the point where the tools of NCW – the networks and computers – are being organised using the same concepts. While the Vision document includes the need to protect the GIG, it does not acknowledge that global interoperability opens the door to global failure, as demonstrated by Buckshot Yankee.

The creation of USCYBERCOM, the US DoD's response to growing concern over cyber incidents (particularly Buckshot Yankee, according to William Lynn), can be traced to the rapid realisation, on the part of the military, that the move to NCW had exposed them to network attack. After several gyrations USCYBERCOMM was 'stood up' on 21 May 2010, under a four-star General (Warner, 2013: 35).

By tracing the evolution of USCYBERCOM it is possible to understand some of the reasons that the military has focused almost completely on network defence and cyber-attack while being unaware of the need to address the vulnerabilities in systems that could be exploited in future conflicts against technologically capable adversaries. It is a problem mirrored in most organisations. The network security staff are separate from the end-point security staff who manage desktops through patch and vulnerability management tools, and ensure that software and AV signatures are up to date. Meanwhile, the development teams who create new applications, web services, and digital business ventures work completely on their own with little concern for security. The analogous behaviour observed in the military is the creation of new weapons systems, ISR platforms, precision targeting and C2 capabilities without ensuring that they are resistant to the types of attacks that USCYBERCOM and the NSA have been researching and deploying.

USCYBERCOM had its genesis in NCW thinking. First, the military worked to participate in the information revolution by joining their networks together. Then it recognised the need for protecting those networks (now termed 'cyberspace'). The concept that a strong defence requires a strong offence, carried over from missile defence and Cold War strategies, led to a focus on network attack and less emphasis on improving resiliency of computing platforms and weapons systems.

Cyber arming in other states

Before a change in the methods of war fighting becomes apparent it is the norm to first see the rise of the technology underpinning it, followed by organisational changes in the military to accommodate the new technology; it is usually only then that we see the widespread incorporation of the new weapons into tactical and even strategic orders of battle. Thus, the rapid creation of cyber units within major militaries – representing the 'organisational change' phase in this process – is an important indicator of the future use of cyber warfare. While the United States has made the biggest public commitment to its cyber war-fighting organisation, it is important to note that many other states have begun this process too.

United Kingdom

In May 2013 the Ministry of Defence established the Joint Forces Cyber Group and a Joint Forces Cyber Reserve to provide support to the two Joint Cyber Units: one in Corsham, the other in Cheltenham. The United Kingdom has not moved as quickly towards a cyber warfare 'fighting stance' as has the United States. While funds have been budgeted for cyber defence, there has not been the same focus on creating a separate cyber command. The Ministry of Defence's Global Operations and Security Control Centre (GOSCC) has taken the lead in coordinating network defences (i.e. it has taken more of a traditional IT security role) and there is a separate Joint Cyber Unit within GOSCC to coordinate cyber defence across all three Services and the Government Communications Headquarters (GCHQ).

The Defence Cyber Operations Group (DCOG) is under the United Kingdom's Joint Forces Command and will most likely be more focused on cyber war fighting than is the GOSCC's Corsham Joint Cyber Unit – while the Cheltenham Joint Cyber Unit, hosted by GCHQ, has a remit to 'deliver military effects' (Parliamentary Session, 2012–2013).

The Netherlands

The Dutch Ministry of Defence is establishing a cyber command, which will be responsible for defence, intelligence, and attack (Ministerie van Defensie, 2012). One of the top priorities of the Dutch Cyber Strategy is 'the development of the military capability to perform cyber operations ("offensive")' (Koot, 2012).

Germany

Germany operates a Computer Network Operation (CNO) team of 60 people from the Bundesnachrichtendienst (BND)'s Tomburg Joint Services Barracks in Rheinbach (Fischer, 2013). Interestingly, this unit was operating entirely covertly from its inception in 2006 until the German government first acknowledged its existence in 2012. It has also been revealed that the German CNO is particularly mandated to focus on offensive (rather than defensive) cyber operations (Leyden, 2012).

Estonia

After the 2007 attacks against Estonia's infrastructure there was considerable focus put on cyber warfare. Tallinn is the home of NATO's Cooperative Cyber Defence Centre of Excellence. Estonia has taken a 'home guard' approach to cyber defence by establishing a cyber unit within the 11,000-strong Estonian Defence League. Cyber security experts from industry have been working together to ensure that Estonia has sustainable cyber resilience against future attacks (Kaitseliit, 2014).

India

While India has been the target of many cyber-attacks, organisational changes have been limited to discussion about establishing a Cyber Command with the Ministry of Defence (Raghuvanshi, 2013). However, despite pressure coming from within the Indian military establishment for the government to set up such a command (see Sagar, 2014), this has not yet occurred.

Israel

Israel has suffered its share of cyber-attacks from a variety of sources. Unit 8200 of the Israel Defense Force (IDF) is responsible for Signals Intelligences, and personnel who have come out of Unit 8200 have gone on to found leading security vendors such as Check Point Software and Imperva. Media reports credit Unit 8200 with active cyber-attacks including participation in Operation Olympic Games (Sanger, 2012) and interfering with Syria's air defences during the attack and destruction of that state's nuclear reactor (Operation Orchard) (Markoff, 2010).

China

China's PLA has been accused of perpetrating many cyber-espionage incidents in the United States: a number of examples were set out above. The Mandiant APT1 report identified Unit 61398 as the group responsible for many such attacks (Mandiant, 2013) and, in May 2014, the US Justice Department indicted five members of Unit 61398 (*United States v. Wang et al.*, 2014). In June 2014, CrowdStrike, a US cybersecurity vendor, published a report providing attribution of cyber-attacks to another unit: Chinese PLA, 3rd Department, 12th Bureau Unit 61486 (Hartley, 2014). It is no surprise that Chinese academic thinking on IW has evolved into active cyber espionage. The volume of attacks and the increasingly vocal response from the United States is a symptom of growing capability within China's military.

Overall, it is clear that bespoke cyber commands are proliferating throughout the states of the world. A notable number of states now have such organisational structures in place, and many of those that do not are currently looking to set up something of a similar sort. This fact suggests that we are quickly moving towards a true 'age of cyber warfare': all states are now fully aware of cyber threats and are taking active steps to limit these threats, while an increasingly large number of states are also becoming meaningfully engaged with the *offensive* possibilities that cyberspace can offer.

Conclusion

The history of cyber warfare is intimately bound up with the history of cyber-attacks from the earliest experimental or nuisance worms and viruses to sophisticated attacks on consumer banking applications to economic and diplomatic espionage. It was only when governments and militaries began to be highly networked that the threats against those systems began to materialise. Lessons are still to be learned by most organisations, and the responsibilities of supporting the information technology infrastructure include the need to harden these systems well in advance of the inevitable attacks.

A contemporaneous history of cyber warfare must look at analogous systems to identify signs of emerging threats that will materialise in attacks that can be strictly classified as 'war-like'. Information operations in support of efforts to project force by states can be as broadly categorised as citizen hacker attacks, PSYOP efforts to control the story of a conflict (including disinformation) and 'comment armies' such as those employed by Russia and China.

Acts of electronic warfare – the jamming of radio frequencies for communication and ISR, and the application of stealth technology to avoid detection – are more closely related to future cyber warfare then perhaps are the viruses and worms used to steal banking credentials. But even radar systems are becoming increasingly digitised and linked via networks that are susceptible to attack. Using cyber espionage to learn the weaknesses of radar, ISR, communication systems, drone platforms and precision targeting systems is the precursor to the use of cyber-attacks during future battles. When weapons systems are disabled, ISR is misled and command and control communications are disrupted or tampered with, cyber warfare will have become an integral part of all future war fighting.

References

Allison, R. (2008), 'Russia resurgent? Moscow's campaign to "coerce Georgia to peace"', *International Affairs*, vol. 84, no. 6, pp. 1145–71.

CBSNews (2010) 'Iran confirms Stuxnet worm halted centrifuges', 29 November [online], available: www.cbsnews.com/news/iran-confirms-stuxnet-worm-halted-centrifuges/ [25 September 2014].

Cebrowski, A.K. and Garstka, J.J. (1998), 'Network-centric warfare: its origin and future', January, *Proceedings Magazine* [online], available: http://mattcegelske.com/wp-content/uploads/2012/04/ncw_origin_future.pdf [25 September 2014].

Dai, S. and Shen, F. (1996) *Information warfare and information security strategy*, Beijing: Jincheng Publishing House.

Drummond, D. (2010) 'A new approach to China', 12 January, *Google Official Blog* [online], available: http://googleblog.blogspot.com/2010/01/new-approach-to-china.html [25 September 2014].

Evron, G. (2008), 'Battling botnets and online mobs: Estonia's defense efforts during the Internet war', *Georgetown Journal of International Affairs*, vol. 9, pp. 121–6.

Fischer, M. (2013) 'German armed forces equipping for cyber war', 22 May, *Stars and Stripes*, [online], available: www.stripes.com/news/europe/german-armed-forces-equipping-for-cyber-war-1.222156 [25 September 2014].

F-Secure (2008) 'Threat description: Worm:W32/Agent.BTZ' [online], available: www.f-secure.com/v-descs/worm_w32_agent_btz.shtml [25 September 2014].

Fung, B. (2014) 'The mysterious disappearance of China's elite hacking unit', 10 April, *Washington Post* [online], available: www.washingtonpost.com/blogs/the-switch/wp/2014/04/10/the-mysterious-disappearance-of-chinas-elite-hacking-unit/ [25 September 2014].

Gibish, J.E. (ed.) (1996) *Revolution in military affairs: A selected bibliography*, Carlisle Barracks: US Army War College Library.

Gjelten, T. (2011) 'Security expert: U.S. "leading force" behind Stuxnet', 26 September, *NPR* [online], available: www.npr.org/2011/09/26/140789306/security-expert-u-s-leading-force-behind-stuxnet [25 September 2014].

Gorman, S., Cole, A. and Dreazen, Y. (2009) 'Computer spies breach fighter-jet project' 21 April, *Wall Street Journal* [online], available: http://online.wsj.com/articles/SB124027491029837401 [25 September 2014].

Green, J.A. (2010), 'Passportisation, peacekeepers and proportionality: The Russian claim of the protection of nationals abroad in self-defence', in Green, J.A. and Waters, C.P.M. (eds), *Conflict in the Caucasus: Implications for international legal order*, Basingstoke: Palgrave Macmillan, pp. 54–79.

Green, J.A. (2014) 'Editorial comment – The annexation of Crimea: Russia, passportisation and the protection of nationals revisited', *Journal on the Use of Force and International Law*, vol. 1, no. 1, pp. 3–10.

Grimes, J.G. (2008), 'Department of Defense NetOps strategic vision', December, *Department of Defense Chief Information Officer* [online], available: http://dodcio.defense.gov/Portals/0/Documents/DIEA/DoD_NetOps_Strategic_Vision.pdf [25 September 2014].

Harley, J. (ed.) (2008) 'Information operations newsletter', US Army Strategic Command G39, *Information Operations Branch*, vol. 8, no. 19, pp. 1–33 [online], available: www.oss.net/dynamaster/file_archive/080815/ab3b6c26d8dc916d6b93bf2956afe888/20080814%20IO%20Newsletter%20v8%20no%2019.doc [25 September 2014].

Hartley, N. (2014) 'Hat-tribution to PLA Unit 61486', 9 June, *CrowdStrike Blog* [online], available: www.crowdstrike.com/blog/hat-tribution-pla-unit-61486/ [25 September 2014].

Hoover, J.N. (2012) 'NSA chief: China behind RSA attacks', 27 March, *Information Week* [online], available: www.informationweek.com/news/government/security/232700341 [25 September 2014].

'House Hearing, 112 Congress, 2011': 'Improving the readiness of U.S. forces through military jointness' (2011), Hearing before the Subcommittee on Readiness of the Committee on Armed Services, House of Representatives, 112th Congress, first session, United States Government Printing Office [online], available: www.gpo.gov/fdsys/pkg/CHRG-112hhrg65804/html/CHRG-112hhrg65804.htm [25 September 2014].

Hutchins, E.M., Cloppert, M.J. and Amin, R.M. (2010) 'Intelligence-driven computer network defense informed by analysis of adversary campaigns and intrusion kill chains', 21 November, *Lockeed Martin* [online], available: www.lockheedmartin.com/content/dam/lockheed/data/corporate/documents/LM-White-Paper-Intel-Driven-Defense.pdf [25 September 2014].

'IIFFMCG Report, 2009': The Report of the Independent International Fact-Finding Mission on the Conflict in Georgia 30 September 2009), 30 September [online], available: www.ceiig.ch/Report.html [25 September 2014].

JTA (2013) 'Snowden says Israel, U.S. created Stuxnet virus that attacked Iran', 19 July, *Haaretz* [online], available: www.haaretz.com/news/diplomacy-defense/1.534728 [25 September 2014].

'Kaitseliit, 2014': 'Estonian Defence League's Cyber Unit' (2014) Kaitseliit website of Estonian Defence League [online], available: www.kaitseliit.ee/en/cyber-unit [25 September 2014].

Kehoe, B.P. (1992) *Zen and the art of the Internet: A beginner's guide to the Internet*, free e-book, 1st edition [online], available: www.cs.indiana.edu/docproject/zen/zen-1.0_10.html#SEC91 [25 September 2014].

Koot, M.R. (2012) 'The Dutch defense cyber strategy', translation, 18 July, blog [online], available: https://blog.cyberwar.nl/2012/07/nl-uk-translation-of-the-dutch-defense-cyber-strategy/ [25 September 2014].

Krepinevich, A.F. (1994) 'Calvary to computer: The pattern of military revolutions', *The National Interest*, Fall, 30–42.

Leyden, J. (2012) 'Germany reveals secret techie soldier unit, new cyberweapons', 8 June, *The Register* [online], available: www.theregister.co.uk/2012/06/08/germany_cyber_offensive_capability/ [25 September 2014].

Liaropolous, A.N. (2006) 'Revolutions in warfare: Theoretical paradigms and historical evidence – The Napoleonic and First World War revolutions in military affairs', *Journal of Military History*, vol. 70, pp. 363–84.

Lynn, W.J. III (2010) 'Defending a new domain: The Pentagon's cyberstrategy', *Foreign Affairs*, vol. 89, no. 5, pp. 97–108.

Mandiant (2013), 'APT1: Exposing one of China's cyber espionage units', *Mandiant publication* [online], available: http://intelreport.mandiant.com/Mandiant_APT1_Report.pdf [25 September 2014].

Markoff, J. (2010) 'A silent attack, but not a subtle one', 26 September, *New York Times*, 26 [online], available: www.nytimes.com/2010/09/27/technology/27virus.htm [25 September 2014].

Microsoft Security Advisory 2934088 (2014) 'Vulnerability in Internet Explorer could allow remote code execution' 19 February [online], available: http://technet.microsoft.com/en-us/security/advisory/2934088 [25 September 2014].

Ministerie van Defensie (2012) 'Cyber commando' [online], available: www.defensie.nl/onderwerpen/cyber-security/inhoud/cyber-commando [25 September 2014].

Moore, D., Paxson, V., Savage, S., Shannon, C., Staniford, S. and Weaver, N. (2003) 'The Spread of the Sapphire/Slammer Worm', January, *Cooperative Association for Internet Data Analysis* [online], available: www.caida.org/publications/papers/2003/sapphire/sapphire.html [25 September 2014].

Nakashima, E. (2011) 'Cyber-intruder sparks massive federal response — and debate over dealing with threats', 8 December, *Washington Post* [online], available: www.washingtonpost.com/national/national-security/cyber-intruder-sparks-response-debate/2011/12/06/gIQAxLuFgO_story.html [25 September 2014].

Nakashima, E. (2012) 'Stuxnet was work of U.S. and Israeli experts, officials say', 1 June, *Washington Post* [online], available: www.washingtonpost.com/world/national-security/stuxnet-was-work-of-us-and-israeli-experts-officials-say/2012/06/01/gJQAlnEy6U_story.html [25 September 2014].

Nakashima, E. (2013) 'Confidential report lists U.S. weapons system designs compromised by Chinese cyberspies', 27 May, *Washington Post* [online], available: www.washingtonpost.com/world/national-security/confidential-report-lists-us-weapons-system-designs-compromised-by-chinese-cyberspies/2013/05/27/a42c3e1c-c2dd-11e2-8c3b-0b5e9247e8ca_story.html [25 September 2014].

Nakashima, E. and Wan, W. (2014) 'U.S. announces first charges against foreign country in connection with cyberspying', 19 May, *Washington Post* [online], available: www.washingtonpost.com/world/national-security/us-to-announce-first-criminal-charges-against-foreign-country-for-cyberspying/2014/05/19/586c9992-df45-11e3-810f-764fe508b82d_story.html [25 September 2014].

Naraine, R. (2010) 'Stuxnet attackers used 4 Windows zero-day exploits', 14 Septmeber, *ZDNET* [online], available: www.zdnet.com/blog/security/stuxnet-attackers-used-4-windows-zero-day-exploits/7347 [25 September 2014].

Owens, W.A. (2000) *Lifting the fog of war*, New York: Farrar, Straus and Giroux.

Parliamentary Session (2012–2013) 'hc 106 defence and cyber-security', supplementary written evidence from the Ministry of Defence following the private evidence session

on 18 April 2012 [online], available: www.publications.parliament.uk/pa/cm201213/cmselect/cmdfence/writev/106/m01a.htm [25 September 2014].
Radio Free Europe (2007) 'Newsline', 3 May [online], available: www.rferl.org/content/article/1143864.html [25 September 2014].
Raghuvanshi, V. (2013) 'India debates establishing cyber command', 22 November, *Defense News* [online], available: www.defensenews.com/article/20131122/DEFREG03/311220008/India-Debates-Establishing-Cyber-Command [25 September 2014].
Raiu, C. (2010) 'Stuxnet signed certificates frequently asked questions' 21 July, *Securelist* [online], available: www.securelist.com/en/blog2236Stuxnet_signed_certificates_frequently_asked_questions [25 September 2014].
Reuters (2014) 'NATO agrees cyber attack could trigger military response', 5 September [online], available: http://uk.reuters.com/article/2014/09/05/us-nato-cybersecurity-idUKKBN0H013P20140905 [25 September 2014].
Rosen, S.P. (2010) 'The impact of the office of net assessment on the American military in the matter of the revolution in military affairs', *Journal of Strategic Studies*, vol. 33, no. 4, pp. 469–82.
Rosenberg, B. (2009) 'Army CIO sets sights on improved data sharing', 10 August, *Government Computing News* [online], available: http://gcn.com/articles/2009/08/10/gcn-interview-sorenson-army-cio.aspx [25 September 2014].
Sagar, P.R (2014) 'India readies cyber command service to combat espionage threats online', 15 January, *DNA* [online], available: www.dnaindia.com/india/report-india-readies-cyber-command-service-to-combat-espionage-threats-online-1950997 [25 September 2014].
Sanger, D.E. (2012) 'Obama order sped up wave of cyberattacks against Iran', 1 June, *New York Times* [online], available: www.nytimes.com/2012/06/01/world/middleeast/obama-ordered-wave-of-cyberattacks-against-iran.html [25 September 2014].
SecDev Group (2009) 'Tracking GhostNet: Investigating a cyber espionage network', 29 March [online], available: www.scribd.com/doc/13731776/Tracking-GhostNet-Investigating-a-Cyber-Espionage-Network [25 September 2014].
SecDev Group (2010) 'Shadows in the cloud: Investigating cyber espionage 2.0', 6 April [online], available: www.scribd.com/doc/29435784/SHADOWS-IN-THE-CLOUD-Investigating-Cyber-Espionage-2-0 [25 September 2014].
Sevastopulo, D. (2007) 'Chinese hacked into Pentagon', 3 September, *Financial Times* [online], available: www.ft.com/intl/cms/s/0/9dba9ba2-5a3b-11dc-9bcd-0000779fd2ac.html [25 September 2014].
Shane, S. and Lehren, A.W. (2010) 'Leaked Cables Offer Raw Look at U.S. Diplomacy', 28 November, *New York Times* [online], available: www.nytimes.com/2010/11/29/world/29cables.html?pagewanted=all&_r=0.
Shen, W. (1995) 'Focus of contemporary world military revolution – Introduction to information warfare', 7 November, *Jiefangjun bao (PLA Daily)*, p. 6.
Shen, W. (1997) *On new war*, Beijing: Renmin chubanshe.
Singer, P.W. (2009) *Wired for war: The robotics revolution and conflict in the 21st century*, New York: Penguin Press.
Stiennon, R. (2010) *Surviving cyberwar*, Lanham: Government Institutes.
Thomas, T.L. (2007) *Decoding the virtual dragon*, Fort Leavenworth: Foreign Military Studies Office.
Thornburgh, N. (2005) 'The invasion of the Chinese cyberspies: An exclusive look at how the hackers called TITAN RAIN are stealing U.S. secrets', 29 August, *Time Magazine* [online], available: http://courses.cs.washington.edu/courses/csep590/05au/readings/titan.rain.htm [25 September 2014].

Tikk, E., Kaska, K., Rünnimeri, K., Kert, M., Talihärm, A.-M. and Vihul, L. (2008) 'Cyber attacks against Georgia: Legal lessons identified', November, *Cooperative Cyber Defence Centre of Excellence*, Tallinn, Estonia [online], available: www.carlisle.army.mil/DIME/documents/Georgia%201%200.pdf [25 September 2014].

United States v. Wang et al. (2014) Case 2:14-cr-00118-CB, United States District Court, Western District of Pennsylvania, 1 May.

Varma, R., (2012) 'Combatting Aurora', *McAfee Labs* [online], available: https://kc.mcafee.com/resources/sites/MCAFEE/content/live/CORP_KNOWLEDGE-BASE/67000/KB67957/en_US/Combating%20Threats%20-%20Operation%20Aurora.pdf [25 September 2014].

Wang, Q. (1993) *Modern military-use high technology*, Beijing: AMS Press.

Warner, M. (2013) 'US cyber command's road to full operational capability', in Seidule, J.T. and Whitt, J. (eds), *Stand up and fight! The creation of US security organizations, 1942–2005*, United States Military Academy, under review at AUSA Press (on file with author).

Zhu Y., Feng Y. and Xu De. (1994) *Information war under high tech conditions*, Beijing: AMS Press.

2 Understanding cyber-attacks

Duncan Hodges and Sadie Creese

Introduction

While the concept of cyber warfare (or 'cyber conflict') is arguably commonly understood in the abstract, and is undoubtedly difficult to define in both military and civil paradigms, it can also easily be argued that it does not constitute 'war' in a traditional military sense (Ridd, 2013). Yet it is unquestionable that there are actors that can (and regularly *are*) launching missions in cyberspace as part of both intelligence and military missions and corporate espionage. There is not a large amount of information in the public sphere surrounding the success (or failure) of overtly state-sponsored cyber-attacks; attackers have good reputational, political and technical reasons to not publicise their actions or methods and a state is unlikely to claim responsibility or to disclose impacts felt where it has been a victim. However, within the public domain there have been a number of attacks that appear to have been state-sponsored (or at least state-influenced). We have seen disruption of communications in order to attempt an informational superiority, notably before the involvement of Russia in both Georgia and Ukraine; we have also seen attacks looking to disrupt nuclear research progress (Falliere *et al.*, 2011), national media (NSHC, 2013) and nationalised industry (Bronk and Tikk-Ringas, 2013), and corporate espionage looking to reduce a military capability gap (Gorman *et al.*, 2009; Fritz, 2008).

This chapter considers what, in effect, a cyber-attack actually *is* and sets out a taxonomy of the characteristics of attacks to provide a context in which it is possible to understand cyber-attacks. The taxonomy is intended to explore, manage and understand the consequences of each action. As we decompose these characteristics we provide a number of examples of different cyber-attacks. These examples have been chosen to give an indication of the breadth of attack that a state could launch to achieve a particular mission, rather than to provide a comprehensive list of all possible attacks. Of course, the attack characteristics discussed herein are not restricted to instances of 'cyber warfare' as defined in this volume's Introduction, nor are the examples discussed necessarily of an 'interstate nature' (especially because, as noted, there is limited data on such attacks). However, the key characteristics of cyber-attacks are explored to highlight the actual (and potential) nature of cyber warfare.

From the outset, it is important to define a 'cyber-attack'. There are many definitions of cyber-attacks but we will use one that is built upon the understanding of 'cyber warfare' as outlined in this volume's Introduction, consistent with the aims of this chapter (with a view to being inclusive of a number of atypical, but increasingly common, attacks).

We define a cyber-attack as:

> An electronic attack to a system, enterprise or individual that intends to disrupt, steal or corrupt assets where those assets might be digital (such as data or information or a user account), digital services (such as communications) or a physical asset with a cyber component (such as the process control system found in a building, aircraft or nuclear refinement facility). Typically such attacks seek to compromise the confidentiality, integrity or availability of digital assets, and so cyber security controls seek to preserve these properties in some way.

In this definition of a cyber-attack the term 'electronic' refers to the use of energy to transmit information (in contrast to 'electrical' which is the use of energy to create movement or perform the attack itself – hence using a railgun is not an 'electronic attack'). An electronic attack also includes the electronic data that is applied to the system during the attack (for example, some attacks require carefully crafting specific code to compromise a system).

The remaining terms 'confidentiality', 'integrity' and 'availability' form a classic triad of information security and typically represent the 'goals of security' (Anderson, 2008). There has been some discussion over the last decade as to the inclusion of other fundamental aspects such as 'non-repudiation', 'authenticity', etc. A compromised system will have had at least one of these key principles violated.

Confidentiality is probably the most intuitively desirable characteristic of a secure cyber system. Confidentiality ensures that data and information is only available to those who are authorised to view it. In some cases confidentiality may also include not only the content of a communication but also the fact of a communication (Anderson, 2008). It should be noted that data and information requiring protection take many forms. This can include data associated with preserving access controls across a system or enterprise – i.e. data that is utilised in delivering cyber security. It also includes those assets that would be considered as business-critical and whose confidentiality is essential to maintaining market position.

Integrity can be thought of as relating either to information or an actual service. Information integrity refers to the fact that the information has not been transformed in a manner that is different from the way in which the service was designed, or against the intention of the authorised creator(s). Service, or 'functional', integrity relates to the integrity of the function performed by the service: for example, a system controlling a power plant could have its integrity compromised in order to reduce its efficiency or so that it cannot produce enough power.

Availability refers to the need for it to be possible to use the service or software, when required, in a manner that enables it to perform the function for which it was designed (Anderson, 2008). A client that cannot access a service (or can access only a service that has been degraded so much that it cannot perform the function for which it was designed) has had the 'availability' and, hence, the security of the service compromised.

Despite the fact that cyber-attacks occur within a non-tangible environment, it is worth keeping in mind that these missions will generally appear to be having an effect in the natural world. This is particularly the case in relation to state-sponsored cyber-attacks, where the attacker is likely to be a rational actor (i.e. there will, in most cases, be a 'goal' underpinning the attack). The desired effect in the natural world could simply be to complement, to de-risk or enable a traditional kinetic attack or, as in the case of intelligence gathering, it could be to improve knowledge of a given target.

The low cost of entry to cyberspace and an ability to craft attack software and protocols potentially affords any nation state the ability to launch cyber-attacks. While richer states may be able to launch more sophisticated attacks, it is undeniable that any actor with a modest budget and a small team could be a significant player in a conflict in cyberspace. Given that the barrier to entry into cyber conflict is very low, many commentators (e.g. Denning, 2009) compare the cost of causing comparable effects by way of kinetic attacks with the smaller cost of cyber-attacks; however, this is perhaps an odd comparison since cyberspace has a greater affordance for some results than others. Insurgents looking to create a culture of terror may currently be perceived to prefer a suicide bomber, so as to cause a significant loss of life, rather than a cyber-attack. Having said this, in the future we may see cyberspace offering more affordance for cyber-enabled terror attacks.

This 'affordance' of cyber-attacks could be a strong motivation for some state actors to take to cyberspace in order to provide a capability that, for political or financial reasons, they cannot possess in the natural space. The 'Machete' targeted attack campaign (GREAT, 2014), for example, has targeted embassies, intelligence services and military targets across a number of Latin American states. This particular campaign appears to use the Social Engineering Toolkit (SET), an open-source toolkit that can be downloaded along with significant documentation and a large volume of tutorials all aimed at helping a novice get started with the tool. In this example an entire campaign compromised a significant number of relatively high-value targets throughout an entire continent with a toolset that required little (if any) technical ability. To achieve the same outcomes without using cyberspace would involve a higher risk and be very costly, yet it would have a much lower chance of success.

Another good example of a state-influenced actor is the rise of the Syrian Electronic Army (SEA), which in a relatively short period of time has developed from being a minor nuisance to a group that has, in the last year, compromised parts of Reuters, RSA conference, the *Sun*, the *Sunday Times*, Forbes, Facebook, eBay UK, Paypal UK and Microsoft (HPSR, 2013). Increasingly, despite this group's attacks being relatively simple, it has achieved significant success; and, from this success, it has achieved significant publicity, which has been well-managed so as to elevate the SEA to being a major actor in the cyber skirmishes motivated by geopolitical events in the Levant.

Having set out our core definition of a 'cyber-attack' and noted the increasing prominence of such attacks at the interstate level, we now turn to the technical environment in which cyber-attacks take place.

The technical environment in which cyber-attacks take place

In order to understand cyber-attacks it is necessary to explore the technical environment in which they occur. The section will provide a technical primer to the non-technical reader: the idea will be to provide as much knowledge as is required for understanding both the nature of these attacks and the context in which they occur.

We can define 'cyberspace' as the environment within which electronically mediated communication occurs; it traditionally includes both notionally 'public' areas, such as the Internet, and notionally 'private' networks, such as a corporate networks or a home WiFi network. We can simplify most of these communications using conceptually simple models.

Initially, we focus on a 'service': this is an entity in cyberspace that performs a particular function. This function could be – amongst other things – a data-store (such as a file-hosting service, e.g. DropBox), a social media space (where users can store and share information), a business intelligence product (providing information about a business's stock level, etc.), controlling parts of a power system, a display board in an airport, or a media outlet providing streaming entertainment.

A service is hosted on an infrastructure; this forms the physical facilities and various interacting smaller services that enable the service to function. A data-store service may require an infrastructure that involves a number of machines, interconnected to provide a single 'cloud service'. Other services may simply require a single machine, normally called a 'server', in order to function. Often servers will host multiple services. For example, a web server may host websites, and provide remote access, which allows the developers to connect into the machine and also a mechanism to upload files to the server.

In order to use the service clients must connect to it. In general, communications between two clients are mediated by the service in some way – for example, email between two clients will use a set of services so as appear as peer-to-peer (P2P) communication. Another example is Skype, because, although the content (i.e. the sound and video) is streamed from one client directly to another, the call is initiated via the Skype service – this also provides other functionality such as an address book.

There are few services that are genuinely P2P (i.e. involve no central service provider or node that provides some sort of management services). Some services that can be argued to be P2P include file-sharing services such as BitTorrent, some digital currency such as bitcoin and various malware networks (which use P2P communications to provide a system for communications that protect the malware writers and provide a difficult-to-disrupt communication channel).

In order to enable communication between services (or between clients and services) there is a 'communication protocol'. This protocol defines how information is 'packaged up' to be transmitted across a network; it also defines how infrastructure is labelled to enable traffic to be routed to the correct service. The most common type of communication protocol is the Internet Protocol suite, more commonly called TCP/IP (Transmission Control Protocol/Internet Protocol). This can itself be broken down into four simple 'layers', making it easier to understand. Since the TCP/IP defines how most information is transmitted it is important to understand conceptually that cyber-attacks can occur at all of these levels.

Figure 2.1 shows an example of how a simple request for a website can be broken down into these layers.

The top layer is the application layer – this represents the service itself. For example, if a user is making a request to a website, the application layer on the client side represents the web browser (e.g. Internet Explorer or Chrome). This is where the information is 'understood' and the service is provided to the user; in this example the service is the web server, which understands how to provide the information made in the request. It is important to understand that the application layer has no understanding of how to send this information to the client – it simply knows how to process the request for service.

The raw data from the application layer is then passed to the transport layer, which provides the basic communication channel for the application. In the case of TCP it also provides flow control, connection establishment and the reliable transmission of data. This ensures that, as the information is broken down into small 'packets' of information that the network uses, these packets can be reassembled in the correct order. It also provides the ability to retransmit packets that are in error or have gone missing.

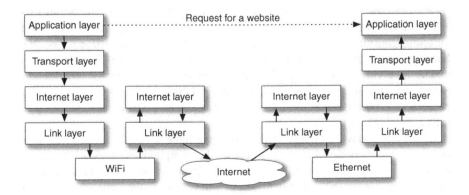

Figure 2.1 A request for a website broken down into the four layers of the Internet Protocol suite (TCP/IP).

The packets from the transport layer are then passed to the Internet layer, which has the task of moving these packets around the network. It provides a networking interface abstracting the actual method of moving the packets: in other words, it essentially defines the Internet. This layer defines the global addressing and routing used in the network (meaning, in the example set out in Figure 2.1, IP addresses). The job of this layer's routing is simply to transport packets to the next point in the network that is closer to the final destination. This way a packet, which contains a small chunk of our information, hops its way across a network to its final destination. It should be noted that the picture in Figure 2.1 only shows the first and last hops – in actuality the Internet is made up of a number of these hops. Each hop requires the packet passing up to the Internet layer to work out the next hop and then the passing down to the link layer to work out how to send the packet to that destination.

The final link layer defines how the network functions within the scope of the local network link; it understands the local network layout and how to transmit the packet onto the medium that carries the information. In the example provided in Figure 2.1, we have further differentiated the link layer for the home WiFi, which understands how to send the packet to the WiFi Access Point/router (having been told by the Internet layer that this is the next hop). The router then understands how to send the information along a copper wire (or optical fibre) to the router at the local exchange, which in turn understands how to send the information to the Internet Service Provider (ISP) router, etc. If we had made our request from a mobile phone then our link layer understands how to control the phone's radio and send the packets to the local base station.

Of course, the human actor should not be overlooked, not least because humans can provide essential elements of a successful cyber-attack. For systems that are hard to attack from the outside (such as hacking in from the Internet) a person with physical access to the internal systems can often provide the essential toe-hold required to launch an attack. This might be via delivery of a piece of malicious code (malware) to a computer inside the system – possibly downloaded from an email or loaded onto the computer from a Universal Serial Bus (USB) drive. These actors are considered 'insiders', and may be involved in a conscious capacity or may, perhaps, be acting without the knowledge of the risk that they are introducing. Many recent security threat reports note a rise in attacks involving insiders. The Stuxnet worm attack launched on the Iranian nuclear refinement facility involved the use of a USB stick to insert malware into the system – although it is not known whether this involved a malicious insider or an accidental act.

By breaking down systems in this way, we have a simple set of tasks that each layer has to perform in order to create the complexity that exists in cyberspace. We can map attacks onto each of these layers in order to understand how these attacks compromise a system: that is, how they violate one or more of a cyber system's confidentiality, integrity or availability.

Cyber-attacks often go beyond the purely technical spaces considered in the definition of cyberspace, so we can enrich the technical scope of the

Understanding cyber-attacks 39

cyber-attacks with two new layers: business and people. The people layer represents the users of a particular client. These are the users of a service in cyberspace. The top level represents the business function. The use of the word 'business' here is perhaps a misnomer, as this represents the overall function that the user is trying to perform: for example, in a power station the 'business function' is to safely provide a certain amount of power at a certain efficiency.

Attack stages

Having explained the environment in which cyber-attacks can occur we can now start to consider different attacks. There is a large range of different 'types' of attack that a defender could face; however, these attacks typically have a number of common stages. These common stages have been extracted in a number of different models, such as the 'Cyber Kill Chain' (Hutchins *et al.*, 2011), the OWASP model of attacks (OWASP, 2013) or the Common Attack Pattern Enumeration and Classification (CAPEC) (MITRE, 2014). The idea of these models is to enable a defender to 'cast' an attack into a model that can then be used to defend or understand the attack. In this section we present a simplified version of an attack that can be used to contextualise the process of performing a cyber-attack.

A typical attack can be split into a number of stages: these are shown in Figure 2.2, across the layers of cyberspace that we have previously introduced.

Reconnaissance

A typical attack will start with a reconnaissance phase. During this phase the intention is to learn as much about the target as possible; this can include information about all the levels of the target as shown in Figure 2.2.

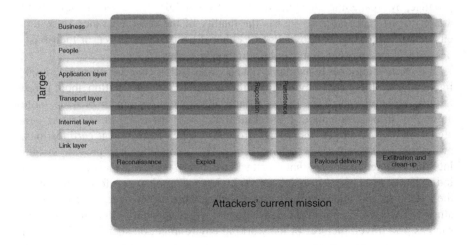

Figure 2.2 A simplified model of attack steps.

The technical infrastructure includes the target's projection into cyberspace, including Internet layer information, such as the IP address ranges associated with the target infrastructure or the application layer services running on the infrastructure that is observable (for example, database servers, web servers, web-proxies, remote access end-points – such as Virtual Private Network (VPN) servers). An understanding of the software providing these services (and the associated software version) will help to identify the most successful avenues to exploitation. This information can be gathered relatively covertly over a period of time using a mixture of port-scanning and banner-grabbing. These are technical processes, where an attacker starts to make a connection to a service (often not completing it properly) and the responses from the server can be used to identify the service, and often the name and version of the software providing that service.

In addition to the technical infrastructure forming the target, it is also important to understand the mitigations that a target may have in place: for example, the target may be employing email filtering (often given away in email headers), the edge protection offered by remote access (for example, two-factor authentication). Also of interest are the business processes that a target may have in place in order to mitigate attacks. Simple unsophisticated attacks can be launched – for example Distributed Denial of Service (DDoS) attacks can be purchased for as little as 30 cents for a 10-minute period from criminal groups (Krebs, 2013) – either to provide cover for more sophisticated attacks or, indeed, to probe the business processes an organisation may have in place to mitigate cyber-attacks.

Reconnaissance surrounding the individuals associated with a target is also important; indeed, in some cases, the individuals may be the actual target of the attack. These social engineering attacks manipulate the people layer in order to release information or perform an action that causes a compromise of security (confidentiality, integrity or availability), or provide an opportunity for a compromise, by weakening the cyber defences (Mann, 2012). For social engineering attacks to be successful the key is the quality of the reconnaissance since this ensures the attacker has knowledge of either the individual target, or their business processes, in order to make the situation believable.

Research using openly available data sources (often called open-source intelligence, or OSINT) can provide a significant amount of information about given targets. Networks such as LinkedIn and StackOverflow can a provide large amount of information about the technical ability of the cyber-defenders associated with a given target (including information such as technical certifications, programming languages, experience, etc.). This knowledge can provide insight into the technical defences that an attacker is likely to face. At a social level, an individual's presence on social network sites will point to information about their hobbies and interests, which may help enable an attacker to better target attacks looking to compromise the individual's user accounts. Other information, such as past travel, pictures of the working environment on social media (which often includes indications an individual's degree of physical security) can provide a rich vein for information gathering.

A good, thorough knowledge of both the individuals using, and the technical infrastructure of, the target, will dramatically improve the chances of the attack being successful. This phase is generally very covert and remote from the target, allowing a significant amount of information to be gathered before there is any form of engagement with it: the attacker can then use this information to preposition themselves before engagement. Depending on the mission (and its desired effect) this period of reconnaissance could be anything from a period of hours to one of months.

Exploit delivery

Once the attacker has gathered enough information and prepositioned themselves, the next stage is to deliver the exploit. This is the stage where a machine or individual is actually compromised – where the target's defences are actually penetrated.

These exploits are unlikely to be unique for specific missions but, rather, to be reused for different missions. An exception to this is when 0-day exploits are used; these are exploits that target bugs in software for which there is no known mitigation. These 0-day attacks are often serious as, for many individuals or organisations, the only mitigation is to not use a particular software product – a mitigation that is often not acceptable.

Thankfully, 0-days are relatively rare occurrences, although there is a healthy underground market within the criminal fraternity for these 0-day exploits and many large cybercrime activities, such as the Zeus botnet, often leverage these new exploits. Since these large activities tend to not be targeted but more indiscriminate in their actions, cyber-defenders such as anti-virus (AV) providers are typically able to learn how to identify these quickly. However, it is worth noting that when these 0-day exploits are used sparingly in targeted attacks the ability of cyber-defenders to identify and arrange mitigations is dramatically reduced. It is nonetheless still noteworthy that many cyber-attacks do not use these esoteric, complex exploits but rely on relatively simple, well-known attacks (OWASP, 2013). Indeed, resorting to 0-days can often highlight the fact that the attacker is an 'advanced' threat. Any attack that uses high-value exploits should therefore be very carefully planned since as soon as a 0-day is identified, its value in attacking 'hard-targets' is dramatically reduced, although targets with lower-skilled defenders may still be vulnerable.

Outside of technical exploits, an attacker can exploit the business and people levels using a variety of different techniques. If the attacker has performed a successful reconnaissance phase against the target they are already in a position where they may be able to exploit vulnerabilities in either the 'business' processes or the individuals associated with the target. Examples of these exploits could be deliberate insider placement where a malicious individual is placed within the target with the covert mission of compromising the target. This individual may be directly responsible for the compromise or may facilitate it, for example by deliberately reducing the defensive capability of the target.

In addition to the placement of individuals in an organisation, it is also possible to place malicious technology within organisations, often through supply chain compromise. This also need not necessarily be overtly 'malicious' technology: it could, for example, involve the use of security appliances (such as firewalls) or cryptographic products that have weaknesses or 'backdoors' that allow access. Backdoors can be incredibly covert: for example, it could be possible to create an Internet router that forwarded particular elements of Internet traffic to an attacker but only after a certain combination of packets were sent to the router. Accusations of these sorts of attacks have been levied at both the United States (alleging the National Security Agency deliberately weakened cryptographic appliances and protocols, see Menn, 2013) and China (where allegations have been made against the state-owned manufacturer Huawei, see Simpson, 2014).

Payload injection

Once the target is compromised, the payload is injected into the compromised machine. This payload stage is where the tasks of achieving the attacker's mission are performed. For some missions, for example intelligence-gathering missions this may involve further exploitation to maintain footholds and move laterally within infrastructure to further improve the attacker's positioning, for example pivoting to reach previously inaccessible parts of a network or to compromise further user accounts. For other missions there may not be a requirement for a lateral movement as the compromised machine or account may include all the resources or access required for the current mission specifics.

During a successful mission there is often an opportunity to maintain a more permanent presence on a system. This 'persistence' allows future access to the compromised systems or user accounts in order to perform future missions (in effect, removing the requirement of an exploit in order to deploy a payload). There are many ways of covertly maintaining presence on a system; however, if the presence is discovered it will alert the target to the fact that it is, in fact, a target and potentially alert it as to other compromised systems that use the same techniques to maintain presence. Despite these risks, it will still be the case that most attackers will create a form of persistence on the compromised system, since the most difficult part of a cyber-attack will, in general, be the exploit phase (hence, having gained access, persistence is often worth the risk for the attacker). Persistence on systems is also often worthwhile as the target's infrastructure will change over time, software will be patched, users will leave or change credentials, hardware will be swapped out, machines will be removed, networks will change – all of these things could threaten the ability to exploit a system in the future where it was once successful.

Persistence is particularly interesting when compromising laptops or other mobile devices (such as smartphones and tablets), as these are very dynamic objects and may appear in many different locations. Here, persistence can potentially provide access into very high-value environments where access would otherwise prove very challenging. However, again, a trade-off must be made in that the initial risk of the mission may be low because the device is in an environment where persistence is unlikely to be detected (for example, at a target's home), but if the device is then moved into a different environment the risk of the persistence being detected may increase (indeed, the risk of action being taken based on this detection may also increase).

The payload associated with each attack will be mission-specific and, for many state actors, will be unique for a given mission (or, at least, be encoded so as to appear unique – there are many ways of changing a piece of software so that it performs the same function but appears to be different to both a machine and a human observer). This massively reduces the risk of the payload being detected by typical end-point security systems, and if it *is* detected by such systems it will be difficult to attribute purely based on this single attack. Where attribution has been achieved, this has generally been through detecting patterns in multiple attacks, or through the detection of common infrastructure, i.e. through the examination of tradecraft (see Chapter 3 of this volume for an examination of the most successful ways of technically attributing cyber-attacks).

Iteration

As with all missions, it is unlikely that attacks will follow a simple flow through all these stages. Some cyber-attacks will involve a level of persistence on a target system that allows for some serendipity and discovery of new assets of interest. This can mean that attacks follow an iteration through the stages in order to formulate onward attacks against potentially new targets. In other cases the attack vehicle is specifically designed to reconfigure itself in order to exploit aspects of a system as they are discovered – again resulting in an iteration through the stages. In this kind of attack a remote control system is required in order for a reach-back mechanism to access new exploits and payloads required to conduct new aspects of the attack. Flame (CrySys, 2012) is a good example of a polymorphic attack, where malware that was focused on gathering intelligence essentially took advantage of any potential communication channels available and was able to carry out many different types of operation, depending upon the target itself.

A taxonomy of attack characteristics

The remaining sections of this chapter will examine the 'exploit stage' of a cyber-attack in some detail, as this essentially constitutes the 'weaponry' of the attack. The exploit stage is also where we can explore the effect of an attack on those individuals who are not associated with the target but are involuntarily targeted in the attack. The 2010 Stuxnet attack can be taken as an example (Falliere *et al.*, 2011). Here, a number of individuals were exploited (i.e. had their security compromised) but the payload searched for the presence of particular control equipment before looking to perform its sabotage mission. In other circumstances it looked to perform different intelligence-gathering missions, and this polymorphism makes it difficult to explore the whole set of possible missions.

We continue by exploring the characteristics that are associated with the exploit stage. There are many taxonomies that look at identifying commonalities in cyber-attacks (Kotenko and Chechulin, 2013; Simmons et al., 2014). However, they tend to focus on similarities in the technical characteristics of attacks – i.e. what *sort* of attack is it? In other words, what is the vulnerability that is to be exploited and the process by which the exploit works. For many applications it is valuable to determine this: for example, classifying attacks based upon the weaknesses that they exploit is important in order to provide insight into the best approaches for mitigating particular attacks and understanding the threats that a defender is currently facing.

Rather than look to classify the attack based on a technical characteristic, we look to consider the characteristics associated with the attack. These characteristics can then help us to consider the effect of attacks on the target, individuals associated with the target but who are not actively a target themselves (often called cyber non-combatants) and the general public; for most audiences, this is more valuable than the technical classifications.

It is worth briefly noting, before turning to the immediate set of six characteristics examined in this section, that there is a further crucial characteristic to any cyber-attack: this is the probability that the attack is ultimately successful. The probability of success is a very important characteristic, as this helps to assess the proportionality of the attack (in combination with the other factors) given the value of the target. In our assessment, an exploit should be considered 'successful' if it provided a suitable platform from which the mission payload could be deployed. We do not consider this within the immediate set of 'characteristics' discussed in this section, since the success of a mission depends on the attack's lateral movement and positioning post-exploit, and also the success of the payload. Therefore, it is difficult to isolate the probability of the attack's success as related only to the exploit stage, as it is a function of the entire mission. Nonetheless, the probability of success is an important factor.

The six characteristics of a cyber-attack at the exploit stage can be assessed by considering the following questions:

1 How *targetable* is the exploit?
2 How much *control* does the attacker has over the exploit?
3 How *persistent* is the exploit?
4 What is the *effect* of the exploit?
5 How *covert* is the attack?
6 How *mitigatable* is the exploit?

This chapter will now consider each of these characteristics and take the opportunity to use some example attacks to illustrate the extremes of each characteristic. These examples will also illustrate the diversity of attacks that are common

Understanding cyber-attacks 45

in cyberspace from the trivial through to the complex. Typically the exploit will depend on the target, the attacker's position and the desired mission (some mission requirements are likely to render certain attacks unsuitable for delivering a payload for that specific mission). We will explain more as we progress through the remainder of the chapter.

Targetability

The first main characteristic we consider is that of targetability. This represents the ability of the attacker to target the exploit at a small-set of system components (such as individuals or infrastructure). When considering any attack, the ability to exploit just the target is significant; a particularly targeted attack that has a very small compromise is easier to control and is arguably more ethically acceptable and more covert.

For state attackers or other advanced threats that are actively targeting mission-specific targets (rather than cybercrime syndicates, which are more concerned with the number of compromised machines), being able to reduce the number of targeted system components can have significant benefits. The most striking technical benefit is a reduction in the effectiveness of traditional endpoint security. Traditional AV products use a set of signatures to look for malicious activity – if an attacker is able to use exploits only on a small number of targets then the likelihood of the exploits being discovered and signatured can be reduced. More complicated AV behavioural analysis, which is aimed at detecting malicious activity based on behaviour rather than on a static set of signatures, is still in its infancy and does not have a good record of protecting against sophisticated targeted attacks (although there are a number of research initiatives around the globe seeking to address this limitation). The targetability characteristic is shown in Table 2.1.

An example of an attack that rates low on the targetability characteristic would be an attack that used a cross-site scripting (XSS) attack on a second-party website. These attacks exploit the application layer of a service by attacking a poorly written website into which an attacker can introduce their own malicious code: many sites are vulnerable to these attacks and hence compromises through them are very common (OWASP, 2013). This malicious code can then attempt to compromise any users visiting the second-party website – while it is possible to steer targets to this particular site using any number of social

Table 2.1 The targetability characteristic

Very high	Can be targeted to an individual user, machine or piece of infrastructure
High	Can be targeted to a reduced known subset of users, machines or pieces of infrastructure (e.g. IP range, corporation)
Medium	Can be targeted to a wider set of users, machines or pieces of infrastructure, but the set is largely unknown
Low	Cannot be targeted

engineering approaches, it is impossible to constrain the attack just to one's target, meaning that any visitor will have the exploit delivered to them. These types of attacks have been seen at state-actor level (Waqas, 2013).

Controllability

The next characteristic that is associated with targetability (although subtly different) is the controllability of the attack. This represents the degree of control that an attacker has on a given attack at any time. This characteristic is shown in Table 2.2.

An example of attacks that rate low in controllability are attacks on the Border Gateway Protocol (BGP) routing tables. These tables are used to route traffic at the Internet Level from one ISP to another. Attacks on these tables are not uncommon (normally through accidental misconfigurations of routers). The result of such attacks is that Internet traffic is rerouted incorrectly into other networks (Cowie, 2010; Beijnum, 2008). These types of attacks are very difficult to control and once a route has been added to the BGP table it cannot be removed (though it can, of course, be overwritten). The routes take an unpredictable amount of time to propagate through the network of routers forming the core Internet. It is also incredibly difficult to predict the effect of a given route on the overall routing table, meaning the controllability of this attack is very low.

In contrast, Structured Query Language (SQL) injection attacks on services are a notably controllable form of cyber-attack: SQL injection attacks target the application layer of a service. SQL injections exploit the incorrect parsing of information provided to a service by a client in order to execute commands on the server hosting the website, effectively by disguising executable commands as content. These attacks are the most common form of attacks seen on the Internet (OWASP, 2013) and, although it is easy to mitigate these attacks, they are still frequently successful. Injection attacks are easily controlled as, typically, the attack is interactive – i.e. the attacker is actively involved in the attack. There are some automated tools that de-skill the attack; it is, however, still very unlikely for a situation to occur where the attacker cannot control the attack.

Persistence

Associated with controllability is the persistence characteristic. It is worth remembering that we are here considering the persistence of the initial exploit

Table 2.2 The controllability characteristic

Very high	Complete control of all aspects during all phases of the attack
High	Complete control of all aspects during phases of the attack
Medium	Some control of some aspects during phases of the attack
Low	No control of any aspects of the attack

rather than the payload. Depending on the mission, the *payload* may last for a significant amount of time (and often it may be mission-critical to retain a permanent presence on a system). Indeed, most of the discovered high-profile missions (APT1, Stuxnet, etc.) involved payloads that exhibited significant levels of persistence: this was both a mission requirement and also a contributing factor to their discovery.

From an exploit perspective, we use 'persistence' to refer to the amount of time that it takes for an attack to stop, i.e. the amount of time the attacker is still able to exploit targets once they have decided to finish the exploit phase of the attack. Persistence in this sense can be considered an aspect of controllability, however it is a very important factor associated with any attack since it is key to managing the effect on cyber non-combatants. The persistence characteristic is shown in Table 2.3.

Persistence is also one of the characteristics that a defender can actually influence. Lots of standard defence mechanisms are not necessarily aimed at stopping attacks but at reducing the impact of an attack; one of the key ways this is done is to reduce the period of time for which the attack can succeed. Promptly updating software and regularly changing passwords are both standard security 'good practice', aimed at reducing the window of opportunity for attackers.

An example of an exploit with a low persistence is brute-forcing attacks on online credentials such as usernames and passwords. Brute-force attacks try usernames and passwords over and over again until successful (rather than targeting specific software vulnerabilities). These tend to focus on application-layer services and look to compromise the attack access points into a corporate network: for example, VPN access, email accounts, etc. These attacks attempt to guess the service's authentication tokens (typically passwords). In general these types of attacks will use dictionaries of common passwords; these common passwords can be either from other breaches, or tailored to a given target exploiting knowledge from the reconnaissance of both individuals and business processes/policies (including password policies within corporate targets – this can massively reduce the difficulty of these attacks). While these attacks are unsophisticated they are often successful, particularly if a good level of reconnaissance has been performed.

There are two competing motivations associated with these sorts of attacks targeting online credentials. The first is that the attacker may need to check thousands or millions of potential passwords against the target, which implies that they need to check potential passwords as fast as possible. However, an attempt

Table 2.3 The persistence characteristic

Very high	Exploit phase of attack continues for an unknown period of time
High	Exploit phase of attack continues for in excess of ~ hours
Medium	Exploit phase of attack stops in a short period of time and that period is understood (~ hours)
Low	Exploit phase of attack stops immediately (~ minutes)

to quickly identify a password will be easily detectable by even a low-skilled defender. A more covert approach is to slow down the 'guessing' so that the attacker is less likely to be detected, but then the attack will take a significant amount of time. Whichever of these approaches is taken the persistence is low: slower attacks are easily stopped instantaneously while fast, distributed, multi-threaded attacks are unlikely to take longer than a few minutes to stop. As discussed above, the cyber defender can influence the persistence of this particular attack; using credentials in a way that is uncharacteristic for a given user can be detected (e.g. logging on to remote end-point late at night) and the account temporarily suspended. Alternatively, requiring users to periodically change their passwords reduces the availability of the exploit.

In contrast to the brute-forcing attacks, techniques such as supply chain compromise display a high level of persistence. These are sophisticated attacks that look to compromise systems by supplying infrastructure that has, for example, compromised cryptographic subsystems thus making the target easier to attack, or, indeed, building a backdoor into a subsystem (in effect meaning that the subsystem is supplied exploited). These attacks look to compromise the integrity of the target, either by providing technology that is pre-exploited or by making it easier to compromise the target if the attacker has the requisite knowledge of the backdoor/weakness.

Such supply chain compromises can be difficult to detect, and backdoors and compromised crypto can be subtle and notably covert. A large number of allegations have been made against both the United States (Menn, 2013) and China (Simpson, 2014), to the effect that these states have provided compromised systems in this manner. These attacks rate very high on the persistence characteristic – it is very difficult to know for how long the attack will continue once it has been launched, and infrastructure may stay in use for a significant period of time after the mission has been completed.

Effect

The next characteristic that helps to explore cyber-attacks is that of the effect, meaning the *consequences* of the attack. At this point it is worth reiterating that in this section we are discussing the effect of the exploit and not of the payload. The effect of the payload may be significant and may often *be* the mission. For example the goal of Stuxnet appears subtly (but fundamentally) to change the performance of the centrifuges employed in the Iranian nuclear processing plants (Falliere et al., 2011). We have also seen attacks on South Korean broadcasters and banking institutes (Branigan, 2013) and the Saudi Aramco (Bronk and Tikk-Ringas, 2013): both of these attacks had missions that appeared to be to destroy data and systems in order to reduce an organisation's ability to undertake a mission.

The effect of the exploit is perhaps the hardest characteristic to quantify, as an observer, because the victim of an attack is unlikely to disclose its full effect (particularly if that victim is a corporation or a state). In some situations, such as where a large amount of Personally Identifiable Information (PII) has had the confidentiality compromised, there may be a legal requirement for the release to

Understanding cyber-attacks 49

be disclosed. However, for states, it is unlikely that the effect of a cyber-attack would be disclosed to the general press (or, indeed, to anyone who was unable to directly action a response). State actors, unlike low-skilled attackers (often called 'script kiddies'), are also unlikely to announce that an attack has been *successful*. After all, one of the affordances of cyberspace for offensive operations is that attacks can be kept secret (on the issue of attributing cyber-attacks to a state in either a factual or a legal sense, see Chapter 5 of this volume).

It can also be difficult to predict the wider effects of an exploit; counteracting the defences of a target can have unpredictable results, not only for the target but for others that are associated with the target (but are, themselves, not actively a target), an example of which could be other users of a shared infrastructure. These cyber non-combatants can be affected to the same degree as a target but for no legitimate or operational reason, other than that they share use of a particular server or communication channel.

Table 2.4 explains the effect characteristic associated with exploit phase of cyber-attacks.

An example of an attack that has little effect is 'DNS poisoning'. The Domain Name System (DNS) provides the process by which a networked device resolves a domain name (e.g. bbc.co.uk) to an IP address (e.g. 212.58.244.18). Individual machines can be compromised by altering the DNS records local to the machine or whole networks can have false records injected into their DNS tables. With a poisoned DNS cache in place, devices can have traffic to specific websites redirected to the attacker. The attacker can then view (compromise the confidentiality) or interfere (compromise the integrity) of the system with this information before relaying it to the original service. For the user or the infrastructure this will, in general, have little effect other than a slightly increasing the flight time for some network activity.

There are many exploits that have the potential to do damage to a machine. Typically this is likely to not damage hardware (although some attacks may inadvertently disable cooling fans, etc.) but will commonly crash applications, or – when not successful – an exploit can cause kernel panics (the 'blue screen of death' on Windows machines), which can often damage operating systems.

Some attacks require a high degree technical proficiency. This is particularly the case, for example, in relation to exploits that target technical errors in products, such as 'buffer-overflows' (that is, the targeting of mistakes in the code that makes up a program, allowing an attacker to alter the behaviour of the program in order to execute their own code in another part of the machines memory). The technical nature of attacks of this sort necessarily means that they will not be

Table 2.4 The effect characteristic

Very high	Significant damage to infrastructure or machines
High	Some damage to infrastructure or machines
Medium	Users inconvenienced
Low	No observable effect

successful all of the time, and when they are unsuccessful they will commonly crash applications or potentially hang machines. This is an example where the attack has failed and yet the target is still affected.

There can also be unexpected effects even when an attack is successful – an example is the DDoS attacks on Boston Hospital, which were attributed to the Anonymous collective as part of #opJustina (although it should be noted there was some public disagreement within Anonymous and the attack is often referred to as coming from a 'fringe element'). These attacks resulted in several related sites being taken down, including sites that patients and doctors use to check test results and manage appointments, as well as the main hospital's donation site. The attack was more or less successful, in that it resulted in several websites being taken down (although, ironically, the main hospital site was kept up). The mission can also arguably be seen as being successful because there was an increase in awareness of Justina Pelletier's case: however, the attack had significant effects on the hospital and ultimately the patients that it serves. In addition, the attack has undoubtedly damaged the public profile of Anonymous.

Covertness

For many attackers the ability to perform covert attacks is particularly desirable, both at a political level and at a mission-enabling level. Covertness is a requirement of a number of missions – it will generally be the case that the target should not be aware they are being compromised. Indeed, where a cyber-attack is enabling (or de-risking) a physical action – whether a covert action as part of an intelligence operation or an overt action such as a kinetic attack – it is critical to the mission that the exploit is covert. In our definition of covert we are not concerned about *attribution* (i.e. who is performing the attack) but the question of the extent to which the victim is aware that an ongoing attack is being perpetrated. Table 2.5 shows the characteristics associated with the covertness.

An example of a covert attack is the QUANTUM family of attacks, which were allegedly used by the US National Security Agency (Weaver, 2014). These allegedly form an Internet-scale man-in-the-middle (MITM) attack: the QUANTUM family appears to identify the connections that are of interest (for example, the downloading of Jihadist material) and then performs some action upon these connections. Different members of the QUANTUM family perform different actions upon the connection, for example inserting malicious code on a webpage (QUANTUMINSERT) (Farivar, 2013). These attacks are particularly covert as it is impossible to identify that an exploit is occurring.

Table 2.5 The covertness characteristic

Very high	Impossible to identify an attack is ongoing
High	Difficult to identify an attack is ongoing
Medium	Some work is required to identify an attack
Low	Attack is easy to identify

An example of an attack that is not covert is a phishing attack. Phishing is the act of providing a client with fake login page to a service and tricking the user into surrendering their authentication and identification information, and such attacks are a common threat to any Internet connected individual. Typically this is done by sending a fake email although it is also often done through fake wireless access points (particularly where physical access to a target area can be achieved).

A phishing attack looking to target a specific user or set of users, which is the most likely scenario for state-sponsored attacks, is generally going to be more sophisticated than a simple attack looking to acquire Facebook data or generic email accounts. More sophisticated attacks will look to mimic the end-point services provided by an organisation (e.g. the cloning of a corporate webmail login page) and will often purchase domains and certificates closely resembling either the target domains or matching the 'story' associated with the email. For example, an email purporting to come from the human resources department at Widget Corp. asking an employee to login into check their pension statement at www.secure.pension-widget.com is likely to be very successful. This is another example where a good reconnaissance can act as a significant force-multiplier in an attack. Phishing attacks are self-evidently not covert, indeed, they are designed to be as overt as possible covering as many users as possible. This will undoubtedly make this sort of attack unsuitable for some missions.

Mitigatable

The final characteristic that needs to be considered is how mitigatable a particular attack is. This can be thought of as the level of difficulty in preventing the attack, which is therefore something that is also related to an attack's covertness. An especially covert attack that is impossible to detect is also likely to be difficult to mitigate, however it is often possible to take precautionary measures to mitigate attacks. For example, a supply chain compromise may be difficult to detect but can be mitigated, to some degree, by using a small set of trusted suppliers. Table 2.6 defines the mitigatable characteristic.

An example of an attack that is incredibly difficult, if not impossible, to mitigate is an amplified DDoS attack. Denial of Service (DoS) attacks are those that aim to stop a system or service from assisting its intended users. At their earliest inception DoS attacks would come from a single point, exploiting a number of weaknesses in the Internet protocol stack to render a service unusable; however, attacks from a single point are relatively easy to block using standard end-point

Table 2.6 The mitigatable characteristic

Very high	Impossible to mitigate
High	Difficult to mitigate by an organisation, impossible for a home user
Medium	Mitigatable by a knowledgeable user
Low	Mitigatable by any user or organisation

security appliances. In order to circumvent such defences these attacks grew in complexity to become distributed; with coordinated attacks occurring from a number of different sources. This coordination can either be social arrangements of groups of individuals performing attacks to create an ad-hoc distribution of attacks (as seen, for example, in the attacks by the Anonymous group that formed Project Chanology and Operation Payback) or technically coordinated attacks using a large distributed architecture such as a botnet. The latter are dramatically more successful since it is difficult to identify malicious traffic from genuine traffic and hence the defensive response can often also contribute to the DoS by blocking genuine traffic.

With the advent of cloud technologies it is harder for DDoS to block service to users, since these technologies allow the spreading of the traffic volume across a scalable number of machines that allows the service to be provided to the users. The ability to spread the volume of the attack across a significant number of machines has led to the arrival of amplified DDoS attacks.

Amplified DDoS attacks create very large volumes of traffic to be directed to a target in the hope that even cloud infrastructures cannot mitigate the load or that the connection to or from the infrastructure is overloaded. In effect these attacks amplify their volume using misconfigured technology in order to achieve very high volumes of attack. The Spamhaus attack in early 2014, for example, used a reflected DNS amplification to achieve volumes in excess of 300 gigabytes a second, which was sustained for around half an hour, the next day an attack of around 290 gigabytes a second was sustained for nearly 75 minutes (Cumming, 2014). This was an unprecedented volume of traffic, the equivalent of downloading around 1.2 million HD (high definition) movies over the period. The Spamhaus attack only required one controller using 10 compromised servers on three different networks that allowed 9 Gbps to the DNS networks in order to generate in excess of 300 Gbps of attack traffic.

Other more efficient amplification techniques can exploit Network Time Protocol (NTP) servers, and this has the potential to generate more attack traffic than DNS attacks with significantly less compromised infrastructure; theoretically Simple Network Management Protocol (SNMP) amplification could offer another order of magnitude on these attacks.

While some expensive dedicated technologies – such as that provided by CloudFlare, for example – claim that they can mitigate some of these sorts of attacks, a coordinated large DDoS attack could still cause enough disruption to degrade a service to the degree that it is effectively denied and the mission is successful.

Other potentially unmitigatable DDoS attacks could target mobile telephone networks. Cellular networks are very fragile and built on technology that is now approaching 25 years old; even 3G technology shares elements of the underlying GSM networks, particularly for backhaul connections from base stations. At the time of writing a number of smartphone-based botnets are appearing; this platform of compromised phones could easily limit the functionality of a cellular network. A small number of phones in a number of cells could degrade the ability of a network to handle new phones entering the area or correctly distribute phones to neighbouring cells.

It is, of course, worth noting – given the focus of this volume – that DDoS attacks have been used in a number of high-profile instances of seemingly state-orchestrated (or state-sponsored) acts of cyber warfare. The DDoS attacks against Estonia in 2007, and those launched in the context of the Russia–Georgia armed conflict of 2008, are two notable examples (see Chapter 1 of this volume for discussion of these particular DDoS attacks). The difficulty in mitigating DDoS attacks understandably makes them particularly appealing to state actors seeking to maximise the impact of attacks on the virtual battlefield.

Examples of attack characteristics

In the previous section, we examined six characteristics in order to help describe cyber-attacks. In so doing, we explored the extremes of the 'scales' for each characteristic, so as to elucidate the particular characteristics themselves. In this section, we provide three separate examples of attacks broken down into their constituent characteristics. The first of these examples is a traditional simple attack used for everything from script kiddies, through cybercrime to state attackers looking to target high-profile individuals. The second example is a very sophisticated attack of the sort that (while, in theory, almost any significant actor could launch it) few actors other than states are likely to be able to turn into a platform for a mission. The final example attack is one that looks to exploit the people layer of a target in order to gather intelligence.

Example 1

The first example is a relatively simple drive-by attack, which is one of the easiest cyber-attacks to perpetrate. Given their simplicity, drive-by attacks are often employed by cybercriminals as a way of dropping payloads on machines. However, state actors have also used this sort of attack against a number of (presumably) lower-value targets. Drive-by attacks are generally launched from a compromised website: that is, a website that has been poorly designed (and/or poorly written), which allows an attacker to add their own code to the site. This code will generally either attempt to automatically download the payload to the target's machine or trick the user into downloading the code (for example, using a popup with an OK button which then downloads the file). The attacker then looks to trick the target into running the payload.

The drive-by download attack displays the following characteristics:

> **Targetability** – *Medium*. These attacks generally use compromised legitimate websites, meaning that it can be difficult to target individual users. If a good degree of reconnaissance has been performed then it should be possible to target a restricted group of users with the malicious content. Technical filtering could reduce exposure to the set of IP addresses from which

visitors should have the malware delivered, however this level of complexity will not necessarily constrain the attack just to individual users or machines, except in exceptional circumstances.

Controllability – *Medium*. While they are adding the code to a website the attacker has full control over the code that is added. However, once the code is on the compromised site there may be no way of altering or correcting the code should there be an error. It may also be difficult to switch to a different payload should the mission evolve over time.

Persistence – *Medium/High*. The ability to stop an attack is highly dependent on the nature of the compromised site. For example, if the website is a blog with comments that are not correctly sanitised then it will be possible to upload malicious code within a comment. If this occurs, then whenever the comment is displayed on screen the malicious code has the opportunity to download the payload to the user's machine. At the end of the engagement it may be possible to delete the comment and hence stop the attack; however it may also be impossible to delete comments, in which case the attack will continue indefinitely.

Effect – *Low*. The attack itself is unlikely to do anything to inconvenience the user, the mission-specific payload may do damage or cause inconvenience but the drive-by download is unlikely to inconvenience the user in any way.

Covertness – *Low*. The attack is in no way covert – it is very clear that there is something happening. Instead, the attack relies on the target either being poorly trained or ignoring their training.

Mitigation – *Low*. The attack can technically be mitigated by any user or organisation. However, as with any attack there is still a chance that a well-targeted attack built on a good level of reconnaissance could be successful.

The characteristics of this simple cyber-attack indicate that it will be most appropriate for low-value targets in general missions.

Example 2

In contrast to a simple drive-by attack, we can consider Border Gateway Protocol (BGP) routing attacks, which have been touched upon above. To reiterate, the BGP table controls how traffic is routed from one ISP to another. More specifically, the Internet can itself be thought of as a collection of Autonomous Systems (ASs), all of which have their own AS Number (ASN). An AS is a collection of routing prefixes that presents a clearly defined routing policy to the rest of the Internet (RFC1930), 1996], typically an ISP may have one or more ASNs. BGP tables control how traffic is routed from one AS to another, and form the core process by which traffic is routed around the Internet.

This routing system is susceptible to a number of attacks that can allow an attacker to advertise or adjust routes. This has happened a number of times in the past simply because of operational errors at ISPs (Beijnum, 2008); however, a suitably skilled attacker can perform these attacks and reroute portions of the Internet. While the attack itself is not difficult to perform, managing the result of the attack and being able to generate a platform to launch a successful mission potentially requires a large amount of resources.

An attack on the BGP routing tables is likely to exhibit the following characteristics:

> **Targetability** – *Low/Medium*. While it is possible to target a particular route from one AS to another, there will be a knock-on effect to other ASs, particularly if it is multi-homed (meaning connected to more than one AS) or a transit AS (used by other ASs to relay traffic). While it is arguably possible to get a rough idea of the effect of changing a particular route, it is difficult to be confident when a new route is added.
>
> **Controllability** – *Low*. Once the new route is added to the BGP table, it is impossible to control the effects. The only way to change is to add a new route to the table, effectively overwriting the original route.
>
> **Persistence** – *Very High*. It is impossible to predict the persistence of a particular route. The routing table is massively complex and no single site ever has perfect visibility of the entire table, meaning that it is not possible to fully predict the effect of a single malicious route.
>
> **Effect** – *Low*. The attack has the effect of redirecting traffic through a different route. It is unlikely that this will inconvenience the user in any way – there will be a slight increase in the latency of the connection but the attack itself is unlikely to inconvenience the target. However, an attack like this can result in a large amount of traffic for the attacker to deal with, and the mission itself may significantly delay the processing of traffic (which, in turn, may lead to users being inconvenienced or indeed their traffic being black-holed and not reaching its intended destination). However, a BGP routing attack is unlikely to damage any infrastructure.
>
> **Covertness** – *High*. These attacks are covert, in that it is difficult for most users to understand if an attack is ongoing. It is one of the few attacks where it is possible to look back at an attack and get a relatively good picture of what happened, but it can take some time to collect and process the information surrounding the complete set of route changes. Hence it is difficult to triage while an attack is ongoing, and individuals and, indeed, enterprises are unable to identify or explore these attacks.

Mitigation – *Very High*. To all intents and purposes it is impossible to mitigate against BGP routing attacks. Even ASs that are Tier 1 – meaning that any other AS can be reached without purchasing an IP transit or paying settlements – may still rely on other networks to deliver their traffic to other ASs: as such, there is a dependency on others. There are many legitimate reasons to update the routing table, which makes identifying malicious changes in real time a very challenging (if not impossible) task.

Example 3

The final example of an attack is one that targets the people layer. This attack is a social engineering attack that looks to exploit online social networks. It involves the attacker creating a fake profile on a social network imitating the target. Attacks of this sort have been identified as targeting senior NATO commanders (Hopkins, 2012). In one case, for example, the attacker created a number of profiles pretending to be Admiral James Stavridis. The intention behind such attacks is to lure individuals into making contact or 'friending' the fake account and then using this contact to gather intelligence about the target. These sorts of targeted attacks are trivial to launch and can be very successful.

The characteristics associated with this particular attack are:

Targetability – *Low*. It is impossible to control who is likely to find the profile and 'friend' the profile, it is possible to increase the targeting to specific individuals by sending them messages. However, in general, social networks are very good at suggesting users who may be associated with the target and hence there is a good chance that other individuals may be inadvertently targeted.

Controllability – *Medium*. As this attack is interactive there is a degree of control over the exact constituents of the attack, however there is an initial untargeted nature to the attack which makes it difficult to control all aspects of it.

Persistence – *Very High*. It is almost impossible to estimate the persistence of these attacks. The attack will continue until the target (or a designated authority) identifies the fake page, notifies the social network and the social network actions the request. This process can take an undetermined length of time.

Effect – *Low*. The effect of the exploit phase of the attack on the victims and the target is low. However the wider consequences of the success are significant. The attack may also involve those friends and family of the target (potentially children), which may also have the effect of further attacks being perpetrated against them.

Covertness – *Low*. The attacks are not covert, as it will be very difficult to conceal the attack from the target.

Mitigation – *Low*. Although the attacks are not covert, the geographically distributed nature of social networks in cyberspace mean that it can be difficult to alert all potential victims that an attack is ongoing and to avoid the fake profiles of the target.

Influences on attack tool choices

Given the large amount of potential attacks that can be used to achieve a mission, it is interesting to explore the factors affecting this choice. An initial factor is the mission goal and the payload that the attack is going to deliver; this ultimately sets the level of access required by the exploit. Some attacks can be disregarded immediately by a would-be attacker because the result of the attack will not be a platform from which the payload will can be launched.

There is also a requirement for attackers to understand the defences and technical capability of the target: in other words, to fully understand the threat to the discovery of the mission. For example, an attack on an embassy's IT system is likely to have a higher risk of discovery than one targeted at an individual's home computer. This threat of discovery can be reduced by the choosing an attack with a higher degree of covertness, and should also be evaluated in the context of the action that a defender could take following discovery. If a state defender discovers a 0-day exploit then it is likely to be able to action more in the way of a defence (including alerting AV vendors of appropriate signatures). This could render an expensive attack (and signature of 'tradecraft') unsuitable for high-value targets. In contrast, in the unlikely event an individual discovers a 0-day exploit from state malware, they are unlikely to be able to action a response that will have such consequences.

As with all forms of attack (in both the natural space and cyberspace) the key decision in relation to the means and methods of the attack is the value of the mission versus the value of the assets that could be lost. In the case of cyber-attacks, the assets are the exploit, exploit delivery method and payload. In addition to these assets, an attacker has to balance the risk of exposing their tradecraft. This is the way that an attacker goes about building the attack. It is the sum of weak signals in the coding of the exploit, the infrastructure used to deliver the exploit and the goals of the mission payload. This tradecraft is correlated over a number of attacks in order to build up a picture of the attacker; this is typical behaviour for any defender in a hostile environment. Good examples of collected data on the tradecraft of particular attackers include the Symantec report on Stuxnet (Falliere *et al.*, 2011) and the Mandiant report on APT1 (Mandiant, 2013).

The attacker must always fundamentally balance this risk of compromise with the value of the mission, in addition to choosing the simplest exploit that is required to get a mission achieved successfully. There is no merit in risking high-value assets and high-value tradecraft on a low-value mission. We see many state-sponsored (or at least state-influenced) missions that use open-source attack tools such as the Poison Ivy Trojan or use parts of the Zeus crimeware. A recent targeted attack campaign dubbed 'Machete' (GREAT, 2014) targeted embassies, intelligence services and military targets across a number of Latin American appeared to use the Social Engineering Toolkit (SET) and proved to be very successful.

Balancing the resources of a state arsenal between a greater number of low-value targets and a smaller number of high-value targets is one of the challenges in state-on-state cyber activity. Many states use sponsored (or at least influenced) groups to perform their low-value attacks. This insulates their high-value assets from risk, while not compromising the ability of the state to perform attacks on low-value targets.

Conclusion

In this chapter we have introduced a number of different attacks and placed them in context by defining the characteristics of each attack. The six characteristics (and the probability of mission success) not only allow an observer to explore the context of a particular cyber-attack but also help us to understand an attacker's rationale in the choice of a particular attack.

We have highlighted a number of attacks that are difficult to target precisely and those that are very persistent. It is worth reiterating that we have only considered the exploit phase of the attack, i.e. the element of the attack that punches through the target's defences. The next phase of the attack, the payload delivery, is the part of the attack where the mission is actually conducted, whether this mission involves intelligence gathering, the degradation of a target's ability to defend itself or, indeed, the causing of a physical effect. It is worth noting that if the exploit is well targeted, then the payload will be delivered only to the target and – although a payload is likely to have some additional fallout – it is likely to be better constrained within the target. A better targeted attack therefore not only has 'cyber humanitarian' benefits but also may improve the covertness of an attack (which, in turn, improves the likelihood of both the exploit and payload delivery being successful, and hence increases the likelihood of a mission success).

Throughout this chapter we have assumed a certain skill level for the attacker and a good level of reconnaissance consistent with what we know about state actors. It is worth noting that both the effectiveness of attacks, covertness and the degree of targetability and controllability are entirely dependent on the *ability* of the attacker to design and construct the exploit and payload. An unskilled or unresourced attacker may not be able to achieve these goals and, as such, attacks may be poorly executed resulting in a greater collateral damage, and significant second- or third-order effect.

It is perhaps these poorly executed cyber-attacks from unskilled or unresourced attackers that pose the greatest threat to the open, stable Internet that now forms so much of the financial, cultural and social fabric of our lives. In the context of interstate cyber-attacks, however – for all of the 'levelling' affect that conflict in cyberspace has for 'weaker' states – success commonly remains dependant on the skill level and resources of the attacker.

References

Anderson, R. (2008) *Security engineering: A guide to building dependable distributed systems*, 2nd edition, Indianapolis: Wiley.

Beijnum, I. (2008) 'Insecure routing redirects YouTube to Pakistan', 25 February, *Arstechnica* [online], available: http://arstechnica.com/uncategorized/2008/02/insecure-routing-redirects-youtube-to-pakistan/ [23 September 2014].

Branigan, T. (2013) 'South Korea on alert for cyber-attacks after major network goes down', 20 March, *Guardian* [online], available: www.theguardian.com/world/2013/mar/20/south-korea-under-cyber-attack [25 September 2014].

Bronk, C. and Tikk-Ringas, E. (2013) 'The cyber attack on Saudi Aramco', *Survival*, vol. 55, no. 2, pp. 81–96.

Cowie, J. (2010) 'China's 18-minute mystery', 10 November, *Renesys* [online], available: www.renesys.com/2010/11/chinas-18-minute-mystery/ [25 September 2014].

Cumming, J.C. (2014) 'Understanding and mitigating NTP-based DDoS attacks', 9 January, *CloudFlare* [online], available: http://blog.cloudflare.com/understanding-and-mitigating-ntp-based-ddos-attacks [25 September 2014].

CrySyS (2012) 'sKyWIper (a.k.a. Flame a.k.a Flamer): A complex malware for targeted attacks', 31 May, *Laboratory of Cryptography and System Security (CrySyS Lab)* [online], available: www.crysys.hu/skywiper/skywiper.pdf [25 September 2014].

Denning, D.E. (2009) 'Barriers to entry: are they lower for cyber warfare?', *IO Journal*, vol. 1, no. 1, pp. 6–10.

Falliere, N., Muchu, L. and Chien, E. (2011) 'W32.Stuxnet Dossier', February, *Symantec Security Response* [online], available: www.symantec.com/content/en/us/enterprise/media/security_response/whitepapers/w32_stuxnet_dossier.pdf [26 August 2014].

Farivar, C. (2013) 'UK spies continue "quantum insert" attack via LinkedIN, Slasdot pages', 10 November, *ArsTechnica* [online], available: http://arstechnica.com/tech-policy/2013/11/uk-spies-continue-quantum-insert-attack-via-linkedin-slashdot-pages/ [25 September 2014].

Fritz, J. (2008) 'How China will use cyber warfare to leapfrog in military competitiveness', *Culture Mandala: The Bulletin of the Centre for East–West Cultural and Economic Studies*, vol. 8, no. 1, Article 2.

Global Research and Analysis Team (GREAT), Kaspersky Labs (2014) 'El machete', 20 August, *SecureLIST* [online], available: https://securelist.com/blog/research/66108/el-machete/ [25 September 2014].

Gorman, S., Cole, A. and Dreazen, Y. (2009) 'Computer spies breach fighter-jet project', 21 April, *Wall Street Journal* [online], available: http://online.wsj.com/news/articles/SB124027491029837401 [25 September 2014].

Hopkins, N. (2012) 'China suspected of Facebook attack on NATO's supreme allied commander', 11 March, *Guardian* [online], available: www.theguardian.com/world/2012/mar/11/china-spies-facebook-attack-nato [25 September 2014].

HP Security Research (HPSR) (2013) 'Understanding the Syrian Electronic Army (SEA)', 24 April, *HP Security Research Blog* [online], available: http://h30499.www3.

hp.com/t5/HP-Security-Research-Blog/Understanding-the-Syrian-Electronic-Army-SEA/ba-p/6040559 [25 September 2014].

Hutchins, E.M., Cloppert, M.J. and Amin, R.M. (2011) 'Intelligence-driven computer network defense informed by analysis of adversary campaigns and intrusion kill chains', in Ryan, J. (ed.), *Leading Issues in Information Warfare and Security Research*, vol. 1, Reading: Academic Publishing International, pp. 78–104.

Kotenko, I. and Chechulin, A. (2013) 'A cyber attack modeling and impact assessment framework', in Podins, K., Stinissen, J. and Maybaum, M. (eds), *2013 5th International Conference on Cyber Conflict (CyCon)*, Tallinn: NATO CCD COE Publications, pp. 1–24.

Krebs, B. (2013) 'DDoS services advertise openly, take PayPal', 13 May, *Krebs on Security* [online], available: http://krebsonsecurity.com/2013/05/ddos-services-advertise-openly-take-paypal [4 September 2014].

Mann, M.I. (2012) *Hacking the human: Social engineering techniques and security countermeasures*, Aldershot: Gower.

Mandiant (2013) 'APT1: Exposing one of China's cyber espionage units', *Mandiant Intelligence Center Report* [online], available: http://intelreport.mandiant.com/ [25 September 2014].

Menn, J. (2013) 'Exclusive: secret contract tied NSA and security industry pioneer', 20 December, *Reuters* [online], available: www.reuters.com/article/2013/12/21/us-usa-security-rsa-idUSBRE9BJ1C220131221 [24 October 2014].

MITRE (2014) 'Common attack pattern enumeration and classification', *MITRE* [online], available: https://capec.mitre.org/ [24 October 2014].

NSHC (2013) '3.20 South Korea Cyber Attack', 22 March, *Red Alert Research Report* [online], available: http://training.nshc.net/KOR/Document/virus/20130321_320Cyber TerrorIncidentResponseReportbyRedAlert%28EN%29.pdf [25 September 2014].

OWASP (2013) 'OWASP Top 10–2013', *Open Web Application Security Project* [online], available: http://owasptop10.googlecode.com/files/OWASP%20Top%2010%20-%202013.pdf [25 September 2014].

Weaver, N. (2014) 'A close look at the NSA's most powerful Internet attack tool', 13 March, *Wired* [online], available: www.wired.com/2014/03/quantum/ [25 September 2014].

'RFC1930, 1996': Hawkinson, J. and Bates, T., 'Guidelines for creation, selection, and registration of an Autonomous System (AS)', March 1996, Request for Comments: 1930 BBN Planet, BCP: 6, Best Current Practice MCI [online], available: http://tools.ietf.org/pdf/rfc1930.pdf [24 January 2015].

Rid, T. (2013) *Cyber war will not take place*, London: Hurst.

Simmons, C., Shiva, S., Bedi, H. and Dasgupta, D. (2014) 'AVOIDIT: A cyber attack taxonomy', 9th Annual Symposium on Information Assurance (ASIA'14), 3–4 June, Albany [online], available: www.albany.edu/iasymposium/proceedings/2014/6-SimmonsEtAl.pdf [25 September 2014].

Simpson, P. (2014) 'British government drops Huawei devices amid security concerns', 14 January, *South China Morning Post* [online], available: www.scmp.com/news/world/article/1405044/british-government-drops-huawei-devices-amid-security-concerns [24 October 2014].

Waqas, (2013) 'Tunisian cyber army founds XSS vulnerability on Pentagon websites', 10 March, *HackRead* [online], available: http://hackread.com/tunisian-cyber-army-founds-xss-vulnerability-on-pentagon-website/ [25 September 2014].

3 The attribution of cyber warfare[1]

Neil C. Rowe

Introduction

When I discuss the planning of cyber-attacks on the United States by other states, the usual reaction of military officers is: 'why can't we attack them back?' Usually counterattack is a key strategy and tactic in warfare, providing an important deterrent against attacks, but it is hard to do in the context of cyber warfare. In part, this is due to the difficulty of assessing the damage of cyber-attacks and the difficulties of controlling a cyber-counterattack (Rowe, 2010). An even more significant problem, however, is determining who attacked you and proving it to the world (Goel, 2011).

The United States recently indicted some alleged Chinese hackers for stealing important business secrets by cyber espionage (Nakashima, 2014), but proving these allegations will be very difficult because of the ease of faking data in cyberspace. Establishing responsibility for cyber warfare is a similar problem. On the other hand, when the Russian army invaded Crimea in 2014, Russia's initial denial of involvement did not convince anyone since it was the only neighbouring state and the invaders were speaking Russian. Similarly, when aircraft drop munitions on another state, their flight paths can be traced and usually a single state can be identified as their source. Attribution in the context of cyber warfare presents unique difficulties that are not apparent in other conventional means and methods of armed conflict.

Several factors contribute to the difficulty of cyber warfare attribution:

- Cyber weapons have considerably more variety than conventional munitions, since there are many ways that computers and networks can be disabled. This means that searching for cyber weapons and their use is considerably harder than searching for other kinds of weapons and their use.
- Cyber weapons do not require physical proximity of the attacker to the victim (Brenner, 2007). Since information is automatically and quickly forwarded on the Internet to wherever it needs to go, it is almost as easy to cyber-attack a site on the opposite side of the world as a geographically proximate site.
- Cyber-attacks will be unlikely to come with intrinsic attribution data, unlike uniforms for military personnel and markings for military vehicles.

- Cyber weapons do not leave persistent traces like chemical residue, fingerprints, or perpetrator DNA since digital data can be easily overwritten to leave no trace of the original data.
- Cyber weapons are easy to conceal because they are just abstract patterns of bits, looking just like legitimate data and programs until subjected to detailed inspection. This means they can easily be trafficked across the Internet, making them accessible to small or less powerful states, as well as terrorist groups.
- Cyber weapons can easily implement delayed effects after they are installed, waiting for the right conditions or specified times to act. This means that the relationship the between cause and effect of a cyber weapon can be difficult to see.
- Cyber weapons technology is very similar to cyber espionage technology: the main challenges for both are to gain access to adversary computer systems and establish a foothold. This means that it is difficult to distinguish counterattack-justifying behaviour from routine espionage.

These difficulties in attribution make cyber weapons appealing for many countries, and suggest that we will see the increasing use of such weapons by nation states (Geers et al., 2013). Despite the abovementioned difficulties, however, attribution of cyber-attacks is definitely possible. The evidence will always be circumstantial in the legal sense since cyber-attacks cannot be witnessed inside computers directly. Nonetheless, strong legal cases can be made from circumstantial evidence, and much progress has been made in the techniques of data mining from computer science (Mena, 2003) to construct such cases.

Attribution of files

One approach to attribution is to examine the artefacts left in a computer or digital device that is the victim of a cyber-attack. Legitimate software usually contains attribution information to provide recourse for the end-users of faulty products. But even without explicit attribution, we may recognise malicious software ('malware'). Anti-malware software that identifies known malware is widespread, and libraries of malware are available such as the Open Malware site (oc.gtisc.gatech.edu:8080) for which matches can be quickly found using the hash values for the entries. A hash value is a many-to-one mapping from a set of bits to a much smaller set of bits, and is often used for indexing data. We may also be able to recognise parts within malware even when we do not recognise their whole; cyber warfare specialists within each state will tend to reuse some code sequences because it saves time and improves attack effectiveness. We can identify pieces of code through sub-file hashing methods (Garfinkel et al., 2010) and we can recognise overall similarities through functional analysis of the code (Aquilina et al., 2008). We can also undertake stylistic analysis of cyber-attack programs or data (Kothari et al., 2007; Rosenblum et al., 2011), analogous to stylistic analysis of prose, to get clues to authorship. This can allow us to find similar coding patterns such as proportions of certain kinds of instructions or sequences. This was used to establish sources, within Russian organised crime, of some of the cyber-attacks against Georgia in 2008 (US-CCU, 2009).

Once we have established a similarity between new and previous malware, we can guess that an attribution to the previous malware will also apply to the new malware. Given sufficient time, most previous malware is thoroughly investigated and a good deal is learned about it, including its origins. However, identifying a similarity between malware only provides a *probability* of authorship rather than a certainty, and this does not prove attribution since a person or state can buy or steal another's malware.

Attribution is much more feasible if we can obtain a computer or device (and its peripheral devices, since they often have most of the data) that we suspect is responsible for the planning or execution of a cyber-attack (such as by seizing it in a military operation). We may then be able to match the malware used in the attack to malware on the computer or device, or examine the logs of activity on the computer to show that the attack was launched from there. This provides strong evidence of responsibility for an attack, particularly if the malware is unusual or we also find tools for controlling and testing malware. We can also find user names and other personal identifying information to indicate who was using the computer or device, to enable us to possibly hold them legally or politically responsible.

Attribution of network traffic

Another approach to attribution is to examine network traffic to see where an attack is coming from. Internet traffic is comprised of 'packets' of information. While there are many protocols, the common IPv4 protocol is typical. IPv4 packets specify in order the type of software the packet supports, the packet length, sub-packet information if the packet has been split, 'time-to-live' or the number of forwardings allowed, the protocol used, the code for error detection, the source address, the destination address, additional options and the actual data transmitted. Only the source address gives information about where the packet is from, in the form of an 'IP address' given as four eight-bit numbers. This was originally supposed to be the address of the computer sending the packet, but as there are now more computers than possible addresses in IPv4, the address of a proxy server often handles many customers simultaneously. It is not difficult to fake ('spoof') an address, since packets generally pass through many routers on their way across the Internet, and routers could deliberately change the packets to conceal their origins. In fact, 'anonymisers' for the Internet like Tor (www.torproject.org) do this for legitimate purposes such as protecting user privacy when browsing. It is very likely that deployers of cyber weapons, like cyber criminals, will falsify their originating sites since otherwise automated responses can quickly thwart control of the attack by blocking traffic from there. This means that the direct method of attribution of checking packet source addresses will fail for cyber weapons.

Backward tracing of traffic

To check if an Internet address has been spoofed in packets, it is helpful to attempt to contact the alleged address immediately with a simple request such as a ping or 'are-you-there' request. If the site does not respond, or responds with a packet ID number or time-to-live value that is very different from that of the original packet, this suggests spoofing (Templeton and Levitt, 2003). Routers also can recognise some spoofing directly because they can know when the last-given source address is external to a local-area network and must be incorrect. Other kinds of spoofing can be inferred if one knows the rules by which sites forward their packets and knows also that the data provided with the packet violates those rules (Cohen and Narayanaswamy, 2004). Any spoofing that is detected is rare and suspicious activity, and warrants more detailed investigation.

Even with spoofing, we may be able to determine the true address by backward tracing or 'backtracing' the packet across the Internet. This is particularly feasible if the attack has some distinctive packets. To do it, we contact the site administrator of the last site, have them retrieve the cached origin information, contact that site in turn, and repeat until the original source is found. Records of packet data are only kept for a limited time, so backtracing needs to be done quickly after an attack. If an intermediate site has been attacked to facilitate the transmission of malware, contacting the site administrator is valuable help for them in indicating security problems that they need to fix.

If we can characterise a known malicious packet at the attack target, we can search cooperative Internet sites to find earlier occurrences of the same packet even without backtracing. We may be able to guess sites involved in the attack because of the data in the packet or the history of similar previous attacks, so we can start with those. Most Internet sites are cooperative with international law enforcement. The emergence of broad-area routers for regions of the world means that those router sites are good places to look for information, and they have already been directed to collect information useful for backtracing criminal malware and scams. We are seeing increasing international cooperation on the tracing of criminal activity in cyberspace starting with the Budapest Convention on Cybercrime (2001) and including recent initiatives by Europol and NATO. Much of this cooperation will be effective in tracing state-sponsored cyber-attacks that traverse the Internet as well.

Massive attacks, such as Distributed Denial of Service (DDoS) attacks, are easier to trace than single-packet attacks because they provide plenty of data. With such attacks, large portions of Internet space are commandeered, likely including some sites with good backtracing capabilities. Massive attacks can also be done with botnets: large numbers of maliciously controlled computers and devices (Elisan, 2012). Although the botnet computers may be scattered over the world, they need to be controlled from a central site, and the central site can usually be tracked down without much difficulty from observing the odd messages sent to and from it.

The major challenge in backward tracing and searching of sites is dealing with the huge volume of data. Carefully designed methods can speed detection of strings of interest (Haghighat et al., 2013). It can also help to store signatures of packets or files in the form of cryptographic hash values computed on them by hash standards like SHA-1. A SHA-1 signature, 160 bits appearing to be random, is very unlikely to coincide for any two packets or files, since on the average it will take 10 to the 48th power tries to match a given signature. Another challenge is that a given signature needs to be confirmed as part of a cyber-attack to make it worth searching for, and that confirmation may take so much time that the tracing information will be lost by then.

A countermeasure to backtracing is for attackers to vary their code so that the attack appears different each time: what are termed 'polymorphic' attacks. However, to reduce code writing, many of the pieces must be the same, and this common code can be recognised by sub-packet or sub-file hashing. In fact, large data files sent across the Internet are split into small packets anyway, so malware may well have recognisable hashes for some packets even if the attacker uses polymorphism. In addition, many attackers view mounting polymorphic attacks as undesirable, because it is hard for the different versions of the attack to recognise one another and consequently they tend inefficiently and repeatedly to re-infect the same machines.

Alternatives to backward tracing

Even if we cannot backtrace an attack, correlation of information between attacks can be a helpful step towards later attribution. Attackers, both criminal and those engaged in cyber warfare, tend to repeat particular methods of attack (modus operandi) (Kong et al., 2013), as well as attack codes. An attacker's modus operandi will often include the apparent planning of the attack, the pre-surveillance methods used, the type of weapon, the timing of the attack, the precautions taken by the attacker and the volatile (main-memory) clues left (Turvey, 2011). We can develop a model from a similar set of attacks and use it to recognise new attacks from the same source, something that can be done automatically with a variety of machine-learning techniques (Pfeffer et al., 2012). Then, if we obtain additional clues, such as through catching a spy from a particular state who possesses code for a previously seen attack, we can infer that it applies to similar attacks.

Correlation can also be done with network data even if we cannot backtrace. Intermediate sites seeing earlier or large amounts of traffic for an attack are likely closer to the source than other sites (Thonnard et al., 2010), and we can combine multiple pieces of uncertain evidence to get stronger evidence (Kalutarage et al., 2012). We can also use the 'time-to-live' (the permitted number of forwardings, limiting the 'lifespan' of data in a computer network). For instance, Figure 3.1 shows a network. If site A receives a denial-of-service packet from site B with a time-to-live of 62, and an identical packet from C with a time-to-live of 61, then if we assume a common source for both packets, the source must

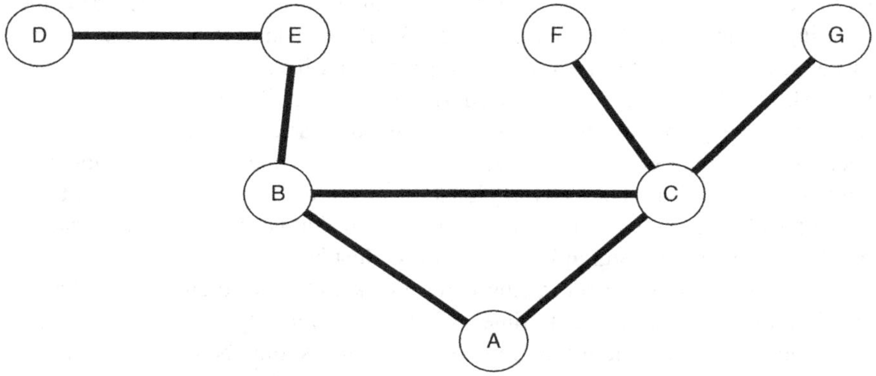

66   N.C. Rowe

Figure 3.1 An example network.

be closer to B than to C because time-to-live is decremented at each step. Assuming that the initial time-to-live was 64, a common initial value, we can infer that the packet must come from E and not D, F or G, even if the source address is being spoofed.

Planting beacons

Backward tracing can be made easier if the source of the cyber-attack can be induced to provide identifying information. Cookies for web browsing are one example, where data from a web destination site is sent back to the browser source site to save time on subsequent reconnections (Brain, 2000). A website that is a victim of a cyber-attack could send back a cookie with a unique identifying code to the cyber-attacker to enable recognition of the attacker on subsequent activity, to aid in attribution. However, this only works for web protocols, and requires the attacker to accept cookies, which – of course – they may well choose not to do.

More can be accomplished if we can put specialised software onto the attacker's computer, since cookies cannot include executable code. We may be able to induce the attacker to download an executable file, particularly if they are trying to steal secret data anyway. Then, when the executable file is run, it could send messages including the name, Internet address, software present and other identifying information about the attacker site. Executables can also be sent back to an attacker by 'drive-by downloads' using techniques of malicious websites, or spies could also plant executables on possible attacker computers or attach wireless hardware. However, these methods would themselves be illegal in most states, going well beyond the legally acceptable responses to a crime by being cyber-attacks themselves.

A counterintelligence technique that can provide a beacon in a more legal way is to offer distinctive false information to attackers. An example is when the attacker is trying to steal something like a password; we can give them a distinctive false password, and then look for its use. Backtracing can then be focused more narrowly.

Countermeasures for beacons involve trying to detect the beacon signal and stopping it. This can be done by anomaly analysis in outgoing network traffic. Then the beacon source can be disabled or, better, transferred to another computer to provide a decoy target. However, most attackers do not have time to do this.

Attribution to a state

The focus of this book is on cyber warfare (meaning interstate cyber-attacks). While most of the foregoing analysis is relevant to cyber-attacks both by individuals and states (or state-sponsored actors), the particular issue of technically attributing a cyber-attack to a *state* is an especially pertinent one in the context of this volume. It is desirable to attribute cyberwar-type attacks to a state to enable settlement of the conflict and fair clean-up and reparations. However, even if we can attribute an attack to a particular computer or device in a particular state, we cannot necessarily attribute it to that state. And even if we have enough evidence to attribute it to a state, we need to collect evidence through carefully employing a validated 'chain of custody' and carefully documented standard procedures (Casey, 2011) so that our evidence will reach an acceptable legal standard (on the problem of attaining a legal standard of evidence for state cyber-attacks, see Chapter 5 of this volume). Despite these difficulties, proving attribution of a damaging cyber-attack can be beneficial to the world community in much the same way as trials for war crimes (Ellis, 2001) and has benefits in establishing international standards of cyber conflict even if state responsibility is not sufficiently established.

Semantic analysis of cyber-attacks for attribution

One obvious clue to attribution is analysis of which states could benefit from an attack. If one state is engaged in a conventional war with another state, or is on the brink of one, then cyber-attacks are more likely to originate from the two warring parties as tactical ploys. This was the case for the cyber-attacks against Georgia by Russia in 2008, which were followed by – and continued in the ongoing context of – conventional military action. Such knowledge narrows the search over the Internet for clues; however, it is rather different in the case of criminal cyber-attacks, which could generally come from anywhere. However, such obvious or 'semantic' clues may be misleading, because a third party may actually be responsible and be trying to provoke a war. This is more likely to occur with cyber warfare than with traditional warfare because the low cost of mounting cyber-attacks makes them available to states with limited resources. For example, we can see a good deal of third-party involvement today in the Israeli–Palestinian conflict (Okuniewska, 2013).

Levels of national responsibility

In many cases, a state has disclaimed responsibility for cyber-attacks because it has claimed that the responsible computers or devices within its borders were used to attack without approval of the state, as with criminal cyber-attacks. In such instances, it is the responsibility of the state in question to stop the attacker and impose penalties, much as the state is responsible for terrorists within its borders (Värk, 2006; see also James A. Green's discussion of the legal obligation of 'cyber due diligence' in Chapter 5 of this volume). If the state does not police cyber-attacks emanating from within its territory, it is likely to be in breach of a key principle of international law, although this does not necessarily mean that the state is legally responsible for the attacks themselves. Healey (2011) distinguishes ten progressive levels of national responsibility for cyber-attacks: state-prohibited, inadequately-state-prohibited, state-ignored, state-encouraged (as by editorials), state-shaped (as by actively recruiting independent attackers by social networking (Johnson, 2014)), state-coordinated, state-ordered, state-rogue-conducted (as by people in the government not acting by government order), state-executed, and state-integrated (including both the government and other people). Different observers can disagree as to where in this list true national responsibility beings. Nonetheless, threshold events can be tied to this spectrum: for instance, whether a state prosecutes its citizens who have been responsible for an attack is a good threshold event for distinguishing inadequately-state-prohibited from state-ignored attacks, and evidence from bulletin boards can distinguish state-encouraged from state-shaped attacks. Evidence from the attack computers, and devices in their messages and downloads, can more convincingly prove state coordination.

For widely distributed attacks such as those carried out by botnets, backtracing the botnet communications is essential to reduce the possible sources to a small number. But all the states harbouring the bots or sub-attackers should take measures to stop the attack machinery within their borders because it is stealing their resources as well, and it is in their interests to cooperate internationally to share information about the attack even if they have no legal obligation. A complicating issue is that the nationality of the owner of an attacking computer or device may not be that of the state in which they reside or operate. However, visitors to a state are, of course, still subject to its laws.

Proving attribution to the international community

A key problem with attributing cyber aggression is that much of the evidence will likely be circumstantial and will not meet the legal requirements for assigning state responsibility (O'Connell, 2012). Thus even if a state is entirely sure who attacked it, the victim state may be unable to justify a counterattack to the international community. The evidence will usually be circumstantial because data can be changed easily in cyberspace without leaving traces, through spoofing for instance. The sophistication of an attack generally does not rule out any particular states, since 'sophistication' is very much in the eye of the beholder (Guitton and Korzak, 2013) and a primitive state can buy sophisticated technology at a reasonably low cost.

Another issue is that, even if we capture a computer that was used in cyber-attacks and show by its records that it initiated the attacks, this may be insufficient legal proof because the computer records may have been modified to incriminate (FIDIS, 2006). Having said this, there are standard procedures for cybercrime investigations that should be followed, and these can be similarly employed in attributing interstate cyber-attacks. These include scripted steps for interacting with devices whose accomplishment can be confirmed by log files, operating only on copies of the original data and installing 'write blocker' software on the analysed computer to prevent evidence being tampered with. If these procedures are followed, the evidence obtained can be strong.

It is worth noting that illegal methods can also support attribution. If someone breaks into the computer or device used to launch the attack, they can search around for evidence of who owns it. They may be able to find personal identification of the owner such as names, addresses, phone numbers, personal identification numbers and so on, and do so more easily than if the owner knows their machine is to be seized. They may also be able to find clues to government involvement in cyber-attacks. However, it should go without saying that breaking the law to investigate crimes is not acceptable in most states.

Experts may very well disagree on a question of attribution. Ranum (2011) argues that attribution questions should be decided publicly using experts from all sides of a conflict, who should use accepted, standard and open-source methods so that the international community can be convinced. It is useless to establish attribution of a cyber-attack by secret methods, because the necessary next step – proving it to the international community – would reveal such methods.

Explicit attributability

Various proposals have been made to increase the attributability of Internet activity by attaching stronger information to packets, such as requiring every computer and device to embed a hardwired identification code in its packets. However, Clark and Landau (2010) point out that these methods will not usually help against well-organised adversaries such as states engaging in cyber-attacks because, if they wish, large organisations can use sophisticated methods to conceal themselves well, even with increased attribution measures. For instance, states can put their attacks into modified computer chips (integrated circuits) installed on systems, or transmit attacks to hidden receivers attached to systems, so that no malicious traffic need traverse Internet connections.

Nonetheless, I have argued elsewhere (Rowe, 2010) that voluntary attributability is desirable for cyber-attacks to provide better political effects, for how can a state be effectively coerced if it does not know who is attacking it? This could be analogised to the wearing of uniforms and the placing of distinctive markings on military vehicles. It is undesirable to attach obvious indications of the source of an attack to its attack code, as then it could be more easily blocked. As such, steganography (Fridrich, 2009), or hidden data, is necessary for voluntary attributability. There are many methods of achieving this: for instance, the attribution text can be hidden in every eleven hundred and eighty-third character, for example, or put in the lower-order bits of a picture. Attribution can be made provable later by the attacker if they provide information about the steganographic method used, and can use a cryptographic signature so it cannot be forged. However, there is a close connection between espionage and cyber warfare, and attribution is not desirable in espionage; this makes it hard for cyber warfare planners to understand the value of attributability.

Conclusion

The attribution of cyber-attacks in cyber warfare is a difficult but not impossible problem. The large scale and effectiveness of the attack often provides opportunities for tracing and analysis that are not possible with common criminal cyber-attacks that we see more regularly on the Internet. Still, the evidence that we obtain will generally be circumstantial and difficult to use in legal proceedings unless computers and devices of the alleged attackers can be searched. It does not appear that this assessment will change anytime soon even with major technological changes, so the major invasions of Internet privacy that some people propose to keep us safe (e.g. those described in Angwin, 2014) appear unjustified.

Note

1 This work was supported by the US National Science Foundation under grant 1318126 of the Secure and Trustworthy Cyberspace Program. The views expressed are those of the author and do not represent those of the US Government.

References

Angwin, J. (2014) *Dragnet nation: A quest for privacy, security, and freedom in a world of relentless surveillance*, New York: Times Books.

Aquilina, J., Casey, E. and Malin, C. (2008) *Malware forensics: Investigating and analyzing malicious code*, Burlington: Syngress.

Brain, M. (2000) 'How Internet cookies work', 26 April, *HowStuffWorks* [online], available: http://computer.howstuffworks.com/cookie.htm [12 July 2014].

Brenner, S. (2007) 'At light speed: attribution and response to cybercrime/terrorism/warfare', *Journal of Criminal Law and Criminology*, vol. 97, no. 2, pp. 379–475.

Casey, E. (2011) 'Handling a digital crime scene', in Casey, E. (ed.) *Digital evidence and computer crime*, 3rd edition, Waltham: Elsevier.

Clark, D. and Landau, S. (2010) 'The problem isn't attribution; it's multi-stage attacks', *Proceedings of Workshop on Re-Architecting the Internet*, Philadelphia, November, Article 11.

Cohen, D. and Narayanaswamy, K. (2004) 'Attack attribution in non-cooperative networks', *Proceedings of the IEEE Workshop on Information Assurance*, West Point, June, pp. 436–7.

Convention on Cybercrime (2001) Budapest, Hungary, 2296 UNTS 167, 23 November.

Elisan, C. (2012) *Malware, rootkits, and botnets: A beginner's guide*, New York: McGraw-Hill Osborne.

Ellis, A. (2001) 'What should we do about war criminals?', in Jokic, A. (ed.) *War crimes and collective wrongdoing*, Oxford: Wiley-Blackwell.

FIDIS (2006) 'Forensic implications of identity management systems', January, WP6, D6.1 [online], available: www.fidis.net/resources/deliverables/forensic-implications [2 July 2014].

Fridrich, J. (2009) *Steganography in digital media: principles, algorithms, and applications*, Cambridge: Cambridge University Press.

Garfinkel, S., Nelson, A., White, D. and Roussev, V. (2010) 'Using purpose-built functions and block hashes to enable small block and sub-file forensics', *Digital Investigation*, vol. 7, pp. S13–S23.

Geers, K., Kindlund, D., Moran, N. and Rachwald, R. (2013) 'World War C: understanding nation-state motives behind today's advanced cyber attacks', *FireEye* [online], available: www.fireeye.com/resources/pdfs/fireeye-wwc-report.pdf [7 April 2013].

Goel, S. (2011) 'Cyberwarfare: connecting the dots in cyber intelligence', *Communications of the ACM*, vol. 54, no. 8, pp. 132–40.

Guitton, C. and Korzak, E. (2013) 'The sophistication criterion for attribution', *RUSI Journal*, vol. 158, no. 4, pp. 62–8.

Haghighat, M., Tavakoli, M. and Kharrazi, M. (2013) 'Payload attribution via character dependent multi-bloom filters', *IEEE Transactions on Information Forensics and Security*, vol. 8, no. 5, pp. 705–16.

Healey, J. (2011) 'Beyond attribution: seeking national responsibility for cyber attacks', Issue Brief, *Atlantic Council* [online], available: www.fbiic.gov/public/2012/mar/National_Responsibility_for_CyberAttacks,_2012.pdf [4 April 2014].

Johnson, C. (2014) 'Anti-social networking: crowdsourcing and the cyber defence of national critical infrastructures', *Ergonomics*, vol. 57, no. 3, pp. 419–33.

Kalutarage, H., Shaikh, S., Zhou, Q. and James, A. (2012) 'Sensing for suspicion at scale: a Bayesian approach for cyber conflict attribution and reasoning', *Proceedings of the 4th International Conference on Cyber Conflict*, Tallinn.

Kong, D., Tian, D., Pan, Q., Liu, P. and Wu, D. (2013) 'Semantic aware attribution analysis of remote exploits', *Security and Communications Networks*, vol. 6, no. 7, pp. 818–32.

Kothari, J., Shevertalov, M., Stehle, E. and Mancoridis, S. (2007) 'A probabilistic approach to source code authorship identification', *Proceedings of the Fourth International Conference on Information Technology*, pp. 243–8.

Mena, J. (2003) *Investigative data mining for security and criminal detection*, Burlington: Elsevier Science.

Nakashima, E. (2014) 'Indictment of PLA hackers is part of broad US strategy to curb Chinese cyberspying', 22 May, *Washington Post* [online], available: www.washingtonpost.com/world/national-security/indictment-of-pla-hackers-is-part-of-broad-us-strategy-to-curb-chinese-cyberspying/2014/05/22/a66cf26a-e1b4-11e3-9743-bb9b59cde7b9_story.html [25 September 2014].

O'Connell, M.E. (2012) 'Cyber security without cyber war', *Journal of Conflict and Security Law*, vol. 17, no. 2, pp. 187–209.

Okuniewska, E. (2013) 'The role of third parties in Israel and Palestine', *Palestine–Israel Journal of Politics, Economics and Culture*, Blog, 19 May [online], available: www.pij.org/details.php?blog=1&id=201 [12 August 2014].

Pfeffer, A., Call, C., Chamberlain, J., Kellogg, L., Ouellette, J., Patten, T., Zacharias, G., Lakhotia, A., Golconda, S., Bay, J., Hall, R. and Scofield, D. (2012) 'Malware analysis and attribution using genetic information', *Proceedings of the 7th International Conference on Malicious and Unwanted Software*, Fajardo, Puerto Rico, October, pp. 39–45.

Ranum, M. (2011) 'Cyberwar: about attribution (identifying your attacker)', 21 October, *Fabius Maximus* [online], available: http://fabiusmaximus.com/2011/10/21/30004/ [3 June 2011].

Rosenblum, N., Miller, B. and Zhu, X. (2011) 'Recovering the toolchain provenance of binary code', *Proceedings of the International Symposium on Software Testing and Analysis*, Toronto, pp. 100–10.

Rowe, N.C. (2010) 'The ethics of cyberweapons in warfare', *International Journal of Technoethics*, vol. 1, no. 1, pp. 20–31.

Templeton, S. and Levitt, K. (2003) 'Detecting spoofed packets', *3rd DARPA Information Survivability Conference and Exposition*, Washington, DC, April, pp. 164–177.

Thonnard, O., Mees, W. and Dacier, M. (2010) 'On a multicriteria clustering approach for attack attribution', *ACM SIGKDD Explorations*, vol. 12, no. 1, pp. 11–20.

Turvey, B. (2011) 'Modus operandi, motive, and technology', in Casey E. (ed.) *Digital evidence and computer crime*, 3rd edition, Waltham: Elsevier.

US-CCU (United States Cyber Consequences Unit) (2009) 'Overview by the US-CCU of the Cyber Campaign against Georgia in August of 2008', August, *US-CCU Special Report* [online], available: www.registan.net/wp-content/uploads/2009/08/US-CCU-Georgia-Cyber-Campaign-Overview.pdf [12 August 2014].

Värk, R. (2006) 'State responsibility for private armed groups in the context of terrorism', *Juridica International*, vol. 11, pp. 184–93.

4 The strategic implications of cyber warfare[1]

Danny Steed

Introduction

Cyber warfare is strategically misunderstood. Those seeking authoritative analysis on the subject will, instead of finding conceptual guidance, become buried under an avalanche of loosely connected and disparate literature. Academic thinking on the subject of cyber warfare finds itself therefore in a quandary; the literature has thus far been unable to provide useful guidance to an activity that in the practitioner's world is not only rife, but has been labelled, in the case of the current UK Government, a 'Tier One national security issue' (UK Government: 27). There is no agreement on how important cyber warfare is, what effects it can generate, how to go about waging such warfare or, most critically, what political consequences and interpretations cyber warfare will provoke. The scholarly thinking to date has instead been dominated by speculative argumentation that generally either makes the case of a dramatic change in the character of war as we know it, or seeks to temper the hyperbole and argue the case for the normalcy of strategic affairs: simply, affairs that are conducted in a 'cybered' world.

The scale of dispute can be seen from the argument of Colin Gray, who states that 'we do know enough now ... to make strategic sense of cyber' (Gray, 2013: 4). This is incorrect: Gray's earlier categorisation is that the essence of strategy 'lies in the realm of the *consequences* of actions for future outcomes' (Gray, 1999: 18, emphasis added). By following this earlier, extremely robust reasoning, it can be seen that, as we do not yet understand the political consequences of cyber warfare in detail, we are unable to understand its occurrence in a rigorously strategic manner. Indeed, we now know a great deal about its technical details, the tactics of cyber warfare, through works such as Carr's *Inside cyber warfare* (Carr, 2011) and Andress and Winterfield's *Cyber warfare* (Andress, Winterfield, 2011), but this technical understanding has not yet been bridged to political meaning. Until we can reliably understand the political consequences and political interpretations of cyber warfare, the strategic understanding of cyber warfare remains incomplete.

The argument made in this chapter is simple: this 'pre-strategic' (Cornish, 2012: 2) state of affairs that currently afflicts thinking on cyber warfare results from a lack of considered engagement with the empirical evidence available on the occurrence of cyber warfare. The proliferation of conceptual thinking, which places little consideration on the analysis of case studies of cyber warfare, leaves the strategic understanding of cyber warfare in a weakened state. It must now be recognised that the occurrence of cyber warfare should no longer be considered a stranger to thinkers; a once barren plain devoid of empirical evidence to consult is no longer so. Kello (2013: 15) is right in stating that compared to other notable technological fields, such as the nuclear and biological cases, there are now enough examples of cyber warfare to work with. We have enough evidence to begin making strategic *sense* of cyber warfare, but a considered approach must be taken to identify the strategic *implications* of cyber warfare to date.

The approach taken in this chapter will be that of a comparative case study. After reviewing the current state of strategic thinking on cyber warfare, and identifying why there is a lack of strategic understanding on the subject, we will analyse three primary case studies in order to draw out the implications substantiated by the practical application of cyber warfare. The cases to be considered are the cyber-attacks against Estonia in 2007 and against Georgia in 2008, and the use of the Stuxnet virus against the Iranian nuclear programme in 2010. While other candidate cases could be considered, these have been chosen due to the volume of evidence available concerning them. They also represent the most cited cases of cyber warfare, but have not so far been analysed from a comparative strategic perspective.

Current thinking on cyber warfare

The current state of scholarly thinking suffers from an acute contradiction that carries far-reaching consequences. That contradiction is simply that while literature on cyber warfare is plentiful in volume, it is also desperately impoverished in terms of its quality, particularly in generating strategic understanding. Writing on all matters associated with the security implications of cyberspace has increased exponentially, definitively replacing counterinsurgency as the current decade's *vogue* subject. Despite this, there is quite clearly no established consensus on the strategic value of cyber warfare.

The trend of the discourse within the literature can generally be described as the hyperbolic versus sceptical schools of thinking on the importance of cyber warfare. It is all but mandatory to cite Arquilla and Ronfeldt's seminal 'Cyberwar is coming!' article from 1993 (Arquilla and Ronfeldt, 1993) as the origin of the hyperbolic thinkers, insisting that warfare will change interstate conflict unrecognisably from that which has occurred before. The thinking from the early 1990s evolved into military–heavy concepts – 'cyberwar' and 'netwar' being the most cited – seeing cyber warfare as the purview of information warfare and information operations (Dunn Cavelty, 2010: 128): such understandings heavily informed early thinking on the subject as well as US military doctrine.

Clarke and Knake are the latest voice of this lineage with their book *Cyber war* following very much the same logic, that cyber war represents the next great threat to national security. This was famously elaborated by invoking the analogy that critical national infrastructure could be targeted with effects on a par with Pearl Harbor (Leon Panetta, quoted in *The Economist*, 2012: 1). In Clarke and Knake's own words:

> With a nation in the dark, shivering in the cold, unable to get food at the market or cash at the ATM, with parts of our military suddenly impotent, and with the original flashpoint that started it all going badly, what will the Commander-in-Chief do?
>
> (Clarke and Knake, 2012: 260)

This view has permeated policy circles to the point that a new analogy has been coined, the 'cyber 9/11' (see e.g. Magee, 2013; Libicki, 2013). The invocation of such analogies is intended to highlight the perceived risks posed by cyber warfare, and to ultimately invigorate more rigorous strategic analysis to cope with its occurrence. This is best put by Arquilla's declaration that the most important question to ask is: '[c]an cyberwar be controlled?' (Arquilla, 2012: 3).

The sceptics counter that the threat is over exaggerated and full of hype. Thomas Rid is the best known of these thinkers, declaring that '[c]yber war is still more hype than hazard' (Rid, 2012: 1). Rid has further developed his thesis in the directly titled *Cyber war will not take place* (Rid, 2013). The analysis in Rid's work focuses on issues of definition, and the idea that cyber warfare is not instrumental violence in the traditional, Clausewitzian sense. Rid goes further in stating that cyber war has not occurred in the past, nor does it happen in the present, insisting that what we are seeing instead is a new manifestation of three very familiar activities: sabotage, espionage, and subversion (Rid, 2013: xiv).

Gartzke follows in the sceptical outlook when he takes issue directly with the basic logic of a cyber Pearl Harbor, arguing that the rationale underpinning any surprise attack lies in what it enables the attacker to do subsequently. His analysis usefully reminds us that no cyber warfare should take place without considering the purpose for its use (Gartzke, 2013: 63), something that the advocates of such analogies fail to do. Unlike Rid's broader scepticism, Gartzke ultimately argues that cyber warfare can be expected to simply complement traditional forms of military power in use and will ultimately remain incapable of delivering decisive effect.

Ultimately, there is a scarcity of quality strategic literature on cyber warfare. Myriam Dunn Cavelty performs an invaluable service in identifying that this is for two reasons. First, this is because most of the previous literature was of a specialised policy nature outside of scholarly theoretical thinking that was very loosely organised. A second reason is the underappreciated fact that the 11 September 2001 attacks focused the attention of strategic thinking and practice away from anything related to cyber warfare, and towards terrorism and counterinsurgency (Dunn Cavelty, 2010: 125). Consequently, while the focus of thinkers and practitioners alike was on Al Qaeda, and the subsequent wars in Iraq and Afghanistan, the development of activities within cyberspace continued at speed.

It has only been since around 2006/2007 that attention has returned to cyber warfare. A form of conceptual lag has therefore developed while real-world practice has been evolving.

The poverty of evidence

The key problem that afflicts current thinking on cyber warfare is simple: it has grown primarily by developing analyses that are devoid of empirical evidence. Arquilla and Ronfeldt's famous 1993 piece was a speculative argument, grounded on no real evidence. Although permeated with historical analogies on the organisational use of information ranging from the Second Punic War to the Mongols, and in present times with *Blitzkrieg* (Arquilla and Ronfeldt, 1993: 32–40), their argument bases its cyber war thinking on little more than rudimentary induction from the case of the 1991 Gulf War. In 1993, this was perhaps understandable, given that no true instances of what this book terms 'cyber warfare' had yet occurred; however, strategic thinking on cyber warfare has continued to proceed by way of analogy, not evidence.

This is a situation similar to early air power thinkers, who made sensational causal leaps in the interwar years, based on extremely limited practical evidence. Betz and Stevens (2011: 84) illustrate this well in saying that both cyber warfare and early air power thinkers were fundamentally 'concerned with restoring decisiveness to war and see in the new technology a potential means for doing so'. These bold causal leaps are best observed through Giulio Douhet's thinking: one of his core conclusions about the rise of air power being that successful offensives by land forces would be rendered impossible by air forces (Douhet, 2003: 24. See also McIsaac, 1986: 630).

The consequence of this inability to engage with evidence of practice is simple: the strategic understanding of cyber warfare is infantile, disorganised, conceptually weak, offering little or no guidance to practitioners. Cornish *et al.* (2010: 32) are correct is describing cyberspace as 'currently beyond the reach of mature political discourse'. They rightly call for the imposition of analytic discipline holistically – meaning both the extension of policy and politics into any consideration of cyberspace and the incorporation of the complexities of cyber warfare, at its technical level, into policy – in order to bound and generate better thinking. As it stands, thinking on cyber warfare remains strategically misunderstood, as it is unable to explain the significance of cyber warfare robustly in political terms. A key example of this is Dunn Cavelty's (2010: 139) concluding statement that '[c]yberwar is not about a game of seeking strategic advantage from a new technology'. This claim sadly reflects the current status of conceptual thinking about cyber warfare, and contradicts basic strategic logic; strategy must match the use of chosen means in purposeful ways to the desired end state, creating advantage(s) in an inherently competitive political environment. If the use of cyber warfare is not to create strategic advantage then what can it possibly be used for? Dunn Cavelty's argument that the fear of 'blowback' in using these methods is not only unsatisfactory, but also runs contrary to the evidence of the use of new technology throughout history, which is typified by replication and modification.

In order to progress, thinking on cyber warfare must move beyond pursuing the two avenues of analysis that have so far typified their approaches: abstract conceptual thinking as the first, and the blind superimposition of historical analogies as the second. Having already dealt with the first approach, it is necessary to briefly deal with the second. As cyberspace lacks a physical nature (although it most certainly has a physical interface with its users, and a physical geography through its underlying infrastructure), simply articulating its effects has proven a difficult task to achieve. As a result, the use of historical analogies has proliferated in the hope of providing wisdom. In the American literature there is a marked preference for using Cold War analogies, most notably comparisons to the nuclear challenge of the Cold War period (see e.g. Krepinevich, 2012; Nye, 2011; Gray, 2013; Goodman, 2010). While not unreasonable, these analogies suffer from the same logical flaw as that of the abstract thinking: they are issued with little or no consideration for empirical reality. This creates a significant weakness in such analysis in that thinking is dislocated entirely from the reality of cyber warfare as it has actually taken place. Until and unless cyber warfare thinking grounds itself in the empirical reality of its occurrence, highly contestable arguments that betray strategic incoherence will proliferate.

This chapter will now move on to establishing its own contribution to cyber warfare. This will be done by exploring several notable case studies in the application of interstate cyber warfare, in order to generate strategic insights based neither on analogy nor on abstract thought, but instead on the record of cyber warfare's occurrence.

Case studies on cyber warfare

Estonia, 2007

Over a period of some three weeks in April 2007, Estonia suffered the worst cyber-attacks yet seen, in what is now popularly dubbed either as 'Web War 1' (*The Economist*, 2010: 24; Blank, 2008) or the 'Estonian cyberwar' of 2007 (Singer and Friedman, 2014: 111). At the time, Estonia was one of the world's most connected states: Rid (2013: 6) notes, for example, that 95 per cent of banking transactions in the country were carried out online. Laasme puts the scale of Estonian connectivity alternatively: '[a]lmost every activity in Estonia is done over the Internet: its society is inundated with e-government, e-voting, e-parking, e-banking, e-identification systems, e-taxes, and live-streaming public television' (Laasme, 2011: 59). While an example of progressive connectivity, Estonia was also extremely vulnerable to cyber warfare due to the scale of connectivity in the state.

This vulnerability was made apparent in the later hours of Friday, 27 April. Tensions between Estonia and Russia were increasing following the Estonian announcement that a Second World War memorial serving as a symbol of

Estonia's liberation from the Nazis by Soviet Russia – the Bronze Soldier – was to be relocated from Tallinn's city centre to the outskirts. The Russian Government, as well as the Russian-speaking population within Estonia, met the announcement with hostility. Riots soon commenced across Tallinn resulting in 1,300 arrests, 100 injuries and one fatality (Rid, 2013: 6).

On the night of 27 April, cyber-attacks began against various points of Estonian cyberspace in the form of Distributed Denial of Service (DDoS) attacks and botnet assaults. Targets included the websites of numerous government departments, the Estonian parliament, banks, newspapers and broadcasters (Dunn Cavelty, 2010: 135). Rid notes a form of escalation in the sophistication of the attacks, beginning as DDoS attacks that progressed to botnets on the night of 30 April in order to increase the impact of the attacks. These attacks came from, at the time, the largest number of attacking computers then seen, around 85,000, which continued their assaults for a period of almost three weeks. The attacks saw their peak on 9 May, 'when Moscow celebrates Victory Day' (Rid, 2013: 6). On that day, the most tangible effects of the attacks could be seen when Estonia's national bank, the Hansapank, had its online services made unavailable for a period of 90 minutes, and for two hours on the following day (Rid, 2013: 6).

At this stage it has been merely implied, through pointing out contextual coincidences, that these attacks were the will of the Russian government being expressed by cyber warfare. The Estonians hold no doubt that the attacks were Russian in origin; Urmas Paet, the nation's foreign minister, firmly accused the Russian Government, and claimed to have traced certain activities to Russian IP addresses (Singer and Friedman, 2014: 111). This brings analysis to the first notable point about the Estonian case, which is that definitive proof of who was responsible has so far proven elusive. No firm evidence is conclusive of the Estonian accusation that the 2007 attacks were Russia's doing and, indeed, opinions vary throughout the available literature on the credibility of the Estonian allegation. In this instance of uncertainty Brenner (2009: 86) very usefully provides a breakdown of what is known about the attacks:

 i They were transnational, originating in Russia and targeting websites and networks in Estonia.
 ii They only targeted websites and networks in Estonia.
 iii They were deliberate, intentional assaults.
 iv The DDoS attacks were massive in scale, both in terms of the data load and the size of the botnets used in them.
 v The attackers in part used botnets rented from cybercriminals.
 vi Those who planned the attacks were fluent in the Russian language.
 vii The attacks followed action by the Estonian authorities that insulted Russian citizens and Estonian citizens of Russian descent.
 viii They targeted critical infrastructure components, not for exploration, theft, or extortion, but specifically to cause damage in the form of disrupted and denied services.

ix Internet addresses belonging to Russian government agencies were used in the attacks.
x   The Russian government publically and repeatedly denied involvement in the attacks.
xi The sequence of attacks included less sophisticated activity, such as putting a moustache on an online photo of the Estonian Prime Minister.
xii Sophisticated computer expertise is no longer a precondition for launching DDoS attacks, even sophisticated attacks; 'commercial' tools are available online that make it relatively easy to assemble botnets and engage in other malicious activity.

The second notable point about the Estonian case lies in the impact of these attacks. Again, opinions vary on this question. For example, Rid (2013: 6) notes that the impact was 'noticeable, but ultimately remained minor'. Singer and Friedman (2014: 99) follow in this vein in saying that, while interference was clear, the attacks 'had little impact on the daily life of the average Estonian and certainly no long term effect'. *The Economist*, in its headline briefing on Cyberwar (2010: 24), labelled the incident as 'more a cyber-riot than a war'.

Such assertions about the negligible impact of the attacks can be held in contrast to views such as Herzog's, who believes that a blockade is a more fitting analogy to explain the events of April/May 2007 (Herzog, 2011: 54). Blank (2008: 240) goes even further suggesting that these kinds of attacks 'represent a new kind of war where the threat lies not in conventional armies but in a wholly asymmetric or unconventional attack deploying one or another form of IW (Information Warfare)'. Ultimately, at this stage, the most notable fact about the Estonian case is that it provides proof of the ability to target elements of a state's critical national infrastructure, while avoiding a definitive attribution of the origin of the attack.

Georgia, 2008

The August 2008 confrontation between Russia and Georgia over the status of the South Ossetia region can easily be seen as an example of twentieth-century war:

> [It was a] border dispute, inflamed by propaganda and whipped-up ethnic tension, [that] resulted in a murky case of who-shot-first, an armoured blitzkrieg, airstrikes, a plea for peace by the defeated, signatures on a piece of paper, and the winner's annexation of some territory.
>
> (Haddick, 2011: 1)

Despite this very familiar feel to the short confrontation, Haddick is right to note that the use of cyber warfare against Georgia gives a very twenty-first-century angle to this case. Some ten days prior to the start of Russian military operations, attacks on a series of Georgian websites began, following a two-tier approach.

First, the defacement of public websites took place, as well as some privately owned ones that ultimately had little effect. Secondly, the most common and successful series of attacks were DDoS and botnet attacks against Georgian public and private systems, focusing first on Government and media websites (Bonner, 2014: 106). Korns and Kastenberg (2008–2009: 64–65) detail that such an attack against the website of the Georgian President, Mikheil Saakashvili, was detected being routed through an American IP address on 19 July. This attack was facilitated utilising software – 'Machbot' – written in Russian and known to be frequently used by Russian hackers. This was only the beginning, however, with another wave of attacks to come that was enabled by the open publication and distribution of malicious software on publicly accessible websites – such as 'StopGeorgia' – with an attendant target list of Georgian websites (Rid, 2013: 9). Bonner (2014: 106) also notes that a deliberate effort was made to target Georgian educational institutions in order to draw the attention of the sole Georgian CERT (Computer Emergency Response Team) away from attacks elsewhere. This attack 'used CERT Georgia's natural response against it to divert and suppress the state's best cyber defences' (Bonner, 2014: 106).

This 'outsourcing' of cyber warfare is an interesting development carrying two primary consequences. First, the volume of attacks can increase dramatically simply by allowing any Russian speaker online to participate in the cyber offensive; secondly, the already troublesome attribution issue is exacerbated by devolving the attacks to an individual level and to perpetrators with no government affiliation. This second wave of cyber-attacks was observed on 8 August (Korns and Kastenberg, 2008–2009: 65), coinciding with Russian conventional military operations. Haddick (2011: 3) argues that this was a deliberate part of Russian planning, intended to optimise the disruption caused by the cyber-attacks to optimise the military, diplomatic and strategic communications offensives underway against Georgia. Rid (2013: 7) also notes that these attacks 'may have been the first time an independent cyber attack happened in synchronisation with a conventional military operation'.

The effects of the attacks on Georgia were further ranging than those of the attacks carried out against Estonia the previous year. Goodman (2010: 115) argues that a strategic-economic impact was real, in that – as well as general disruption having been caused – there was also a diversion of business away from Georgian fuel pipelines, and a reinforcement of Russian military operations through the reduction of access on Georgian electricity grids. Further to this was the impact on information and the ability of the Georgian government to communicate effectively, both internally and to the outside world (Hollis, 2011: 5). Or, as Korns and Kastenberg (2008–2009: 60) put it, 'the Georgian Government found itself cyber-locked, barely able to communicate on the Internet'. Government websites were relocated abroad in order to get services operational again, Google is also said to have helped Georgian private businesses in the same vein (Goodman, 2010: 115).

Bonner (2014: 106) is right in arguing that Georgia experienced a dislocation of data flows, having to relocate data that would normally flow through Internet channels into other conduits, such as telephone and radio. This overloading of data flows was achieved not only by attack codes themselves, but also simply by the volume of data being injected into the Georgian networks, effectively jamming them (Bonner, 2014: 106). Such information disruption prevented the Georgian government not only from communicating its responses to the Russian conventional attacks, but also from participating in the strategic communications narrative that was subsequently dominated by the Russians. Both of these effects provided the Russians with a clear military operational, as well as a strategic, communications advantage.

Although care must be taken to note that the Georgian conflict in 2008 involved far more than cyber warfare and not to over-exaggerate the cyberspace elements of the situation, the conflict provides notable evidence of the growing effectiveness of acts of cyber aggression. A cyber-attack campaign coordinated closely with conventional military operations, with carefully selected targets intended to disrupt basic infrastructure and severely disrupt government communications, relying on significant outsourcing supported by open malware distribution. The cyber warfare used in the Georgian conflict is remarkable for its tactical and operational coordination, as well as its basic strategic conception of disrupting communications.

Stuxnet, 2010

Of all the cases of cyber warfare that have so far occurred, the Stuxnet virus has been engaged with most frequently in the literature. Discovered in June 2010, Stuxnet is argued by some as representing a step change in cyber warfare; indeed, Rid (2013: 43) labels it as 'by far the most sophisticated known cyber attack to date'. Denning (2012: 673) puts this best in saying that compared to previous worms, none had achieved what Stuxnet did 'either in terms of precision targeting or causing physical damage through ICS (Industrial Control System) manipulation'. Stuxnet is allegedly the creation of American and Israeli intelligence services, although definitive attribution has remained elusive. The case for American and Israeli origins is made in David Sanger's book *Confront and conceal*, which argues that the Stuxnet program was part of a broader program, known as *Olympic Games*, the intent of which was to retard the Iranian nuclear program (Sanger, 2012: chapter 8). According to Sanger (2012: 190), the intent behind Stuxnet was twofold:

> The first was to cripple, at least for a while, Iran's nuclear progress. The second, equally vital, was to convince the Israelis that there was a smarter, more elegant way to deal with the Iranian nuclear problem than launching an airstrike that could quickly escalate into another Middle East war[.]

Unlike Estonia and Georgia, which were broader campaigns with considerable outsourcing of the attack effort, Stuxnet is unique for its secrecy and highly focused targeting. By targeting the Natanz nuclear facility within Iran, considerable challenges had to be overcome simply to deliver the virus to the target system. Natanz was not connected to the open Internet: its computer systems were maintained, instead, on a closed network. This created what in IT terms is referred to as an 'air gap' between the target network and the attacker. Infiltrating a closed network therefore requires physically accessing a networked terminal, in *lieu* of being able to send the attack across the Internet. Lindsay (2013: 380–1) details that Stuxnet infections were traced to five industrial companies in Iran, four of which were probably achieved through the use of human agency loading malware through removable media devices. This immediately implies a considerable level of resource ability: to be able to distribute this malware through human agency into a nation that is difficult to penetrate is most certainly the work of intelligence services. Additionally, two stolen digital certificates were also used, as well as several 'zero-day' exploits (Chen, 2014: 7). Not only was considerable resource used in getting the malware into the Iranian network, there was also significant use of previously unused and privileged software exploits.

Once loaded into the intended networks, the virus had then to locate exactly those controlling the uranium centrifuges, which meant locating systems running the Siemens S7 Programmable Logic Controller (PLC) (Peterson, 2013: 2). This is significant, in revealing that Stuxnet was programmed with the ability to *discriminate* amongst the systems that it had been infected into. Instead of mindlessly manipulating whatever system it occupied, 'it had to examine the hardware, software, and settings of each system to determine if they matched those at Natanz, unleashing its payload only when they did' (Denning, 2012: 674). Once the centrifuge PLC was discovered, Stuxnet still did not attack; instead, it ran a form of deception program, intended to deceive the staff at Natanz into believing that all systems were running as usual. It did this simply by recording the normal operating processes and replaying them back to staff. As Rid (2013:45) notes, '[t]he objective was not just to fool operates in a control room, but to circumvent and compromise digital safety systems'. Only then did the real program go to work. Stuxnet began alternating the frequencies of the electrical current powering the centrifuges, 'causing them to switch back and forth between high and low speeds at intervals for which the machines were not designed' (Farwell and Rohozinski, 2011: 24). The ultimate intention of all this was to compromise the centrifuge process for the refinement of uranium on the nuclear program.

Was Stuxnet effective? In the short term, it appears to have had some success. Milevski (2011: 65) notes that some 1,000 centrifuges were destroyed because of Stuxnet, out of a total of 9,000 held at Natanz. In achieving the broader strategic aim of retarding the Iranian nuclear programme and preventing any Israeli conventional aggression (using Sanger's twofold intent), one can claim a measure of success, albeit very fragile. Israel has not launched any attack thus far; Iran has not made significant progress on the nuclear programme, and is also engaged in progressive political talks with the West. Any notion of strategic success attached to Stuxnet ultimately relies on preventing a regional war with

Iran, as well as reaching some kind of political agreement with Tehran over its nuclear programme. The destruction of centrifuges alone through a cyber-attack will not be enough to satisfy these large political objectives.

While the overarching strategic success of Stuxnet can only be judged according to the progress of political events, a high level of success can be taken from what it achieved at the technical level. Stuxnet has proven that highly specific industrial targets can be infiltrated covertly, using physical means of infiltration, and then attacked with a successful level of discrimination to avoid destroying other systems. Ultimately, when compared to the Estonian and Georgian cases, Stuxnet is also unique for the reason that it facilitated *physical* damage to its intended target. Taken together, the value of Stuxnet lies not in its ability to change the course of events in the Middle East, but instead in what it has proven can be achieved in cyber warfare in the long term.

Strategic implications

Having explored our case studies, attention can now be turned to the implications that can be identified from the instances of cyber warfare discussed.

Cyber warfare is presently beyond political understanding

The essence of strategy lies in political consequences and, so far, the political consequences of cyber warfare remain unclear. So long as there remains such a lack of clarity cyber warfare will be extremely difficult to use strategically, for it simply cannot be meaningfully applied. In Estonia – if the attacks against it did indeed originate from Russia – what exactly was the act intended to achieve? With no acceptance of culpability, or definitive proof of Russian involvement, the political consequence that the initiator of the cyber-attacks hoped to achieve remains unclear. The only tangible consequences appear to have been a small-scale public service disruption, provoking Estonian politicians into making allegations against the Russians and catalysing NATO involvement in cyber security matters. How these effects translate into Russian political gain is unclear.

In Georgia – again assuming that the cyber-attacks against it had Russian origins – any notion of political consequence lies not in the cyber-attacks themselves but, instead, in the broader objective of securing South Ossetia. By linking cyber warfare to traditional forms of war Russia appears to have offered the only strategic use of cyber warfare so far. Tangibly, however, it cannot be stated that the use of cyber warfare benefited the Russian objective in this case. This is because it is difficult to prove either the positive effect for Russia of employing cyber warfare or, more importantly, the negative effects on the Russian campaign had it not been used.

With regard to Stuxnet the political consequences are murkier still. Assuming American and Israeli origins, strategic success can only be measured by the broader success in curtailing the Iranian nuclear programme and preventing Israeli military action. The consequences thus far in a highly fluid issue are as unclear as they are fragile; Israel has not launched any pre-emptive raid on Iran, no regional war has begun, and Iran does not yet possess a nuclear weapon. But it is fanciful to attribute these fragile present facts as a direct result of the use of Stuxnet at Natanz. Indeed, a counterargument can be made that Stuxnet has proven strategically counterproductive by drawing attention to the covert actions of the American and Israeli governments, exposing cyber warfare methods to a global audience, setting a precedent for hostile action through cyberspace and, perhaps, provoking the Iranian regime into quicker efforts on its nuclear programme as well as tightening its own cyber security practices. The strategist must judge whether all of the consequences justify the effort, and, beyond its technical achievements, it is very difficult to establish that this was the case with regard to Stuxnet.

Further to the fact that political consequences remain unclear must also be the recognition that the political interpretation of cyber warfare lacks understanding. There is no consensus on what hostile activity in cyberspace looks like, what can be deemed as a use of force, and what a proportional non-cyber reaction to a cyber event would entail. Holding political understanding in a strategic sense must include the ability to judge and communicate a clear position to other actors, commonly known as 'red lines'. For example, in 1957, Israel's Foreign Minister, Golda Meir, stated that interference with Israeli shipping in the Gulf of Aqaba and Straits of Tiran 'will be regarded by Israel as an attack' (Bregman, 2004: 71). This was a clear, communicated red line. In 1982, Britain established a Total Exclusion Zone around the Falkland Islands, warning all that any intrusion would be met with the use of force. Could a similar exclusion zone be established in cyberspace? Could a penetration of the Pentagon's network servers be interpreted as an act of war? What reactions would be judged proportionate to such activities? Not only is political understanding unclear, but also political actors have no agreed basis on which to communicate their interpretations or understand proportionate response in cyber warfare. There are no clear red lines in relation to cyber conflict.

This lack of political understanding is ultimately underwritten by a pervasive and – so far in this chapter – unexplored issue: attribution. In none of the cases explored is there a definitive attribution of responsibility for the cyber-attacks that took place, or credit/responsibility assumed on the part of those states that were accused. The specific issue of successfully attributing acts of cyber warfare to a state has already been explored by Neil C. Rowe in Chapter 3 in this volume, and the related difficulty of *legal* attribution will be discussed by James A. Green in Chapter 5. Suffice to say, here, that attributing any act of cyber warfare to a particular state actor is extremely problematic: technically, politically and legally. This fact exacerbates the issue of political consequence, because without attribution the intent of the attacker will remain unclear. If war is, as Clausewitz (1976: 104) says, an act of force to compel our enemy to do our will, then the enemy must understand both what, and whose, will it is he must fulfil. With no attribution of the act, one cannot fulfil an opponent's wishes. Political, and therefore strategic, understanding of cyber warfare will remain opaque so long as the understanding of the consequences of cyber warfare remains unclear. This lack of clarity logically prevents any notion of a shared interpretation of what is occurring, all of which is underwritten by the anonymity currently enjoyed in cyber warfare.

Cyber warfare is presently beyond legal consensus

Following immediately from the lack of political understanding is the realisation that cyber warfare is also presently beyond legal consensus, reflecting many of the political issues address above. The core of the problem is the applicability of legal frameworks as they currently exist or, as Foltz (2012: 41) says: '[i]f state-sponsored cyber activities constitute a use of force, then international law governing the use of force (*jus ad bellum*) and the Law of Armed Conflict (*jus in bello*) apply'. The *jus ad bellum* is the branch of international law – also called the law on the use of force – that deals with the initial decision of a state to use military force; the *jus in bello*, in contrast, regulates how conflict must be conducted once force has already been initiated (see Waters and Green, 2010: 292).

There is general – if not, perhaps, universal – agreement in the legal literature that both of these two branches of international law are applicable to cyber warfare, but there is a huge amount of disagreement and confusion as to *how* they are applicable. Hughes (2010: 533) offers two reasons for this confusion, which stem 'from both the rapid spread of cyber-warfare and the lack of precedent to guide international regulation of cyberspace intrusions'. Meyer (2012: 14) echoes this with his observation that defining 'legitimate state activity' in cyberspace remains an unfulfilled task amongst the international community. Indeed, the very fact that the title of a speech given by the British Foreign Secretary William Hague (2011), on the subject of cyber security was 'Seeking the rules of the road' is indicative of the lack of certainty, or of any yet-agreed consensus, as to appropriate conduct in cyberspace.

Following from this, and an interesting development from Estonia's 2007 attack, was the accreditation in 2008 of the NATO Cooperative Cyber Defence Centre of Excellence (NATO CCD COE) in the Estonian capital Tallinn, the task of which is to 'enhance NATO's cyber defence capability' (NATO, 2013). In 2009 this organisation began a project to produce a manual on the law governing cyber warfare, published in 2013 as the *Tallinn manual on the international law applicable to cyber warfare*. The project brought together legal practitioners and scholars 'in an effort to examine how extant legal norms applied to this "new" form of warfare' (*Tallinn manual*, 2013: 1). The premise motivating the entire project was that there are no current treaty provisions directly dealing with cyber warfare, but the key conclusion of the project participants was 'that both the *jus ad bellum* and *jus in bello* apply to cyber operations' (*Tallinn manual*, 2013: 5). The rest of the manual proposes a series of rules on how currently existing international law applies to the conduct of cyber warfare. The substance of those rules is beyond the scope of this chapter. The applicability of the *jus ad bellum* to cyber warfare will be explored in Chapter 5 of this volume, and the applicability of the *jus in bello* will be examined in Chapter 6.

However, it is worth noting here the *Tallinn manual's* first rule regarding sovereignty: '[a] state may exercise control over cyber infrastructure and activities within its sovereign territory'. This starting rule serves to set the scene clearly for the applicability of other legal frameworks as guiding provisions on cyber warfare. It is also worth noting here the closing words of the project's director, Michael Schmitt, to the *Tallinn manual*'s Introduction:

> The Manual does not represent the views of the NATO CCD COE, its sponsoring nations, or NATO. In particular, it is not meant to reflect NATO doctrine. Nor does it reflect the position of any organisation or State represented by observers.
> (*Tallinn manual*, 2013: 11)

What this ultimately means is that, while the *Tallinn manual* represents guidance and advice on how the law should apply, it does not reflect any accepted consensus on the legal parameters of cyber warfare by national policymakers or by NATO itself. As a consequence, it is clear that there remain numerous, and large, legal issues to clarify with regard to cyber warfare. The *Tallinn manual* is a significant step forward for a legal understanding of war fighting in cyberspace, but uncertainty still permeates the legal understanding of cyber warfare as a whole. This can be seen in the current disputes over cyber-attacks taking place in the Russian–Ukrainian crisis, where a determination of the legal status of the attacks cannot be made. This is because:

> [W]e do not know whether [the cyber operations] were designed to militarily support Russia to the detriment of Ukraine. What we do know is that the operations in question are not 'attacks', and therefore the rules on targeting do not apply to them, whether or not they have a belligerent nexus.
> (Roscini, 2014: 4)

Cyber warfare is primarily, though not exclusively, a peacetime resort

Thanks to the cumulative uncertainty, both politically and legally, regarding when cyber warfare can be classified as an act of war, a unique strategic consequence presents itself. This is that cyber warfare so far holds most utility as a peacetime resort. Although the Georgian example took place in the context of broader military action, the Estonian and Stuxnet cases were clearly not 'wartime' actions. Even in Georgia, the fact that cyber-attacks began more than one week prior to the start of conventional military hostilities suggests that utility is held in peacetime use, and can potentially act as an instigator of broader hostilities. Sheldon (2013: 310) states that one of cyber power's attributes is stealth, which links to the problem of attribution addressed above. By utilising the stealth that is inherent in virtually all acts of cyber warfare, strategic actors possess a tool that can avoid escalation into full-scale conflict, but can achieve some level of coercion for limited objectives.

Stuxnet is the best example of such use, the intention of that action being to proactively harm the Iranian nuclear programme while avoiding escalation into military action (Sanger, 2012: 190). This logic is most clear when considering alternative options: an air strike is a definitive hostile act and unambiguous legally; the use of special operations forces, while covert in execution, leaves unmistakable evidence of the perpetrator after the fact; intelligence-sponsored sabotage carries the risk of agents being arrested and precipitating a diplomatic crisis. Cyber warfare, by contrast, remains difficult to understand (both in execution and effect), to identify, to attribute, and to base any legal argument upon. The purported American and Israeli resort to cyber warfare through Stuxnet was seemingly based on the logic of taking hostile action without going to war. So long as the political and legal understandings remain uncertain, cyber warfare will hold its greatest utility as a peacetime resort.

Geography still matters

The most common consequence ascribed to the rise of cyberspace is the notion of the demise of geography (Murray, 2006: Chapter 1). While cyberspace, and especially activities *within* cyberspace, clearly impacts geography beyond previous conceptions, the empirical evidence reveals that geography does indeed still matter. This position is based on three arguments. First, cyberspace has three 'layers': the physical, logical and geographical (Blum, 2012: 20). The logical layer refers to the way in which electronic signals carrying code travel; the physical layer comprises the machines and wires through which those signals travel; and the geographical layer refers to signal origins, routes, destinations and locations of the physical layer. Of these three layers, only the logical layer, by which the code-traversing cyberspace is carried, is in the virtual sphere. The argument, therefore, is that cyberspace is ultimately reliant on a physical architecture, which necessarily must exist geographically. Computers must connect via fibre optic cables, which connect to service exchanges, and which send signals through either submarine cables or orbital satellites to equivalent systems on the receiving end of the signal. A physical architecture is a necessary component for cyberspace to exist and, as anything physical must exist geographically, this carries strategic implications.

Second, although one can speculate, probably correctly, that cyber warfare will affect geographical concerns in radical ways when it comes to war fighting, this does not, however, justify the notion that cyber warfare is a phenomenon that goes entirely beyond geographical realities. Stuxnet is a potent illustration of this. Jumping the 'air gap' was a significant difficulty for those trying to infiltrate the Stuxnet program into the target systems. The air gap problem is generally seen as a purely technical issue, meaning that the system being targeted is not connected to the Internet but is, instead, part of a closed network that must simply be infiltrated. Seen in purely technical terms, this is correct: however, if one then considers the fact that the air gap being targeted resides in a totalitarian state, which is part of a widely dispersed and highly guarded infrastructure, the challenge becomes more than a technical computer challenge. Suddenly the resort to cyber warfare methods must take account of how to *physically* infiltrate the virus into the target nation: by which persons, and into which facilities. Geography affected the feasibility of the Stuxnet action significantly, but in ways not yet appreciated. Ultimately, whether the target is the Natanz nuclear facility, Google's primary server farms, the hard drive for the operations room on board an aircraft carrier, or the National Security Agency's data centre, one needs not only the code that can penetrate the system on its logical level, but also the location of the system physically.

Third, reconsidering the Georgian case, the vulnerability of Georgia to cyber warfare, in comparison to Estonia, should have been lower as only some 7 per cent of Georgia's population used the Internet daily (Bonner, 2014: 105). Georgia's vulnerability was based instead on the geographical reality of where its Internet traffic was routed. Quite simply:

> [M]ore than half of 13 connections made to the outside world via the Internet passed through Russia, and most of the Internet traffic to web sites within Georgia was routed through Turkish or Azerbaijani Internet service providers, many of which were in turn routed through Russia.
> (Bonner, 2014: 105)

By having such a large proportion of its Internet traffic routed through systems and services based in Russia, Georgia was vulnerable to Russian cyber-attack. Being a conduit for the Internet traffic of others conveys a significant, and as yet unrecognised, strategic advantage for those wishing to use cyber power: a strategic advantage that is fundamentally based on exploiting sovereign national geography. Another potent example of the advantage that such a position commands can be gleaned from the Snowden revelations concerning the surveillance practices of the US National Security Agency (NSA) and the United Kingdom's Government Communications Headquarters (GCHQ), particularly in the case of Tempora (a GCHQ program). Tempora is a surveillance program for the interception of communications, which is fundamentally enabled by 'attaching intercept probes to transatlantic fibre optic cables *where they land on British shores* carrying data to Western Europe from telephone exchanges and Internet servers in North America' (MacAskill, *et al.*, 2013: 4, emphasis added). The geography of Internet architecture provides American and British intelligence agencies with a formidable advantage in terms of intercepting communications. Without the physical presence of fibre optic cables in British sovereign territory, GCHQ would not be able to have the Tempora program.

Going beyond these examples, the geographical implications of cyber warfare will matter. For instance, if Internet governance does indeed 'Balkanise' (Goldstein, 2014) into more regionally controlled architectures instead of the predominantly American-dominated one at present, how can one guarantee the ability to target those systems unless one can physically access that network? Such a restructuring would dramatically impact programmes such as those carried out by the NSA and GCHQ. This may require broader corporate or diplomatic agreements to access that cyberspace (akin to accessing another state's airspace), through to physically breaking into or infiltrating closed networks. If military operations are to be expected to carry significant cyber warfare components, adversary forces must understand what physical architecture their opponent is using to be able to target it. Ultimately, while there does indeed need to be greater appreciation for the technical aspects of cyberspace, there equally needs to be an appreciation for exactly how geography, particularly in geopolitical terms, impacts upon the use of cyber power. Geography is not dead: it is a permanent and ubiquitous dimension of strategy (Gray, 1999: 41) that has so far been neglected in cyber warfare thinking.

Cyber warfare is in its infancy

Although the empirical evidence is growing on which to base conceptual thinking, it needs to be acknowledged that cyber warfare remains in its infancy. Cyber warfare is, indeed, all about information (Gray, 2006: 315), but uncertainty remains about exactly how cyber warfare methods can be used, with what effects, and to what purposes. Uncertainty abounds about how to match tactics with effects simply within cyberspace itself, yet there is a deeper level of infancy afflicting cyber warfare that has not commonly been appreciated. Sheldon is correct to state that cyber power is pervasive across land, sea, air and space (Sheldon, 2013: 310), yet he neglects to acknowledge that little attention has so far been paid to thinking about 'how to integrate cyber power into conventional military operations' (Bonner, 2014: 103).

Based on the evidence of the three cases consulted, cyber warfare appears to carry most promise when synchronised with conventional military operations, as demonstrated in the Georgia case. Much thinking focuses on cyber warfare as a standalone option, but both the Stuxnet and Estonian examples serve as illustrations of the *limits* of cyber warfare methods to cause tangible and lasting effects when used alone. The cyber-attacks directed against Estonia appear to have been little more than a nuisance on a par with domestic strikes, and Stuxnet's effect can only be considered in the context of the ongoing development of broader political dialogue with Iran. Overall, it must be accepted that cyber warfare remains in its infancy, and will only become better understood through the school of application. Only by generating a body of empirical knowledge, based on experimental application by strategic practitioners, will greater insight be gleaned into how cyber warfare can be used.

Conclusion

This chapter began with the view that cyber warfare is strategically misunderstood: the intention throughout has been to reveal the shortcomings in current thinking associated with cyber warfare and ultimately to redress the balance somewhat. By focusing on cyber warfare as it has actually occurred between state actors, some strategic implications have been identified. The five implications analysed above should not be considered an exclusive list, indeed it is the author's contention that more implications will be identified as the practice of cyber warfare matures. Instead, the argument of this chapter rests on these implications offering a more reliable foundation for strategic thinking to progress in its endeavour to provide cyber warfare with a meaningful link to desired political intent. The primary argument is that the strategic understanding of cyber warfare can only be progressed by first acknowledging how misunderstood it is at present, and how uncertainty currently pervades its activities. By acknowledging a condition of uncertainty, thinking can be more productively focused on redressing the lack of conceptual clarity based on practical application.

Having made the case for why cyber warfare is both strategically misunderstood and strategically uncertain, it is necessary to offer some progressive conclusions beyond the implications identified in this chapter. Despite the uncertainty that pervades the present understanding of cyber warfare, there are three strategic certainties that can guide thinking moving ahead.

Cyber warfare will grow in strategic significance

Cyber warfare is now a permanent fixture on the strategic landscape, despite Gartzke's bold claims (2013: 72) that 'in grand strategic terms, it remains a backwater'. The argument can certainly be made that cyber warfare does not yet command enough capability to generate decisive strategic effect; nonetheless, it would be foolish to dismiss its occurrence on this basis alone. This would be akin to not recognising the significance of either the early impact of air power, which carried little strategic utility for some years but is now indispensable, or the advent of the atomic bomb. Cyber warfare will feature prominently in future warfare: what remains to be seen is exactly how that warfare will be expressed. The empirical evidence proves that refinement of the tools of cyber warfare continues unabated. Estonia, Georgia and Stuxnet all reveal a variation in use, for differing objectives and with differing levels of success. What they also reveal is a consistent utility, and a desire to refine the methods accordingly.

For proof of this consistency one need only consider the Russia–Ukraine crisis, where reports have been gradually emerging of cyber-attacks launched against Ukraine, again with the allegation of Russian origins (Morbin, 2014). These assaults mirror the previous examples in Estonia and Georgia through the use of DDoS attacks and website defacement (Limnell, 2014: 2). In the latter case, specific targeting of the Ukrainian presidential election has been reported (Clayton, 2014). Moreover, similar to the Georgian example, there are reports of more sophisticated attacks against government and military networks, with reports citing viruses known as 'Snake' and 'Turla', which are parts of programs to steal data, and hijack computer terminals if needed (Khandelwal, 2014).

Cyber warfare will not be a strategically decisive instrument

The second conclusion of this chapter is the most speculative, and the most likely to be disputed as much thinking on cyber warfare centres on the notion of bloodless warfare and the ability to cripple one's adversary through catastrophic cyber-attack. The argument, however, rests on the empirical evidence: neither in Estonia, Georgia, Iran, nor presently in Ukraine can the use of cyber warfare be held as being even strategically significant, let alone decisive. In Estonia, while disruptive, the question has to be asked, what political objective was attained? No action carries strategic significance if it does not productively add to one's desired political end state, remembering this basic logic is a necessity. In Georgia, while considerably more significant in application, cyber warfare was not the decisive instrument. Russian military forces may have encountered a more organised response from Georgian forces had the cyber-attacks not compromised data flows as effectively as they did, but it is fanciful to argue that Georgian forces would have prevented Russia from securing its objectives had they not taken place. In the case of the Stuxnet attack, while a highly intriguing example of the development of cyber-attack potential, the big picture must be kept in mind; it was one attack in the context of a broad strategic issue that has progressed for many years. The continued development of the Iranian nuclear programme, and Western reactions and dialogue concerning that development, is an ongoing story that, at the time of writing, will enjoy more decisive input from diplomacy than from other instruments of power.

The empirical record to date proves that cyber warfare holds no decisive input, and it can be expected to remain in this state for another reason. As Gartzke (2013: 72) correctly states, 'cyberwar can achieve neither conquest nor, in most cases, coercion'. Cyber warfare is uniquely troubling because of the fact that it is not an expression of physical violence. Indeed, Rid (2013: 166) goes as far as to argue that it represents an assault on violence itself. The conceptual issue is not what matters here, instead the strategist's most important question – so what? (Brodie, 1973: 452) – should be asked in order to judge the strategic significance of the nonviolent nature of cyber warfare. That significance is simple: cyber warfare cannot by itself hold strategic significance as the other forms of warfare can and, indeed, will deliver greater impact through the application of physical violence.

Cyber warfare will grow in strategic prominence as will its impact as the methods of its application are refined. However, it is a strategic reality that, just as air power alone cannot deliver decisive effect, neither can cyber warfare. It is, at present, a tool of 'mass disruption' rather than mass destruction (Freedman, 2013: 230). Thinking should focus on how to assimilate cyber warfare into existing modes of warfare: generating greater understanding of how cyber warfare impacts and interweaves with land, sea, air, and space power is surely the most fruitful path of inquiry.

Cyber warfare will remain strategically ambiguous

The final conclusion of this chapter must be the recognition of the present and the expected immediate future. Cyber warfare has not generated either clear strategic benefit or blowback on the part of those initiating it. The record to date is therefore one of ambiguity, a record that can be expected to continue. The scale of political and legal uncertainty alone is enough to justify this argument; there is simply not enough understanding of how cyber warfare purposefully contributes to political gain to provide anything less than ambiguity in practice. As Sheldon (2011: 110) says, 'little effort has gone into identifying exactly what it is that cyberpower strategically provides to its employer'.

Further to this is the political interpretation of acts of cyber warfare by other actors. It will be unclear to actors whether the attacks they suffer are part of warlike behaviour or are simply the result of an environment characterised by anarchic anonymity, thereby creating increased risk. They will struggle to articulate the political gains made through cyber warfare (assuming, of course, that they choose to acknowledge the practice rather than benefit from non-attribution); they will struggle to establish, execute, and justify proportionate reactions to cyber assault; and they will struggle to justify policy red lines in the hope of establishing some kind of mutual political understanding. The record will change, and greater strategic clarity to cyber warfare will ultimately emerge. For the time being, however, the record is one of ambiguity. This is a record that will continue, and it is one that will not be dispelled quickly or comprehensively.

To conclude, while much remains to be done in grasping the strategic significance of cyber warfare, there is now enough empirical evidence of its occurrence upon which to begin basing conceptual approaches. The evidence of Estonia, Georgia, Stuxnet and emerging reports of similar incidents in Ukraine reveal a great deal about the use of cyber warfare. The implications of that use have been offered here as a foundation on which to start generating greater strategic appraisal of a practice that can be expected to continue and grow in value. It is the duty of the strategist to identify such lessons, learn from them, and develop guidance, lest they be confronted by another actor who has already developed such an advantage.

Note

1 I give special thanks to two of my students – Dan Sowik and Rob Finch – for making me aware of, and providing timely sources on, cyber warfare incidents in Ukraine.

References

Andress, J. and Winterfield, S. (2011), *Cyber warfare: Techniques, tactics, and tools for security* practitioners, Waltham: Syngress.

Arquilla, J. (2012), 'Cyberwar is already upon us: but can it be controlled?', 27 February, *Foreign Policy* [online], available: www.foreignpolicy.com/articles/2012/02/27/cyberwar_is_already_upon_us [5 July 2014].

Arquilla, J. and Ronfeldt, D. (1993), 'Cyberwar is coming!', in Arquilla, J. and Ronfedlt, D. (eds, 1997), *In Athena's camp: Preparing for conflict in the information age*, Santa Monica: RAND.
Bregman, A. (2004) *Israel's wars: A history since 1947*, London: Routledge.
Brenner, S. (2009), *Cyber threats: The emerging fault lines of the nation state*, Oxford: Oxford University Press.
Betz, D. and Stevens, T. (2011), *Cyberspace and the state: Towards a strategy for cyberpower*, Abingdon: Routledge (for the International Institute for Strategic Studies, Adelphi Series, 51).
Blank, S. (2008), 'Web War I: is Europe's first information war a new kind of war?', *Comparative Strategy*, vol. 27, no. 3, pp. 227–47.
Blum, A. (2012), *Tubes: Behind the scenes at the Internet*, London: Viking.
Bonner III, E.L. (2014), 'Cyber power in 21st-century joint warfare', *Joint Forces Quarterly*, vol. 74, no. 3, pp. 102–9.
Brodie, B. (1973), *War and politics*, London: Cassell.
Carr, J. (2011) *Inside cyber warfare: mapping the cyber underworld*, 2nd edition, Sebastopol: O'Reilly.
Chen, T.M. (2014), *Cyberterrorism after Stuxnet*, Carlisle: USAWC SSI.
Clarke, R.A. and Knake, R.K. (reprinted edition, 2012) *Cyber war: The next threat to national security and what to do about it*, New York: Harper Collins.
Clausewitz, C. von (Paret, P. and Howard, M., trans.) (1976) *On war*, Princeton: Princeton University Press.
Clayton, M. (2014) 'Ukraine election narrowly avoided "wanton destruction" from hackers', 17 June, *Cyber Conflict Monitor* [online], available: www.csmonitor.com/World/Security-Watch/Cyber-Conflict-Monitor/2014/0617/Ukraine-election-narrowly-avoided-wanton-destruction-from-hackers-video [4 July 2014].
Cornish, P., Livingstone, D., Clemente, D. and Yorke, C. (2010) *On cyber warfare*, London: Royal Institute of International Affairs.
Cornish, P. (2012) 'Digital détente: designing a strategic response to cyber espionage', *Public Interest Report*, vol. 65, no. 1, pp. 23–9.
Denning, D.E. (2012) 'Stuxnet: what has changed?', *Future Internet*, vol. 4, pp. 672–87.
Douhet, G. (2003) *The command of the air*, Dehradun: Natraj Publishers.
Dunn Cavelty, M. (2010) 'Cyberwar', in Kassimeris, G. and Buckley, J.D. (eds) *Ashgate research companion to modern warfare*, Farnham: Ashgate.
Economist, The (2010) 'War in the fifth domain', 3 July [online], available: www.economist.com/node/16478792 [7 July 2014].
Economist, The (2012) 'Cyber-warfare: hype and fear', 6 December [online], available: www.economist.com/news/international/21567886-america-leading-way-developing-doctrines-cyber-warfare-other-countries-may [5 July 2014].
Farwell, J.P. and Rohozinsky, R. (2011) 'Stuxnet and the future of cyber war', *Survival*, vol. 53, no. 1, pp. 23–40.
Foltz, A.C. (2012) 'Stuxnet, Schmitt analysis, and the cyber "use-of-force" debate', *Joint Forces Quarterly*, vol. 67, no. 4, pp. 40–8.
Freedman, L. (2013) *Strategy: A history*, Oxford: Oxford University Press.
Gartzke, E. (2013) 'The myth of cyberwar: bringing war in cyberspace back down to Earth', *International Security*, vol. 38, no. 2, pp. 41–73.
Goldstein, G.M. (2014) 'The end of the Internet? How regional networks may replace the World Wide Web', 25 June, *The Atlantic* [online], available: www.theatlantic.com/magazine/archive/2014/07/the-end-of-the-internet/372301/ [4 July 2014].

Goodman, W. (2010) 'Cyber deterrence: tougher in theory than in practice?', *Strategic Studies Quarterly*, Fall, pp. 102–35.

Gray, C.S. (1999) *Modern strategy*, Oxford: Oxford University Press.

Gray, C.S. (2006) *Another bloody century: Future warfare*, London: Phoenix.

Gray, C.S. (2013) *Making strategic sense of cyber power: Why the sky is not falling*, Carlisle: USAWC SSI.

Haddick, R. (2011) 'This week at war: lessons from cyberwar I', 28 January, *Foreign Policy* [online], available: www.foreignpolicy.com/articles/2011/01/28/this_week_at_war_lessons_from_cyberwar_i [24 March 2014].

Hague, W. (2011) 'Security and freedom in the cyber age – seeking the rules of the road', speech given to the Munich Security Conference on 4th February 2011 [Online], Full transcript available: www.gov.uk/government/speeches/security-and-freedom-in-the-cyber-age-seeking-the-rules-of-the-road [7 July 2014].

Herzog, S. (2011) 'Revisiting the Estonian cyber attacks: digital threats and multinational responses', *Journal of Strategic Security*, vol. 4, no. 2, pp. 49–60.

Hollis, D. (2011) 'Cyberwar case study: Georgia 2008', 6 January, *Small Wars Journal*, pp. 1–10.

Hughes, R. (2010) 'A treaty for cyberspace', *International Affairs*, vol. 86, no. 2, pp. 523–41.

Kello, L. (2013) 'The meaning of the cyber revolution: perils to theory and statecraft', *International Security*, vol. 38, no. 2, pp. 7–40.

Khandelwal, S. (2014) 'Sophisticated Russian malware "SNAKE" and "Turla" targets governments and military networks', 7 March, *Hacker News* [online], available: http://thehackernews.com/2014/03/sophisticated-russian-malware-snake-and.html [4 July 2014].

Korns, S.W. and Kastenberg, J.E. (2008–2009) 'Georgia's cyber left hook', Parameters, Winter, pp. 60–76.

Krepinevich, A.F. (2012) 'Cyber warfare: a "nuclear option"?', 24 August, *Centre for Strategic and Budgetary Assessments* [online], available: www.csbaonline.org/publications/2012/08/cyber-warfare-a-nuclear-option/ [5 July 2014].

Laasme, H. (2011) 'Estonia: cyber window into the future of NATO', *Joint Forces Quarterly*, vol. 63, no. 4, pp. 58–63.

Libicki, M.C. (2013) 'Managing September 12th in cyberspace', Testimony presented before the House of Homeland Security Subcommittee, Subcommittee on Cybersecurity, Infrastructure Protection, and Security Technologies on 20 March [online], available: www.rand.org/pubs/testimonies/CT383.html [5 July 2014].

Limnell, J. (2014) 'Ukraine crisis proves cyber conflict is a reality of modern warfare', 19 April, *The Telegraph* [online], available: www.telegraph.co.uk/technology/internet-security/10770275/Ukraine-crisis-proves-cyber-conflict-is-a-reality-of-modern-warfare.html [4 July 2014].

Lindsay, J.R. (2013) 'Stuxnet and the limits of cyber warfare', *Security Studies*, vol. 22, no. 3, pp. 365–404.

MacAskill, E., Borger, J., Hopkins, N., Davies, N. and Ball, J. (2013) 'GCHQ taps fibre-optic cables for secret access to world's communications', 21 June, *Guardian* [online], available: www.guardian.co.uk/uk/2013/jun/21/gchq-cables-secret-world-communications-nsa/print [25 June 2014].

MacIsaac, D. (1986) 'Voices from the central blue: the air power theorists', in Paret, P. (ed.), *Makers of modern strategy: From Machiavelli to the nuclear age*, Princeton: Princeton University Press.

Magee, C.S. (2013) 'Awaiting cyber 9/11', *Joint Forces Quarterly*, vol. 70, no. 3, pp. 76–82.
Meyer, P. (2012) 'Diplomatic alternatives to cyber-warfare: a near-term agenda', *Royal United Services Institute Journal*, vol. 157, no. 1, pp. 14–19.
Milevski, L. (2011) 'Stuxnet and strategy: a special operation in cyberspace?', *Joint Forces Quarterly*, vol. 63, no. 4, pp. 64–9.
Morbin, T. (2014) 'Russia suspected of Ukraine cyber attack', 10 March, *SC Magazine* [online], available: www.scmagazineuk.com/russia-suspected-of-ukraine-cyber-attack/article/337578/ [4 July 2014].
Murray, W.E. (2006) *Geographies of globalisation*, Abingdon: Routledge.
NATO (2013), Cooperative Cyber Defence Centre of Excellence, *Our mission and vision* [online], available: www.ccdcoe.org/about-us.html [7 July 2014].
Nye Jr, J.S. (2011) 'Nuclear lessons for cyber security?', *Strategic Studies Quarterly*, Winter 2011, pp. 18–38.
Peterson, D. (2013) 'Offensive cyber weapons: construction, development, and employment', *Journal of Strategic Studies*, vol. 36, no. 1, pp. 120–4.
Rid, T. (2012) 'Think again: Cyberwar', 27 February, *Foreign Policy* [online], available: http://foreignpolicy.com/2012/02/27/think-again-cyberwar [19 January 2015].
Rid, T. (2013) *Cyber war will not take place*, London: Hurst.
Roscini, M. (2014) 'Is there a "cyber war" between Ukraine and Russia?', 31 March, *OUP Blog* [online], available: http://blog.oup.com/2014/03/is-there-a-cyber-war-between-ukraine-and-russia-pil/ [4 July 2014].
Sanger, D. (2012) *Confront and conceal: Obama's secret wars and surprising use of American power*, New York: Crown.
Sheldon, J.B. (2011) 'Deciphering cyberpower: strategic purpose in peace and war', *Strategic Studies Quarterly*, Summer, pp. 95–112.
Sheldon, J.B. (2013) 'The rise of cyberpower', in Baylis, J., Wirtz, J.J. and Gray, C.S. (eds) *Strategy in the contemporary world*, 4th edition, Oxford: Oxford University Press.
Singer, P.W. and Friedman, A. (2014) *Cybersecurity and cyberwar: What everyone needs to know*, Oxford: Oxford University Press.
Tallinn manual on the international law applicable to cyber warfare (2013) Prepared by the International Group of Experts at the Invitation of the NATO Cooperative Cyber Defence Centre of Excellence (general editor: Schmitt, M.N.), Cambridge: Cambridge University Press.
UK Government (2010) *A Strong Britain in an Age of Uncertainty: The National Security Strategy* [online], available: www.gov.uk/government/publications/the-national-security-strategy-a-strong-britain-in-an-age-of-uncertainty [4 July 2014].
Waters, C.P.M. and Green, J.A. (2010) 'International law: military force and armed conflict', in Kassimeris, G. and Buckley, J.D. (eds) *Ashgate research companion to modern warfare*, Farnham: Ashgate.

5 The regulation of cyber warfare under the *jus ad bellum*[1]

James A. Green

Introduction

Most interaction between cyberspace and 'the law' occurs at the national level (Remus, 2013: 180). This is largely appropriate, as a significant proportion of such actions involve criminal activity by either individuals or private groups for personal gain (Roscini, 2014: 4), or take the form of a plethora of other 'non-criminal' activities in cyberspace (commercial transactions, advertising, defamation, etc.) that are all best regulated by domestic law. Cyber warfare, however, is inherently 'international' in nature, and thus requires an international legal response (Morth, 1998: 581). Yet, at present, there are no specific rules of international law governing the interstate use of cyber force. The only treaty regulating cyberspace per se remains the 2001 Budapest Convention on Cybercrime, and there are no treaties at all that deal directly with cyber warfare, nor are there any specific provisions of customary international law on the topic (Shackelford, 2009: 219).

The first notable works in international law literature relating to the problem of cyber warfare appeared in the late 1990s (e.g. Morth, 1998; Schmitt, 1999; Sharp, 1999), at a time when the discussion over how to deal with interstate cyber-attacks within the framework of international law was largely hypothetical. By the late 2000s, the need for international law to engage with the issue became rather more urgent, particularly following the various Distributed Denial of Service (DDoS) attacks directed at Estonia in 2007 (a series of attacks discussed in detail in both Chapters 1 and 4 of this volume). Nonetheless, international law has not caught up with this modern form of conflict: cyber warfare, at least at first glance, remains insufficiently regulated by the law. On this basis, cyber warfare has been described as existing 'in a legal netherworld' (Hoisington, 2009: 440; see also discussion by Danny Steed in Chapter 4 of this volume).

Having said this, in contrast, the recent *Tallinn manual on the international law applicable to cyber warfare*, prepared by an international group of experts at the invitation of the NATO Cooperative Cyber Defence Centre of Excellence (2013: 5), argues that '[t]his uncertainty does not mean cyber operations exist in a normative void'. Indeed, the *Tallinn manual* represents the majority view in the literature on this point, which is that the existing rules of international law are applicable to the threat posed by cyber warfare (see e.g. Harrison Dinniss, 2012; Benatar, 2009: 395; Schmitt, 2013: 176–7; Tubbs *et al.*, 2002: 15).

This chapter evaluates the potential for legal regulation of the resort to cyber warfare between states under the '*jus ad bellum*'. This branch of international law – also called the law on the use of force – deals with the initial decision as to whether or not to use military force: the question of *when* the use of force by a state may be lawful, if at all. This is as opposed to the legal regulation of the conduct of cyber hostilities under the '*jus in bello*': the question of *how* conflict must be conducted once force has already been initiated (for further discussion of this distinction, see Waters and Green, 2010: 292). The application of the *jus in bello* to cyber warfare is examined by Heather A. Harrison Dinniss in Chapter 6.

In the context of the *jus ad bellum*, the main approach in the existing scholarship to resolve the lacuna left by the lack of specific international legal regulation has been to try to adapt the existing prohibition of the use of force under Article 2(4) of the United Nations (UN) Charter 1945 to cover cyber warfare. Debate in the literature has therefore largely concerned whether cyber warfare falls within the scope of Article 2(4). The first part of this chapter sets out in some detail this debate as to the correct interpretation of Article 2(4) with respect to cyber warfare. The application of Article 2(4) here is obviously somewhat anachronistic: cyber-attacks were not considered by those who drafted the Charter in 1945 (Buchan, 2012: 212–13). It has been traditionally agreed that the prohibition of the use of force in Article 2(4) includes physical armed force, but excludes non-physical acts, such as economic or political coercion. The question is therefore whether the modern phenomenon of cyber warfare should be correctly analogised with physical violence or with 'non-physical' methods of interstate coercion. However, as 'cyber warfare' covers a huge range of actions, it is not a simple matter to analogise it – wholesale – to other 'types' of intervention. It is, thus, extremely difficult to determine whether Article 2(4) clearly encompasses (or clearly *excludes*) the concept of aggressive cyber operations (Kodar, 2009: 138).

This chapter goes on to argue that 'the Article 2(4) debate' often misses the fact that an act of cyber warfare can be considered a breach of a different legal rule: the principle of non-intervention. This principle is a rule of customary international law, rather than being found in the UN Charter, but it is wider in scope than the prohibition of the use of force: for example, it covers economic and political coercion, in addition to physical military attacks. Therefore, irrespective of the applicability of Article 2(4), resort to cyber warfare will in most cases be unlawful under the principle of non-intervention. Yet, there are good reasons why the legal debate has focused upon Article 2(4) and has so often overlooked the principle of non-intervention: most importantly, this is because the principle is a demonstrably 'weaker' norm of international law, which often struggles to restrain state behaviour.

Next, this chapter considers some of the issues in applying either the prohibition of the use of force or the principle of non-intervention to cyber warfare.

In particular, it is argued that there are significant problems in attributing aggressive cyber actions to a state, as a matter of either law or fact. The chapter concludes by reflecting upon proposals for a bespoke cyber warfare treaty and argues that – given the unlikelihood of such a treaty being agreed upon any time soon – the debate should be reoriented to focus on another existing international legal obligation: the duty to *prevent* cyber-attacks, or what is sometimes called the 'duty of due diligence'.

The 'Article 2(4) debate' on cyber warfare

The prohibition of the use of force

Article 2(4) of the UN Charter has long been at the centre of the legal literature on cyber warfare. It is the key legal provision setting out the prohibition of use of force in modern international law:

> All Members shall refrain in their international relations from the threat or use of force against the territorial integrity or political independence of any state, or in any other manner inconsistent with the Purposes of the United Nations.

The prohibition contained in Article 2(4) is unquestionably one of the most fundamental rules of the UN system and is commonly referred to as a 'cornerstone' provision (Dinstein, 2002: 99; Harrison Dinniss, 2012: 40). Additionally, alongside its inclusion in the Charter, the prohibition is also a norm of customary international law, meaning that even non-UN member states (of which there are, in any event, very few), are similarly bound (Bothe, 2003: 228). As such, the prohibition binds all the states of the world.

The prohibition is also a relatively simple rule on its face: Article 2(4) bans the use of force by one state against another (as does the parallel prohibition under customary international law). There are, of course, exceptions to this rule that are found elsewhere in the Charter. Article 51 provides for a right to use force in self-defence and, under Articles 39–42, the UN Security Council can authorise the lawful use of force. Nonetheless, the general rule is that force is prohibited.

It is additionally worth noting that the majority view is that the prohibition of the use of force is a rule of a 'peremptory', or *jus cogens*, nature (see e.g. Orakhelashvili, 2006: 50). In other words, it is usually seen as having achieved a special status within the international legal system, whereby it cannot be altered or derogated from except by a newer rule of the same 'super-norm' sort (VCLT, 1969: Article 53). Rules of international law that have acquired this special peremptory character are extremely rare, and the present author has elsewhere questioned whether the prohibition of the use of force has in fact achieved *jus cogens* status (Green, 2011). In any event, whether or not the prohibition of the use of force is a *jus cogens* norm or not, no state in the world argues against its existence and general applicability.

Viewing cyber warfare through the prism of Article 2(4) presents an immediate problem, however. While a few writers have simply assumed that the prohibition of the use of force covers acts of cyber warfare (Graham, 2010: in general, but particularly at 88), it is, in fact, far from straightforward to apply Article 2(4) to cyber-attacks.

The 'qualifying terms' in Article 2(4)

A preliminary point of concern in relation to the applicability of Article 2(4) to cyber warfare is whether there is a loophole in the wording of Article 2(4) through which cyber-attacks might squeeze. The provision prohibits the 'use of force *against the territorial integrity or political independence of any state*' (emphasis added). On the basis that the prohibition of 'force' is qualified by this language, it may be argued that certain uses of force may not go 'against the territorial integrity or political independence' of the victim state and, thus, would not be covered (Gray, 2008: 31–3). If this interpretation is correct, it could be a particularly acute issue within the context of cyber warfare, which will likely not physically involve territorial incursion in the traditional sense (Schmitt, 1999: 888). For example, the DDoS attacks on South Korea and the United States in July 2009, for which it was alleged that North Korea was responsible, affected thousands of computers in the two states concerned. However, the attack did not involve territorial incursion into either state, at least in a physical sense: the botnet of hacked computers that was the source of the attacks was remotely activated (Sudworth, 2009). One might perhaps argue on this basis that the attacks in question were not 'against the territorial integrity' of either South Korea or the United States.

However, it is actually fairly clear that the prohibition of the use of force was always meant to be comprehensive in nature, in the sense that any and all uses of force fall under its purview (Franck, 2002, 12). The 'qualifiers' in Article 2(4) were intended by the Charter's drafters to be demonstrative of its all-encompassing scope, not exclusionary in this way (see UNCIO vol. VI, 1945: 334–5). It is worth remembering that the terms 'territorial integrity' and 'political independence' are presented in the alternative in Article 2(4) by the use of the word 'or'; it is rather difficult to conceive of a forcible state action, taken without the consent of the state against which it is directed, that does not in some way act against *either* that state's territorial integrity *or* its political independence. Moreover, as the *Tallinn manual* (2013: 43) notes, even if one could identify a forcible action of this sort, Article 2(4) also includes the 'catch-all' phrase 'or in any other manner inconsistent with the Purposes of the United Nations'; and one of the purposes of the UN is the peaceful settlement of international disputes (UN Charter, 1945: Article 1). The majority view, therefore, is overwhelmingly that *all* uses of force fall foul of the prohibition.

The meaning of 'force'

While it can be said that all 'uses of force' are covered by Article 2(4)'s prohibition, this begs a much more problematic question for the regulation of cyber warfare under the *jus ad bellum*: do interstate cyber-attacks qualify as 'uses of force' in the first place? The primary debate in the international law literature, which has raged since the late 1990s, is whether a cyber-attack equates to 'force' as per Article 2(4). If so, then such action is prohibited by that article; if not, rather obviously, it falls outside of its reach. Unfortunately, Article 2(4) itself does not define what it means by 'force'. Long before the advent of cyberspace, states and scholars therefore debated what was included in the term and what was not. In particular, the question was whether actions such as economic and political coercion should be considered 'force' for the purposes of Article 2(4), or whether the provision is restricted to what might be termed '*armed* force' (i.e. troop movements, gunfire, explosives and so on) (on this debate, see Silver, 2002: 80–2).

The starting point for interpreting the meaning of provisions of a treaty is to consider the 'ordinary meaning to be given to the terms of the treaty in their context and in light of their object and purpose' (VCLT, 1969: Article 31). In other words, international law takes a 'common-sense' approach to determining the meaning of terms found in a treaty. A reading of Article 2(4) based on the ordinary meaning of its wording might well suggest that actions beyond just 'armed force', such as coercive economic action, should be covered by its prohibition. It is certainly arguable that aggressive economic sanctions, for example, are 'forcible' under a normal understanding of the word.

Elsewhere in the UN Charter the qualified term 'armed force' is explicitly used (e.g. in the Preamble, as well as in certain articles in Chapter VII). Some scholars have pointed this out in support of a wide understanding of 'force' as used in Article 2(4). This is on the basis that – by deciding to use the term 'force' *in abstracto* in that article, but 'armed force' elsewhere – the drafters intended Article 2(4) to cover actions beyond just armed force (see e.g. Benatar, 2009: 382). Otherwise, those taking this stance argue, why was the term 'armed force' not simply used consistently throughout the Charter?

Other scholars, however, have used the presence of the term 'armed force' elsewhere in the Charter to support an entirely contradictory, narrower understanding of force as being restricted to 'armed force' only. Harrison Dinniss (2012: 41–2), for example, argues that 'force' is also used in an unqualified form in Article 44, an article that refers to the decision of the UN Security Council 'to use force'. Article 44 is directly linked to the powers of the Council to use all measures necessary to avert threats to international peace and security in Article 42, in contrast to its power to authorise 'measures *not involving the use of armed force*' in Article 41 (emphasis added). This strongly indicates that the unqualified use of the term 'force' in Article 44 should be read as meaning 'armed force' and thus, by analogy, so perhaps should the unqualified use of the same word in Article 2(4).

Also potentially supporting a more restrictive reading of 'force' in Article 2(4) is the fact that the 'ordinary meaning' of terms in a treaty must be interpreted in the context of the broader principles and purposes of the convention in question (VCLT, 1969: Article 31). It is evident from reading the preamble to the Charter that its core object and purpose is to limit the use of military force between states (key goals mentioned therein being to 'save succeeding generations from the scourge of war' and 'to ensure ... that armed force shall not be used, save in the common interest'). As such, reading the word 'force' in the context of the goals of the Charter might similarly indicate that it should be limited to armed force (Buchan, 2012: 216).

These various attempts at interpretive gymnastics in the literature are ultimately inconclusive (Roscini, 2010: 104). In the end, Article 2(4)'s 'ordinary meaning' can be read as pointing in either direction. As such, a secondary method of treaty interpretation, when the ordinary meaning is not entirely clear (as is the case here), is to examine the *travaux préparatoires* of the treaty in question: that is, the debates over its drafting involving the drafters themselves (VCLT, 1969: Article 32). When one considers the *travaux préparatoires* of the Charter, it is evident that states at the time took a restrictive view of what they meant by 'force', in that they saw acts of economic or political coercion as falling outside the concept.

Various actions that were of concern in 1945 and that could have been viewed as being 'forcible' – such as economic or political coercion – were explicitly excluded from the generally agreed-upon and understood meaning of 'force' in Article 2(4) in 1945. There were a number of proposals advanced by states in 1945 to include such actions within the scope of the article. The most famous of these was a proposal by Brazil (UNCIO vol. VI, 1945: 334, 558–9), but similar suggestions were also made by Ecuador (UNCIO vol. III, 1945: 399, 423; UNCIO vol. VI, 1945: 561–2) and Iran (UNCIO vol. VI, 1945: 563). All such proposals were firmly rejected by the vast majority of other states at the time (UNCIO vol. VI, 1945: 720; see also Benatar, 2009: 383–4). Reference to the recorded views of the state drafters of the UN Charter, therefore, clearly indicates that the provision was originally intended to cover *armed* force only.

Perhaps more importantly, the drafters' interpretation of 'force' has been repeatedly confirmed in state practice over subsequent years. State practice is the core element of customary international law (Akehurst, 1974), and it is also a factor in determining the correct contextual development of the meaning of treaty provisions (VCLT, 1969: Article 31 3(b)). The restrictive view of the meaning of 'force' subsequently taken by states was particularly evident in the drafting of the UN General Assembly's Declaration on Friendly Relations (UN Doc. A/RES/25/2625, 1970). In that context, states formally debated whether 'economic, political and other forms of pressure against the territorial integrity or political independence of any state were illegal uses of force' (UN Doc. A/7619, 1969: para. 86). While a small number of states argued in the affirmative, the general view of the plenary sessions was clearly that they did not (see UN Doc. A/7619, 1969: paras 86–93). A similarly restrictive understanding of 'force' can also be seen in the UN General Assembly's Definition of Aggression, adopted in 1974 (UN Doc. A/RES/3314, 1974).

Reflecting the position of states, the vast majority of writers now argue – and have done since at least the 1970s – that 'force' in Article 2(4) means 'armed force' and, thus, excludes such activities as economic or political coercion (for the classic expression of this view, see Farer, 1985). Despite ambiguities in the wording of Article 2(4), therefore, for decades there has been little question that economic and political coercion are excluded from the prohibition of the use of force. Armed force is covered, and economic and political 'force' is not.

The meaning of 'armed force'

Simply put, by the 1970s, it was clear: 'force' means 'armed force'. This seems simple enough until one asks: what counts as 'armed force'? Specifically, are cyber-attacks 'armed force', or are they 'non-armed force'? The same textual ambiguities that plagued early interpreters of the Charter in relation to actions like economic coercion today exist within the context of cyber warfare. Those considering the application of the *jus ad bellum* to the emerging concept of technological force therefore began by trying to analogise such actions to existing forms of 'force', where agreement had already been reached as to Article 2(4)'s (in)applicability.

Analogy to the nature of the attack

The traditional way of defining the distinction between 'armed force' and 'other force' was based on armed force being an action of an 'explosive [nature, involving] shockwaves and heat' (noted by Brownlie, 1963: 362). In other words, the distinction was seen as being based upon the physical, kinetic *nature* of the force used. Cyber warfare does not, of course, involve such kinetic, physical action. The nature of (or what might be called the 'act of launching') the majority of cyber-attacks will have rather more in common with economic attacks (Goldsmith, 2013: 133). On this basis, in the early literature on cyber warfare, some writers argued that cyber aggression should rightly be analogised to economic or political coercion and, thus, excluded from the Article 2(4) prohibition (e.g. Kanuk, 1996: 289). In contrast, others took the view that cyber warfare has more, or certainly *can have* more, in common with the destruction caused by physical attacks, and so should be analogised to conventional warfare (e.g. Morth, 1998: 591). Analogising the nature of the force used simply brought the debate to another impasse.

Analogy to the effects of the attack

Long before the birth of the Internet, concerns had already been advanced that the traditional approach to understanding what was covered by the notion of 'armed force' for the purposes of Article 2(4) was insufficient. Most famously,

Brownlie (1963: 362) took the view that a distinction based on the *nature* of the action missed a crucial point, namely its *effects*. Brownlie had in mind actions such as the use of 'bacteriological, biological and chemical devices', rather than cyber warfare, but the point he made is today equally relevant in the cyber context. The use of biological, chemical and radiological weapons can ultimately have devastating physical effects without necessarily being 'kinetic actions' in themselves (Schmitt, 2010: 154). Yet, even when Brownlie was writing in the 1960s, it was already unquestionable that states considered the use of such weapons by one state against another to be a breach of Article 2(4) (Roscini, 2010: 106). As such, Brownlie argued that the distinction should be – or, rather, already *was* – one based on the effect of an attack and not its nature.

It is clear that a majority of writers in the field have adopted an 'effects-based' approach to the meaning of 'force' in Article 2(4), including in the context of cyber warfare (e.g. Goldsmith, 2013: 133; Haslam, 2000: 165; Kodar, 2009: 139; Silver, 2002: 84–92). Certainly, analogising the effects of a cyber-attack seems to better encapsulate the wide spectrum of activities that can be considered 'cyber warfare' than the all-or-nothing categorisation approach of referencing the nature of force used. An 'effects-based' understanding of what constitutes 'force' for the purposes of Article 2(4) provides a more nuanced way of assessing whether cyber warfare qualifies. Instead of analogising cyber warfare to the nature of an existing action (a near impossible task as cyber-attacks have their own unique nature), one can instead look at the results of a cyber-attack and compare this to the results of other types of action. Taking this approach, it would seem that cyber-attacks that have notably injurious consequences would constitute 'force' and, thus, would be a breach of Article 2(4); interstate cyber aggression resulting in less severe damage would not.

However, despite its widespread adoption in doctrine, problems still exist with a test based on the effects of a cyber-attack. One such issue is that by focusing on effects, breaches of the law may in part be determined by the 'durability' of the victim state (Nguyen, 2013: 1124). More powerful states are likely to be better able to defend themselves against cyber aggression, either because their more advanced cyber security programmes can stop an attack prior to its having had any 'effects' at all, or because the infrastructure of the state is better able to deal with the implications of a cyber-attack that does in fact 'hit' (meaning that where one state might suffer devastating effects, another may suffer far less damage from the same sort of attack). If 'effects' are what matter, an attack that might not be considered as falling within the scope of Article 2(4) if directed at a powerful state may incongruously qualify if the victim was a weaker one.

A related concern is that a test based on effects is *reactive* to force rather than *prescriptive*. One cannot know exactly what is prohibited, or – more pertinently – what responses may be available in relation to a violation, until after it has occurred. This is a concern somewhat amplified in the cyber arena by the potentially instantaneous nature of cyber-attacks (Hoisington, 2009: 452).

Perhaps most problematically of all, the effects approach leads the discussion down yet another interpretive rabbit-hole. To the 'effects' of what exactly are the effects of cyber warfare to be analogised? Or, to put it rather more simply: where is the threshold? Writing in the 1960s, Brownlie (1963: 362) indicated that the weapon used needed to cause 'destruction to life and property' to qualify as 'force'. More recently, and specifically in relation to cyber warfare, Dinstein (2011: 88) has argued that 'the term "force" in Article 2(4) *must denote violence*. It does not matter what specific means – kinetic or electronic – are used to bring it about, but the end result must be that *violence occurs*' (emphasis added).

Under such an understanding, a cyber-attack that results in physical damage or physical violence qualifies, and all other cyber-attacks do not. The sorts of 'cyber doomsday scenarios' that are set out in the literature with increasing regularity, such as the use of computers to melt down a nuclear power plant, turn a state's unmanned military drones against it, drop its planes form the sky and so on (see e.g. Clarke and Knake, 2010: 64–8), would clearly be covered. The effects of such actions would equate to, and could even exceed, the physical consequences of a use of traditional military force. Indeed, even below the level of such ultimate doomsday cyber-attacks, actions like the use of the Stuxnet virus against Iran in 2010 would also probably qualify because Stuxnet led to physical damage to property (Buchan, 2012: 219–21; for detailed discussion of the Stuxnet virus, see Chapters 1 and 4 of this volume).

However, the vast majority of interstate cyber-attacks, at least of those that have so far transpired, would probably not meet Dinstein's 'occurrence of violence' version of the effects-based test for inclusion in the Article 2(4) prohibition. Attacks such as those against Estonia in 2007, or Georgia in 2008 (discussed in Chapter 1 of this volume), can be devastating in many ways, of course, but only in terms of the disruption of infrastructure and economic loss (Nguyen, 2013: 1127–8). In instances where no physical destruction results the consequences of the cyber aggression would be analogised to the effects of economic force, which, as has been discussed above, is not covered by Article 2(4).

Dinstein's approach has thus been criticised by a number of writers on the basis that it is 'under inclusive' (e.g. Handler, 2012: 229). Looking only at violent, physical effects is too limiting, it has been argued, as this excludes too many cyber-attacks from the reach of Article 2(4) (Antolin-Jenkins, 2005: 155). For example, a cyber-attack 'that corrupts data on a stock exchange and which in turn causes widespread economic harm but no direct physical damage' would have devastating effects but would not be considered a breach of Article 2(4) (Goldsmith, 2013: 133). Thus, some – still following an effects-based approach – argue that cyber-attacks that are particularly severe *in spite of not leading to physical destruction* should be included (e.g. Waxman, 2011: 435–6).

The counter-argument to this, perhaps inevitably, is that economic actions can also have devastating, albeit non-physical, effects. Purely economic attacks are, as has been noted, excluded from Article 2(4) per se, however severe their consequences. To allow certain acts of cyber warfare to be included in Article 2(4)'s scope on the basis that their (non-physical) effects were particularly devastating would be to arbitrarily ignore the fact that equally injurious actions have long been considered excluded. This could lead to a slippery slope down which any and all 'forcible' action would be included in the prohibition (Hoisington, 2009: 447, at note 64). It can be argued that the strength of Article 2(4) is that it is reserved for the very worst forms of force – physical military action between states – and that it would devalue its normative weight to allow other actions to be included (e.g. Banks, 2013: 163). Indeed, the present author has suggested elsewhere that the debate over whether cyber-attacks with non-physical consequences fall within the prohibition's scope could undermine its apparent *jus cogens* status (Green, 2011: 239–40).

The 'Schmitt criteria'

The most famous attempt to remedy this uncertainty, by providing some guidelines and principled distinction to this interpretive minefield, is a set of criteria developed by Michael Schmitt (1999: 914–15). Schmitt may perhaps be considered the 'father' of the international legal scholarship on cyber warfare, and his criteria have been adopted by numerous scholars writing on the topic (e.g. Moore, 2013: 237; Murphy, 2013: 313; Dunlap, 2011: 85–6; Papain, 2011: 40–5; Remus, 2013: 182). The commentary to the NATO-commissioned *Tallinn manual* (2013: 48–51) similarly references them with approval (although this is perhaps not especially surprising given that Schmitt was the director of the *Tallinn manual* project). Schmitt has also recently restated his criteria in his own work (Schmitt, 2011: 576; Schmitt, 2010: 155–6) and has noted that they have 'generally withstood the test of time' (Schmitt, 2011: 575).

The Schmitt criteria are: (1) *severity* (the effects must be particularly severe – this will most commonly involve physical damage but is not necessarily restricted to it); (2) *immediacy* (the speed of the cyber-attack should preclude resort to a peaceful response); (3) *directness* (the consequences are clearly caused by the cyber-attack); (4) *invasiveness* (the effects should be felt within the target state and be notably invasive); (5) *measurability* (it should be possible to measure the scale and effects of the attack); and (6) *presumptive legitimacy* (cyber-attacks should be presumed to fall outside of the scope of Article 2(4) unless their effects can be equated to those of other prohibited actions, most notably the use of traditional military force).

These criteria give a comparatively detailed, formalised way of justifying why one cyber-attack is included and another is not, because they break down 'many of the underlying characteristics that define an act as armed force' (Nguyen, 2013: 1123). They undoubtedly provide a useful starting point from which to undertake analysis of the lawfulness under Article 2(4) of any given cyber-attack, and the adoption of the criteria by scholars has helped to inject a degree of much-needed coherence into the possible regulation of cyber-attacks by the *jus ad bellum*.

Schmitt has noted that 'severity is self-evidently the most significant factor for the analysis' (Schmitt, 2011: 576): in other words, 'effects' remain his primary benchmark. However, instead of focusing on 'severity' alone – which may to an extent be in the eye of the beholder – the criteria combine this initial criterion with other factors indicative of the overall 'intention' and 'consequentiality' of the attack in question, thus giving a more nuanced means of assessment. It is also worth noting (*Tallinn manual*, 2013: 51–2) that the criteria are presented both as being non-exhaustive (meaning other factors can be taken into account if they can help analysis) and as operating 'in concert' (meaning that an action need not meet *all* of the criteria, just that reference to them, taken together, provides a strong indication of whether or not a cyber-attack falls within the prohibition).

Perhaps the most important point of departure from many other analytical approaches is that the criteria potentially allow for certain cyber-attacks with severe but non-physical consequences to qualify as a breach of the prohibition of the use of force (*Tallinn manual*, 2013: 52). They do so not just by reference to damage caused, however, but by distinguishing such actions from other forms of coercion in a principled way, based upon various factors indicating what 'sort' of action any given cyber-attack really is. On this basis, most non-physical cyber-attacks would probably be excluded, but not all of them.

Extremely helpful as they are, however, it is important to keep in mind that the Schmitt criteria *are not law*. Even the impressive *Tallinn manual*, where they have recently appeared, is not a binding legal document but a set of suggested guidelines prepared by experts (Roscini, 2014: 31). The writings of scholars can be considered an interpretive, secondary source of international law (Statute of the ICJ, 1945: Article 38.1(d)), but they should never be considered formal 'law' as such. Similarly, while there are some suggestions that states have referred to the criteria on a few occasions (see e.g. Remus, 2013: 183), there is nowhere near enough evidence to conclude that states have adopted the criteria with sufficient consistency and regularity for them to have crystallised into customary international law.

It is also worth noting that Schmitt's criteria have come under some academic criticism, particularly on the basis that the last of them – 'presumptive legitimacy' – is self-referential (Barkham, 2001: 85–6; Hoisington, 2009: 452). This criterion bases its test for the legitimacy of cyber force on whether it is analogous to other actions that are considered to be legitimate. This is clearly a circular criterion, which takes things perilously close to previous debates analogising cyber force to other 'forcible' actions. Indeed, other scholars have questioned whether the criteria as a whole are simply another version of the existing 'categorisation-by-analogy' debate. It could be argued that the criteria merely provide *more* ways of analogising cyber warfare to other types of force, without taking sufficient note of the unique nature of cyber operations (see e.g. Harrison Dinniss, 2012: 63).

Perhaps the most notable criticism that can be levelled at the criteria is that, for all the increased certainty that they provide, they are still ultimately rather vague (Benatar, 2009: 391). For example, Nguyen (2013: 1123–4) notes that, in 2011, Schmitt applied his own criteria to the 2007 attacks against Estonia and concluded that five of his six principles were met. On this basis, Schmitt concluded that the DDoS actions against Estonia constituted a breach of the prohibition of the use of force (Schmitt, 2011: 577). Yet, Nguyen himself convincingly applies the criteria to the Estonia attack in a manner that indicates an entirely contradictory conclusion: i.e. he demonstrates that the criteria can credibly be applied to Estonia so as to support the view that it did *not* qualify as a use of force. Nguyen thus concludes that '[t]hese two contradictory interpretations of the same cyber attack demonstrate that Schmitt's six criteria can be too easily manipulated to create results supporting the geostrategic goals of the nation conducting the enquiry' (Nguyen, 2013: 1124). Schmitt himself has conceded that '[t]he criteria are admittedly imprecise' (Schmitt, 2011: 577).

Ultimately, the Schmitt criteria provide helpful guidance, but they are not 'the law', at least not yet; they are the thoughts of just one scholar (however influential they have been). The criteria are also arguably insufficiently precise and not 'cyber-centric' enough. The present author would thus agree with Benatar (2009: 391) that '[a]lthough Schmitt's model remains the most refined theory to date for addressing the legality of cyber attacks under the *jus ad bellum*, this is not to say that it has resolved the issue definitively'. The Schmitt criteria are not 'the answer' to the issue of cyber warfare and the *jus ad bellum* but are, rather, an important instance of interpretative legal triage.

The forgotten rule: the principle of non-intervention

The nature of the principle and its applicability to cyber warfare

The exhaustive and exhausting debate over the applicability of Article 2(4) is the focus of much of the legal literature on cyber warfare, which is why it has formed a significant part of this chapter. However, Article 2(4) is not the only rule of international law that is applicable to the resort to cyber warfare. As Russell Buchan (2012: particularly at 221–6) has importantly discussed, just because a cyber-attack fails to meet the test to constitute a breach of Article 2(4) (assuming that it can be agreed what this test is) *does not mean that it is lawful*. There is another rule of international law – the principle of non-intervention – that most acts of cyber warfare will fall foul of. Buchan (2012: 221) notes that many international law commentators 'have focused exclusively on Article 2(4), failing to consider the wider customary principle of non-intervention'.

The principle of non-intervention is not provided for as such in the UN Charter (other than in Article 2(7), which specifically requires *the United Nations* to refrain from intervening in the domestic affairs of states). The wider principle of non-intervention that applies to states per se can instead be found in customary international law (Schmitt, 2014: 143–5). This customary law principle has been confirmed by the International Court of Justice (ICJ) (*Nicaragua* case, 1986: para. 205), but is perhaps most notably set out in a number of declarations adopted by the UN General Assembly, which – while non-binding in themselves – reflect, and have contributed to the formation of, the binding customary international law rule (see e.g. UN Doc. A/RES/25/2625, 1970; UN Doc. A/RES/31/91, 1976: particularly paras 1, 3 and 4; UN Doc. A/RES/36/103,

1981: paras 1 and 2). For example, the Declaration on the Inadmissibility of Intervention in the Domestic Affairs of States and the Protection of Their Independence and Sovereignty (UN Doc. A/RES/20/2131, 1965: paras 1 and 2) holds that:

> No state has the right to intervene, directly or indirectly, for any reason whatever, in the internal or external affairs of any other state.... No state may use or encourage the use of economic, political or any other type of measures to coerce another state in order to obtain from it the subordination of the exercise of its sovereign rights or to secure from it advantages of any kind.

The principle of non-intervention means that one state cannot intervene in the domestic affairs of another state, so as to coerce it to act in a certain way. As such, both 'forcible' (in the sense of Article 2(4)) and 'non-forcible' coercive measures (such as economic and political interference) are prohibited by the principle. All uses of force in violation of Article 2(4) are also considered prohibited 'interventions', but the non-intervention principle is wider: not all unlawful interventions also breach Article 2(4). Thus, instances of coercive economic or political pressure are contrary to the non-intervention principle but not to the prohibition of the use of force.

In the cyber context, it is likely that most interstate cyber-attacks – *including* those that fall short of being considered a breach of Article 2(4), whether based on the Schmitt criteria or other interpretative approaches – will be considered breaches of the principle of non-intervention. Admittedly, not all interstate cyber operations will violate the principle (Haslam, 2000: 163). For example, 'cyber espionage and cyber exploitation operations lacking a coercive element do not per se violate the non-intervention principle' (*Tallinn manual*, 2013: 44). Only those cyber-attacks that are of a coercive nature (aiming to 'subordinate' another state in relation to matters within the domestic competence of that state) will breach the principle of non-intervention (Roscini, 2014: 65). However, while not all cyber operations will qualify, acts of cyber *warfare* – as defined in the Introduction to this volume – will in virtually all instances.

Why has the debate overlooked the principle of non-intervention?

It is true, as Buchan (2012: 221) argues, that many scholars have entirely overlooked the principle of non-intervention in their analysis of cyber warfare. Barkham (2001: 94), for example, argues that, if found to fall outside of the scope of Article 2(4), 'IW [information warfare], like economic sanctions, *would become a legal act* under international law' (emphasis added). This, of course, entirely misses the fact that neither coercive economic sanctions nor cyber-attacks are 'legal acts' at all: they are breaches of the principle of non-intervention.

However, it is worth noting that the principle of non-intervention has not been entirely ignored in the literature. A number of writers do in fact take note of the principle, and further conclude that most acts of cyber warfare are likely to constitute a breach of it (e.g. Roscini, 2014: 63–5; Harrison Dinniss, 2012: 73; Hathaway *et al.*, 2012: 843; Haslam, 2000: 160 and 163–4; Kodar, 2009: 140; Schmitt, 1999: 123). Yet, as Buchan (2012: 221) points out, 'these authors do not engage in a sustained analysis of how the non-intervention principle may apply to cyber attacks'. Consideration of the principle in the context of the legal regulation of cyber warfare, to the extent that it has occurred at all, has tended to be cursory.

One might well question why this is the case. The principle of non-intervention is wider in scope than the prohibition of the use of force, which means that it is much easier to conclude that the majority of interstate cyber-attacks are covered. If cyber-attacks are ultimately unlawful irrespective of the applicability of Article 2(4), why has the legal debate focused so much on whether such attacks qualify as a use of 'force' for the purposes of that article? After all, a breach of international law is a breach of international law: the principle of non-intervention already exists and, 'on paper' (using that term figuratively, given that the principle is technically a rule of customary international law and, thus, unwritten), would appear to be sufficient to regulate cyber warfare.

The weakness of the principle of non-intervention and the special 'weight' of Article 2(4)

The literature's focus on Article 2(4) stems, in part, from the fact that the principle of non-intervention is often seen by states and writers as a 'weaker' rule of international law. As noted, the principle is a rule of customary international law rather than a treaty-based norm. While custom and treaties are hierarchically equal in the international legal system as a formal matter (Boas, 2012: 47), rules of custom are often, quite understandably, viewed as being inherently vaguer in nature (Sullivan, 2013: 667). Perhaps more importantly, the principle of non-intervention is also a rule that has long been regularly breached by states – at least in relation to the 'non-forcible' actions that it covers – without much in the way of legal, or even political, consequence (Henderson, 2013: 642–5; Krasner, 1999: 20–5). It is a simple matter to identify numerous instances where states 'coerce' one another on matters that theoretically are within their domestic spheres: the principle is regularly breached in the day-to-day reality of international relations.

Of course, Article 2(4) is at times breached too, but the principle of non-intervention is not particularly well 'respected' by states in comparison. On this basis, Banks (2013: 170) has argued that, '[a]lthough the non-intervention norm has the potential to serve as a legal barrier to disruptive cyber intrusions, there is no indication that any state has relied on Buchan's argument, or that any court has credited it in the cyber context.' To some extent, this overstates the matter: just because states (and courts) have not referred to the principle of non-intervention in the cyber context does not mean that it is inapplicable or that they cannot do so in the future. Nonetheless, the basic point that Banks makes is correct. Despite the fact that the principle is a 'universally accepted [legal] norm in inter-state relations' (Wu, 2000: 38), it is a rule that struggles to restrain state behaviour, and has been marginalised both in academia and practice. Its potential to effectively restrain interstate use of cyber force can, therefore, be seriously brought into question.

In contrast, Article 2(4) has special 'weight' within the international legal system. It has already been noted that the prohibition of the use of force is usually viewed as being a 'superior' rule of *jus cogens*, which means that it cannot be altered or derogated from. Whether one accepts the peremptory status of the prohibition or not, there is no question that holding that cyber-attacks contravene Article 2(4) is rather more likely to stimulate state compliance than saying that it breaches the principle of non-intervention (Morth, 1998: 590). This helps to explain why writers have focused on Article 2(4) as the core of the debate: it is a rule that is rather more likely to restrain behaviour in practice. As Schmitt (1999: 909) has phrased this, violating Article 2(4) is a 'normatively more flagrant act' than violating the principle of non-intervention.

Self-defence

Self-defence is an inherent legal right of all states, and constitutes an exception to the prohibition of the use of force in Article 2(4). In simple terms, the right allows states to lawfully use force – which would otherwise be unlawful under the prohibition – in response to an armed attack (or, some would argue, the threat of an imminent armed attack) (see generally, Tibori Szabó, 2011).

Given that the right of self-defence is an exception to the prohibition of the use of force, Article 2(4)'s prohibition acts as an important 'gateway' to the responses available to a state that has suffered a cyber-attack. Violations of the principle of non-intervention do not trigger the right to use defensive force unless they *also* constitute a prohibited use of force (Roscini, 2014: 71). Thus, those who are concerned about states being left with no viable response to a crippling cyber-attack against them must clear the first hurdle of situating such attacks within the framework of Article 2(4). This, then, also helps explain why the core debate has been so focused on that article and not the wider principle of non-intervention.

It is important to note that not all 'uses of force' will trigger the right of self-defence. The responding state must have suffered an 'armed attack' (UN Charter, 1945: Article 51). If an armed attack has occurred, then the state may defend itself with the use of force (Corten, 2010: 402–6), subject to further requirements – stemming from customary international law – that the response be both necessary and proportionate (Alexandrov, 1996: 20). Just as not all 'interventions' are 'uses of force', not all 'uses of force' are 'armed attacks'. The ICJ has made it clear that an 'armed attack' is not the same as any use of force, but represents instead 'the most grave form of the use of force' (*Nicaragua* case, 1986: para. 191; *Oil Platforms* case, 2003: para. 51).

Regulation under the jus ad bellum 111

Figure 5.1 (previously employed by the present author elsewhere, Green, 2009a: 33) usefully demonstrates the relationship between the three concepts of 'armed attack', 'force' and 'intervention'. The widest concept, and outermost circle, is the notion of intervention, within which both of the other two concepts fall; the narrowest concept – armed attack – is represented by the innermost circle, falling within the notion of force (which is itself encompassed by the concept of intervention).

Given that self-defence is only triggered by the occurrence of the narrowest of these concepts – an 'armed attack' – a secondary debate within the *jus ad bellum* scholarship on cyber warfare has been whether an act of cyber warfare can constitute an armed attack, thus allowing for a defensive response (see e.g. Antolin-Jenkins, 2005: 162–72; Waxman, 2013: 110–16; Hathaway *et al.*, 2012: 843–8; Dinstein, 2002: 100–2). In many ways this debate mirrors that concerning Article 2(4)'s applicability to cyber warfare, which has already been discussed, and so will not be repeated in detail here. Simply put, however, the question has been whether the effects of certain cyber-attacks can be seen as severe enough to be treated not just as 'uses of force' but also as *grave* uses of force: that is, 'armed attacks'. If so, then states can potentially respond in self-defence, not just by meeting cyber with cyber, but by defending themselves by means of conventional military force.

The general consensus in the literature is that, at least when it comes to the 'doomsday'-type scenarios discussed above (i.e. attacks with significant physical consequences), cyber-attacks can constitute armed attacks that trigger self-defence (e.g. *Tallinn manual*, 2013: 54–61; Graham, 2010: 90–2). As with the popular 'effects-based' approach to the interpretation of 'force' discussed above, it is argued by a number of commentators that it would undermine the purpose of the right of self-defence to hold that states have a right to respond with force

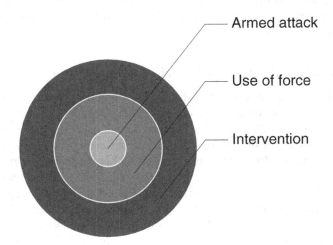

Figure 5.1 The relationship between the concepts of armed attack, force and intervention.

to large-scale conventional attacks leading to death and destruction but not to cyber-attacks that have exactly the same results, simply based on the *method* of attack (e.g. Banks, 2013: 162). In other words, it is commonly argued that the *raison d'être* of the right of self-defence is to enable states to protect themselves from serious attack and, in relation to attacks with severe physical effects, it is illogical to hold that the victim state's defensive imperative is any way lessened just because the attack was perpetrated by cyber (rather than conventional) means.

Therefore, the points of controversy are, as one might expect, at the margins. In particular, what of cyber-attacks that are devastating but 'non-physical' in effect? For example, Harrison Dinniss (2012: 81) argues that only cyber-attacks that cause 'damage to property or persons of sufficient scale' can trigger the right of self-defence; in contrast, Tsagourias (2012: 231–2) takes the view that, so long as its effects are significant, a cyber-attack can be an 'armed attack' irrespective of whether those effects are 'physical'.

It quickly becomes apparent, then, that – other than it involving a somewhat higher threshold – the debate on which acts of cyber aggression should or should not be considered an 'armed attack' triggering self-defence in many ways resembles the debate that has already been examined in detail on whether and which cyber operations qualify as 'force' for the purposes of Article 2(4). Self-defence will therefore not be explored further in this chapter. It should nonetheless be noted that additional issues exist in relation to exercising the right of self-defence in the cyber context, which have all been discussed to varying degrees in the literature. These include: the difficulties in applying the customary international law criteria of necessity and proportionality; whether states can respond in self-defence to cyber-attacks perpetrated by non-state actors; whether a number of comparatively 'minor' cyber-attacks can cumulatively equate to an armed attack; and the possibility of *anticipatory* defensive force being used in response to a cyber-threat (see e.g. Harrison Dinniss, 2012: 82–106, who discusses all of these questions).

Problems with the existing approaches taken in the literature

In previous sections, it has been shown that there exist notable problems in the ability of either Article 2(4) or the principle of non-intervention to effectively regulate cyber warfare. In relation to the former, the unique nature of cyber warfare (in terms of the *range* of activities it encompasses, amongst other things) means that it is extremely difficult to fit such actions within the scope of Article 2(4), created, as it was, without cyber warfare in mind. Despite inventive attempts at interpretation and contextualised analogy, when trying to apply Article 2(4) there remain significant problems of *clarity* and *consistency* – both of which should be high up in any legal regime's bucket list. Similarly, resort to the under-discussed principle of non-intervention seems insufficient for a different reason. The *applicability* of the principle to cyber warfare is relatively straightforward, but the extent to which it will in fact restrain interstate cyber-attacks is highly questionable: it is a comparatively weak rule of customary international law, often violated and rarely leading to condemnation when breached.

The issue of attribution

Beyond the problems already discussed, however, perhaps the biggest issue with regard to the interaction of the *jus ad bellum* with cyber warfare relates to questions of *attribution*. In terms of determining state responsibility for breaches of international law, the International Law Commission's Draft Articles on State Responsibility (which are non-binding in themselves but are largely reflective of binding customary international law) set out in detail how legal attribution is to be established. States are, fairly obviously, responsible for the actions of their organs (ASR, 2001: Article 4), including unauthorised acts (ASR, 2001: Article 7). Thus, cyber-attacks perpetrated by members of a state's armed forces will be considered actions of the state. This also holds true for civilian hackers or programmers working directly for the state (ASR, 2001: Article 4; Roscini, 2010: 98).

In addition, actions of groups or persons 'acting on the instructions of, or under the direction or control of' the state are attributable to that state (ASR, 2001: Article 8). However, there is some debate as to exactly what standard of 'control' is necessary to attribute acts of cyber aggression by a non-state actor to the state (for discussion of this debate, see Shackelford and Andres, 2011: 984–93). Two possible competing tests for the necessary standard of control can be found in case law. The first of these is an 'effective control' test, which requires that the state has specific, practical control over the actor concerned before that actor's actions can be viewed as being attributable to it (*Nicaragua* case, 1986: paras 100–15). The second approach is the wider 'overall control' test, which requires a general level of control – going beyond mere support or provision of funds – but not necessarily specific direction or instruction in each particular instance (*Tadić* case, 1999: paras 116–45).

The present author shares Roscini's view that the *Nicaragua* 'effective control' test is the more appropriate way of attributing cyber operations. This is because the effective control test offers a narrower understanding of what 'control' entails, and so 'would prevent states from being frivolously or maliciously accused of cyber operations', potentially leading to 'abuse of the right of self-defence' (Roscini, 2014: 38). Doubts nonetheless remain as to the appropriate test for determining 'direction or control'. Indeed, Margulies (2013) has recently suggested a third, wider approach of 'virtual control', specifically for attributing cyber-attacks. Under this test, the mere provision of finances or support would amount to sufficient 'control'. At present there is little basis for Margulies' 'virtual control' test in law, however. In any event, despite this fuzziness in terms of its correct implementation, the rule itself is fairly straightforward: the conduct of actors controlled or directed by the state constitutes 'state conduct' as far as international law is concerned.

There is a further legal question in terms of attributing responsibility to the state. This is the necessary *evidentiary standard* required to establish that an act was perpetrated by the state (either directly by one of its organs, or indirectly by an entity under its direction/control). Evidentiary standards for international law generally, and the *jus ad bellum* in particular, are notoriously unclear, and standards have been applied inconsistently (Green, 2009b).

Generally speaking, though, there is a spectrum of three possible evidentiary standards that could be adopted in relation to attributing cyber-attacks to a state. The first, and strictest, possible standard is that the evidence must establish 'beyond a reasonable doubt' that an actor for which the state is responsible undertook the action: the evidence must be indisputable. The second possibility, falling in the middle of the spectrum, is a 'clear and convincing' test: that is, evidence must be *compelling*, but not necessarily indisputable. The third possibility would be a less onerous 'balance of probabilities' standard; under this approach, the evidence would have to establish that it was 'more likely than not' that the state was responsible for the action.

While it cannot be said with any certainty which of these evidentiary standards is the most appropriate for attributing acts of cyber warfare to a state (or which might be adopted in the future in that context), a number of writers have persuasively argued that 'clear and convincing' evidence should be the standard (e.g. O'Connell, 2012: 202; Roscini, 2014: 97–103). In other words, they argue that the compelling-evidence test, which sits in the middle of the spectrum, is the most suitable. Those supporting the adoption of this 'clear and convincing' standard do so on the basis that it is the test most commonly adopted by states and because, from a policy perspective, it is also the most suitable: it avoids an onerous requirement for the evidence to be indisputable, but also guards against 'specious claims and false attribution' (Roscini, 2014: 102). Avoiding such incorrect attribution to a state is a particular issue in the cyber context, as false evidentiary trails are comparatively easy to lay in cyberspace (Kodar, 2009: 140–2).

Thus, if there is 'clear and convincing' evidence that a state organ or entity that the state directs or controls has perpetrated a cyber-attack against another state, then the state will be legally responsible for a breach either of Article 2(4) or of the principle of non-intervention (Schmitt, 2011: 579). The significant difficulty with this, however, is that such *legal* attribution is predicated upon *factual* attribution. Even if it is agreed that the legal standard is that 'clear and convincing' evidence is required, this necessitates that actual evidence of this sort can in fact be obtained.

Questions of factual (or what might also be called 'forensic') attribution of course exist in all attempts to determine state responsibility for breaches of international law, but the problem of obtaining evidence is particularly pronounced in the cyber context (Tsagourias, 2012: 233). As Neil C. Rowe has already examined in Chapter 3 of this volume, there are significant technical uncertainties in attributing cyber activities to any particular actor. This is not the place to discuss these technical issues concerning factual attribution in any detail, but it is clear that, to some extent at least, 'the Internet is one big masquerade ball. You can hide behind aliases, you can hide behind proxy servers and you can surreptitiously enslave computers to do your dirty work' (Brenner, 2011: 32).

As Rowe discusses in his chapter, problems in technically attributing cyber-attacks to any particular actor are not always entirely insurmountable; they are, nonetheless, considerable, and are amplified in relation to technical attribution to a *state*. Thus, even if it can be agreed which actions are covered by Article 2(4) and which are not, and it can then be agreed that the 'clear and convincing' approach is indeed the correct evidentiary standard for legally attributing such actions to the state (directly or indirectly), the chances of that standard being *reached* in terms of reliable forensic evidence will, in most instances in the cyber context, be extremely small (O'Connell, 2012: 202). Legally, '[t]here has to be compelling proof... [meaning that] in these cyber situations, one can point the finger, but not with the needed precision' (Singer and Friedman, 2014: 75). This issue is fundamental to the effectiveness of international law in the cyber context (Goldsmith, 2013: 136) and it is telling that, as yet, *no* act of cyber aggression has conclusively been factually (and, as a consequence, legally) attributed to a state (Harrison Dinniss, 2012: 53).

The militarisation of cyberspace

In addition to the attribution problem, significant concerns may also be raised about what might be termed the 'militarisation' of cyberspace. The *jus ad bellum* is a branch of international law that specifically deals with the use of military force. By situating interstate cyber operations within this area of the law at all, the legal literature can be seen as skewing focus towards a military approach to cyber security. Admittedly, the 'blame' for this cannot be laid entirely at the feet of lawyers: the reality is that states have predominantly engaged with cyber threats through military discourse and procedures, and the legal debate, to some extent, simply reflects that reality. Nonetheless, as has been eloquently discussed by Mary Ellen O'Connell (2012), by focusing on the *jus ad bellum* as the applicable legal regime, there is a real concern that the law is (at least partially) responsible for 'feeding' a cyber arms race and contributing to the potential for military escalation.

In particular, one might argue that the possibility of forcible responses to cyber-attacks occurring under the right of self-defence is troubling in terms of the escalation of the use of force. While few would question that states should have some forcible recourse in response to the most extreme cyber-attacks causing death and destruction (Waxman, 2013: 111), most aggressive cyber operations will probably not come close to causing this kind of effect. By starting from the perspective of situating cyber warfare within the *jus ad bellum*, international law may be inherently inviting forcible responses to non-forcible actions (Tubbs *et al.*, 2002: 16). Once self-defence is entertained as an option – however much the majority of lawyers might say that it must be reserved only for the most devastating scenarios – this opens the door to states considering the 'military option' in response to lesser actions.

After all, as noted previously, the severity of a cyber-attack is in the eye of the beholder: a case can always be made that an attack is damaging enough to require a military response. Furthermore, concerns relating to the escalation of force used in self-defence in response to cyber aggression are amplified when one considers the problems associated with the factual attribution of cyber operations. If a state cannot accurately identify the source of an attack against it, how can it possibly know against which state to launch its responsive strikes?

Conclusion: a shift of focus towards the duty to prevent?

The previous section highlighted a number of issues with current attempts to apply the *jus ad bellum* to interstate cyber-attacks. In response to these sorts of concerns, a number of writers have argued that there is a need for a new bespoke cyber warfare treaty. Indeed, various academic proposals now exist for such a treaty (see e.g. Brown, 2006; Moore, 2013; Hathaway *et al.*, 2012: 880–4). Some states have also produced such plans. Most notably – and somewhat ironically, given its prominent links to cyber (in)security at the international level (Clarke and Knake, 2010: 219) – Russia has been calling for a cyber warfare treaty since the late 1990s (see UN Doc. A/53/576, 1998). Indeed, Russia has recently drawn up a full draft treaty on the subject (Draft Convention on International Information Security, 2011).

Calls for a cyber warfare treaty are worth heeding, at least to an extent. A set of agreed rules on the extent to which the norms of the *jus ad bellum* are applicable – including provisions on what sorts of cyber actions qualify variously as 'force', 'interventions' and 'armed attacks' – would undoubtedly bring an increased level of consistency and certainty to the legal regulation of cyberspace. As noted above, the majority view is that the existing law can, and does, regulate interstate cyber warfare. This view is, in itself, correct, but the intricacies of the debates discussed above show equally that applying the existing law is no easy matter. Just because there is already a law that can be applied to cyber conflict is no reason to avoid reiterating, and providing more specific (and perhaps clearer and more refined) guidance as to how to apply that law in a binding international agreement. Such an agreement would be valuable for the sake of clarity, if for no other reason.

However, while a cyber warfare treaty is appealing in theory, in practice it is extremely unlikely to emerge (Nguyen, 2013: 1111; Waxman, 2011: 426). Getting states to agree to *any* large multilateral treaty is an extremely difficult task, and in the context of an issue that relates directly to questions of national security, the odds of agreement lengthen significantly (Murphy, 2013: 332–3). There are deep rooted differences of opinion as to how the *jus ad bellum* rules should apply, as has been noted; crucially, states have 'divergent strategic interests that will pull their preferred doctrinal interpretations and aspirations in different directions, impeding formation of a stable international consensus' (Waxman, 2011: 425–6). This can be seen by the impasse over Russia's calls for a cyber treaty. In particular, Russia has sought an *arms control* agreement, while the United States favours a very different approach, more in line with the existing *jus ad bellum* rules (Ford, 2010).

The emergence of a treaty confirming the way in which the law is to apply to cyber warfare, at least at present, is therefore something of a pipedream. It is also important to note that a treaty that simply solidifies the majority consensus (to the extent that such a thing can be identified) on the application of the *jus ad bellum* to cyber-attacks would do nothing to alleviate the key issue of *attributing* such attacks to states, even were it to be agreed upon (Barkham, 2001: 98–9).

Placing the notion of a cyber warfare treaty on the legal backburner for the foreseeable future, then, this chapter concludes with a tentative suggestion to try to alleviate some of the issues associated with the application of the *jus ad bellum* to cyber warfare. It is submitted that it would be desirable to promote a reorientation of focus towards another existing rule of international law: the duty that states take appropriate and reasonable steps to protect the sovereign rights of other states. This duty is already legally incumbent upon states. There is an existing requirement in international law that states take reasonable steps to ensure that their territory is not used in a manner detrimental to other states (see, generally, Barnidge, 2006). The ICJ confirmed, way back in 1949, that a state cannot 'allow knowingly its territory to be used contrary to the rights of other states' (*Corfu Channel* case, 1949: 22). This general rule has subsequently been embraced, for example, in the international environmental law context (see e.g. ILA Study Group, First Report, 2014). It could be similarly emphasised in relation to acts of cyber warfare.

The suggestion here is, therefore, not to introduce 'new' law, but to refocus the cyber warfare debate around an existing legal duty. As with the principle of non-intervention, the applicability of the 'duty to prevent' to cyber warfare has been generally overlooked in the literature. Even when it has been referred to, it has, at times, been applied incorrectly. For example, Graham (2010: particularly at 92–6) argues that if a state breaches the duty to prevent, then this in itself means that the state is legally responsible for the cyber-attacks emanating from its territory that it has failed to prevent, whether or not it directed or controlled the perpetrator. This is entirely incorrect: on the basis of this 'duty to prevent', states are legally responsible, not for a breach of the prohibition of the use of force (or the principle of non-intervention) per se, but of a separate duty to take reasonable steps to prevent such attacks (Roscini, 2014: 40). The perpetrator is responsible for the act; the state is responsible for something else: the 'act', as it were, of not taking reasonable measures to stop the act.

A few writers have taken note of the duty in relation to cyber operations and correctly identified its implications (e.g. Tsagourias, 2012: 242; Roscini, 2014: 40, 80–8). The UN General Assembly's 'Group of Governmental Experts' also recently reaffirmed the duty in the context of cyber warfare (UN Doc. A/68/98, 2013: para. 23), as have some individual states (see e.g. the views expressed by India, China and Russia, quoted in Kanuck, 2010: 1591, both in the main text and in note 88). The duty was also recently referenced in the 2013 *Tallinn manual*:

> A state shall not knowingly allow the cyber infrastructure *located in its territory* or under its exclusive governmental control to be used for acts that adversely and unlawfully affect other states.
>
> (*Tallinn manual*, 2013: Rule 5, 26, emphasis added)

Moving the legal focus away from the *jus ad bellum*, towards the more general duty of 'cyber due diligence' has a number of potential advantages. First, it would alleviate the need for analogy to traditional uses of force and problematic categorisation of cyber-attacks so as to 'crowbar' cyber operations into the framework of Article 2(4) and, as a result, would lessen the uncertainty and inconsistency that is so evident in the longstanding 'Article 2(4) debate'. Secondly, it may serve somewhat to conceptually 'demilitarise' interstate cyber security. This would potentially lessen the likelihood of escalation following an aggressive cyber act, at least in relation to all but the most extreme cyber-attacks.

Thirdly, and most importantly, it would help to minimise the inherent attribution problem. The focus of this book is, of course, on *interstate* cyber warfare, but it has already been noted that conclusively attributing cyber-attacks to states rather than 'independent' individuals or non-state groups is extremely problematic. The 'duty of due diligence' requirement means that the *exact* entity conducting acts of cyber aggression would not need to be established, because the rule in question does not relate to the act itself. Instead, states would be inherently responsible for failing to take reasonable steps to prevent attacks from occurring. This would, of course, encompass attacks where the state itself was undertaking or directing the attack, but, importantly, this would not necessarily need to be established.

States themselves would not be able to hide behind attribution issues, because their legal duty does not rest on whether or not they were the perpetrator. One of the reasons that the United States has been reticent about agreeing a cyber warfare treaty with Russia applicable to *states* is that Russia, and other states such as China, are known to rely on independent actors in relation to aggressive cyber operations, the actions of which the state does not endorse but tacitly approves and takes no steps to prevent. The fear, in the United States at least, is that a cyber treaty applicable to states would hamstring the cyber capabilities of the United States while failing to catch many of the attacks emanating from Russia (or China, or elsewhere) within its legal net (Singer and Friedman, 2014: 186). A reorientation of the debate away from its primary focus on Article 2(4) and towards the application of the duty of prevention should help to avoid this lacuna.

As one might expect, relying on the duty to prevent has its own set of problems. First, factual attribution would, of course, still need to be established to the extent that it would have to be 'clearly and convincingly' shown that an act emanated from the territory of the state in question and that the state failed to take reasonable steps, in the context of the situation, to try to prevent its territory being used for cyber-attacks against other states (see Becker, 2006:

Regulation under the jus ad bellum   119

341–5). This is still no easy task. Attribution problems would therefore not be overcome, but they may perhaps be lessened.

Secondly, it is important to note that the duty is not one of strict liability, which would be overly onerous, but rather of due diligence (Roscini, 2014: 87–8). If a state has taken reasonable steps to prevent attacks from occurring from within its territory, then it would not be in breach. Thus, where a state is entirely unable to stop such actions, despite its best efforts, the duty is of little use.

Thirdly, some might question whether this approach would leave a gap in relation to available responses. It was noted above that one reason why the cyber warfare debate has been so consistently framed around Article 2(4) has been that this potentially allows for responses in self-defence (if the nature of the attack is severe enough to raise it to the level of an armed attack). Tsagourias (2012: 242) argues on this basis that 'it would not be of much consolation to the victim [of a large scale, devastating cyber-attack] ... to know that it can hold the host state responsible for breaching its duty of due diligence'. Yet, for all the definitional uncertainty surrounding the *jus ad bellum*'s application to cyberspace, there is widespread agreement that cyber-attacks of the 'doomsday scenario' sort are both 'uses of force' and 'armed attacks' (see e.g. *Tallinn manual*, 2013: 54–61), meaning that in such cases states can respond with force. Indeed, where the defensive necessity to respond is extreme, some would argue that a state can act in self-defence even where the state is not legally responsible for the armed attack (Banks, 2013; Tsagourias, 2012: 242–3). For good or ill, this probably reflects reality, irrespective of legal questions of attribution: states will not refrain from a military response when faced with a catastrophic attack.

The acts of cyber warfare that have occurred in practice up until now have not been of this sort of catastrophic nature, however. While the threat of the 'doomsday cyber-attack' now looms large in the psyche of the developed world, it is likely that the vast majority of cyber-attacks will remain on a much smaller scale in the future. In many cases, therefore, a forcible response will not be appropriate. Instead of debating the extent to which 'non-apocalyptic' acts of cyber aggression may or may not fall within the *jus ad bellum*'s reach, then, the international community may be better served by placing the onus on legal responsibility for good cyber security and communitarian solutions to cyber aggression (see, generally, O'Connell, 2012). This is not to suggest that the *jus ad bellum* has, or should have, no role in the legal regulation of cyber warfare, only that it should be situated at the margins – only called upon where absolutely necessary – rather than being the starting point for the debate.

It is also worth noting that various *non-forcible* countermeasures can lawfully be taken by states in response to breaches of international law (ASR, 2001: Article 22; Buchan, 2012: 226; Harrison Dinniss, 2012: 105–8; Schmitt, 2011: 581–583). There are various restrictions on such countermeasures (see *Gabčíkovo-Nagymaros* case, 1997: paras 83–7) but, in most cases, states will in fact have the option of a response without needing to turn to military force (O'Connell, 2012: 204–5). Such non-forcible options of response should be supplemented by an increased emphasis, at the political level at least – and perhaps increasingly at the legal level (see Sofaer *et al.*, 2010) – on improved international cyber cooperation and information sharing (Hathaway *et al.*, 2012: 882–4). Prevention is, fairly obviously, preferable to response. All this can be combined with the duty for states to take reasonable steps to prevent cyberattacks from emanating from their territory. A breach of this duty will be more easily established because of reduced issues of attribution, and the finding of such a breach – if the duty is better promoted, emphasised and clarified – may help to place political pressure on the state concerned to clean up its cyber act.

Ultimately, the present author supports a 'combination' approach to the cyber warfare problem, which includes resort to the *jus ad bellum*, but which centres on a duty to prevent. The ideal would be for this to all be crystallised in an international treaty, partly to spell out the *jus ad bellum* rules for extreme cases, but more importantly to 'elaborate what [is] required of states' responsibilities in terms of due diligence' (O'Connell and Arimatsu, 2012: 11). Being rather more realistic, however – given the unlikelihood of such a treaty appearing, at least any time soon – international lawyers would at least do well to refocus the debate away from Article 2(4) alone.

Note

1 The author would like to thank Robert P. Barnidge, Jr, Lia Emanuel and Reuven (Ruvi) Ziegler for their invaluable comments on previous drafts of this chapter. He would also like to thank the University of Reading for awarding him research leave in the spring/summer of 2014, which allowed him to conduct the research underpinning it.

References

Documents, treaties and cases

'UNCIO vol. III, 1945': Documents of the United Nations Conference on International Organisation, Volume III: Dumbarton Oak Proposals (Comments and Proposed Amendments) (1945) New York: Library of Congress.

'UNCIO vol. VI, 1945': Documents of the United Nations Conference on International Organisation, Volume VI: Commission I (General Provisions) (1945) New York: Library of Congress.

'UN Charter, 1945': Charter of the United Nations, 1 UNTS 16, 24 October.

'Statute of the ICJ, 1945': Statute of the International Court of Justice, 1945: annexed to Charter of the United Nations, 1 UNTS 16, 24 October.

'*Corfu Channel* case, 1949': *Corfu Channel Case* (*United Kingdom v. Albania*), merits, ICJ Reports 244, 15 December.

'UN Doc. A/RES/20/2131, 1965': Declaration on the Inadmissibility of Intervention in the Domestic Affairs of States and the Protection of Their Independence and Sovereignty, GA Res. 2131 (XX), 20th sess., 21 December.

'VCLT, 1969': Vienna Convention on the Law of Treaties 1155 UNTS 331, 23 May.

'UN Doc. A/7619, 1969': Report of the Special Committee on Principles of International Law Concerning Friendly Relations and Co-operation Among States, GA Official Records, 24th sess., Suppl. No. 19.

Regulation under the jus ad bellum 121

'UN Doc. A/RES/25/2625, 1970': Declaration on Principles of International Law concerning Friendly Relations and Co-operation among States in accordance with the Charter of the United Nations, GA Res. 2625 (XXV), 25th sess., 24 October.

'UN Doc. A/RES/3314, 1974': Definition of Aggression, GA Res. 3314 (XXIX), 29th sess., 14 December.

'UN Doc. A/RES/31/91, 1976': Declaration on Non-Interference in the Internal Affairs of States, GA Res. 31/91, 31st sess., 14 December.

'UN Doc. A/RES/36/103, 1981': Declaration on the Inadmissibility of Intervention and Interference in the Internal Affairs of States, GA Res. 36/103, 36th sess., 9 December.

'*Nicaragua* case, 1986': *Military and Paramilitary Activities in and against Nicaragua (Nicaragua v. United States of America)*, merits, ICJ Reports 14, 27 June.

'*Gabčíkovo-Nagymaros* case, 1997': *Case Concerning the Gabčíkovo-Nagymaros Project (Hungary/Slovakia)*, judgment, ICJ Reports 7, 25 September.

'UN Doc. A/53/576, 1998': Role of Science and Technology in the Context of Security, Disarmament and Other Related Fields, General Assembly, Report of the First Committee, 53rd sess., 18 November.

'*Tadić* case, 1999': *Prosecutor v. Dusko Tadić*, appeal judgment, IT-94–1-A, International Criminal Tribunal for the former Yugoslavia (ICTY), 15 July.

'ASR, 2001': Draft Articles on State Responsibility, International Law Commission, 53 UN GAOR supp. 10, 43, UN Doc. A/56/10.

Convention on Cybercrime (2001), Budapest, Hungary, 2296 UNTS 167, 23 November.

'*Oil Platforms* case, 2003': *Case Concerning Oil Platforms (Islamic Republic of Iran v. United States of America)*, merits, ICJ Reports 161, 6 November.

Draft Convention on International Information Security (Concept) (2011), Yekaterinburg, Russia, 24 September [online], available: www.mid.ru/bdomp/ns-osndoc.nsf/1e5f0de2 8fe77fdcc32575d900298676/7b17ead7244e2064c3257925003bcbcc!OpenDocument [28 May 2014].

'UN Doc. A/68/98, 2013': Report of the Group of Governmental Experts on Developments in the Field of Information and Telecommunications in the Context of International Security, General Assembly, 68th sess., 24 June.

Tallinn manual on the international law applicable to cyber warfare (2013) Prepared by the International Group of Experts at the Invitation of the NATO Cooperative Cyber Defence Centre of Excellence (general editor: Schmitt, M.N.), Cambridge: Cambridge University Press.

'ILA Study Group, First Report, 2014': International Law Association Study Group on Due Diligence in International Law, First Report, French, D. (Chair) and Stephens, T. (Rapporteur), 7 March 2014 [online], available: www.ila-hq.org/en/committees/study_ groups.cfm/cid/1045 [28 May 2014].

Academic works and media reports

Akehurst, M. (1974) 'Custom as a source of international law', *British Yearbook of International Law*, vol. 47, pp. 1–53.

Alexandrov, S.A. (1996) *Self-defence against the use of force in international law*, The Hague: Kluwer Law International.

Antolin-Jenkins, V.M. (2005) 'Defining the parameters of cyberwar operations: Looking for law in all the wrong places?', *Naval Law Review*, vol. 51, pp. 132–74.

Banks, W. (2013) 'The role of counterterrorism law in shaping *ad bellum* norms for cyber warfare', *International Law Studies*, vol. 89, pp. 157–97.

Barkham, J. (2001) 'Information warfare and international law on the use of force', *New York University Journal of International Law and Politics*, vol. 34, pp. 57–113.

Barnidge, R.P. (2006) 'The due diligence principle under international law', *International Community Law Review*, vol. 8, no. 1, pp. 81–121.

Becker, T. (2006) *Terrorism and the state: Rethinking the rules of state responsibility*, Oxford: Hart Publishing.

Benatar, M. (2009) 'The use of cyber force: need for a legal justification?', *Goettingen Journal of International Law*, vol. 3, pp. 375–96.

Boas, G. (2012) *Public international law: Contemporary principles and perspectives*, Cheltenham: Edward Elgar.

Bothe, M. (2003) 'Terrorism and the legality of pre-emptive force', *European Journal of International Law*, vol. 14, pp. 227–40.

Brenner, J. (2011) *America the vulnerable: Inside the new threat matrix of digital espionage, crime, and warfare*, New York: The Penguin Press.

Brown, D. (2006) 'A proposal for an international convention to regulate the use of information systems in armed conflict', *Harvard International Law Journal*, vol. 47, no. 1, pp. 179–221.

Brownlie, I. (1963) *International law and the use of force by states*, Oxford: Clarendon Press.

Buchan, R. (2012) 'Cyber attacks: unlawful uses of force or prohibited interventions', *Journal of Conflict and Security Law*, vol. 17, no. 2, pp. 212–27.

Clarke, R.A. and Knake, R.K. (2010) *Cyber war: The next threat to national security and what to do about it*, New York: Harper Collins.

Corten, O. (2010) *The law against war: The prohibition on the use of force in contemporary international law*, Oxford: Hart Publishing.

Dinstein, Y. (2002) 'Computer network attacks and self-defense', *International Law Studies*, vol. 76, pp. 99–120.

Dinstein, Y. (2011) *War, aggression and self-defence*, 5th edition, Cambridge: Cambridge University Press.

Dunlap, C.J. (2011) 'Perspectives for cyber strategists on law for cyberwar', *Strategic Studies Quarterly*, vol. 5, no. 1, pp. 81–99.

Farer, T.J. (1985) 'Political and economic coercion in contemporary international law', *American Journal of International Law*, vol. 79, pp. 405–13.

Ford, C.A (2010) 'The trouble with cyber arms control', *The New Atlantis – A Journal of Technology and Society*, vol. 29, pp. 52–67.

Franck, T.M (2002) *Recourse to force: State action against threats and armed attacks*, Cambridge: Cambridge University Press.

Goldsmith, J. (2013) 'How cyber changes the laws of war', *European Journal of International Law*, vol. 24, no. 1, pp. 129–38.

Graham, D.E. (2010) 'Cyber threats and the law of war', *National Security Law and Policy*, vol. 4, no. 1, pp. 87–102.

Gray, C. (2008) *International law and the use of force*, 3rd edition, Oxford: Oxford University Press.

Green, J.A. (2009a) *The International Court of Justice and self-defence in international law*, Oxford: Hart Publishing.

Green, J.A (2009b) 'Fluctuating evidentiary standards for self-defence in the International Court of Justice', *International and Comparative Law Quarterly*, vol. 58, pp. 163–79.

Green, J.A. (2011) 'Questioning the peremptory status of the prohibition of the use of force', *Michigan Journal of International Law*, vol. 32, no. 2, pp. 215–57.

Handler, S.G. (2012) 'New cyber face of battle: developing a legal approach to accommodate emerging trends in warfare', *Stanford Journal of International Law*, vol. 48, no. 1, pp. 209–38.

Harrison Dinniss, H.A. (2012) *Cyber warfare and the laws of war*, Cambridge: Cambridge University Press.

Haslam, E. (2000) 'Information warfare: technological changes and international law', *Journal of Conflict and Security Law*, vol. 5, pp. 157–75.

Hathaway, O., Crootof, R., Levitz, P., Nix, H., Nowlan, A., Perdue, W. and Spiegel, J. (2012) 'The law of cyber-attack', *California Law Review*, vol. 100, pp. 817–85.

Henderson, C. (2013) 'The provision of arms and "non-lethal" assistance to governmental and opposition forces', *University of New South Wales Law Journal*, vol. 36, no. 2, pp. 642–81.

Hoisington, M. (2009) 'Cyberwarfare and the use of force giving rise to the right of self-defense', *Boston College International and Comparative Law Review*, vol. 32, pp. 439–54.

Kanuk, S.P. (1996) 'Information warfare: new challenges for public international law', *Harvard International Law Journal*, vol. 37, pp. 272–92.

Kanuck, S.P (2010) 'Sovereign discourse on cyber conflict under international law', *Texas Law Review*, vol. 88, pp. 1571–97.

Kodar, E. (2009) 'Computer network attacks in the grey areas of *jus ad bellum* and *jus in bello*', *Baltic Yearbook of International Law*, vol. 9, pp. 133–55.

Krasner, S.D. (1999) *Sovereignty: Organized hypocrisy*, Princeton: Princeton University Press.

Margulies, P. (2013) 'Sovereignty and cyber attacks: technology's challenge to the law of state responsibility', *Melbourne Journal of International Law*, vol. 14, no. 2, pp. 496–519.

Moore, S. (2013) 'Cyber attacks and the beginning of an international cyber treaty', *North Carolina Journal of International Law and Commercial Regulation*, vol. 39, pp. 223–57.

Morth, T.A. (1998) 'Considering our position: viewing information warfare as a use of force prohibited by article 2(4) of the UN Charter', *Case Western Reserve Journal of International Law*, vol. 30, pp. 567–600.

Murphy, J.F. (2013) 'Cyber war and international law: does the international legal process constitute a threat to US vital interests?', *International Law Studies*, vol. 89, pp. 309–40.

Nguyen, R. (2013) 'Navigating *jus ad bellum* in the age of cyber warfare', *California Law Review*, vol. 101, pp. 1079–129.

O'Connell, M.E. (2012) 'Cyber security without cyber war', *Journal of Conflict and Security Law*, vol. 17, no. 2, pp. 187–209.

O'Connell, M.E and Arimatsu, L. (Wilmshurst, E., chair) (2012) 'Cyber security and international law', 29 May, *Chatham House*, Meeting Summary [online], available: www.chathamhouse.org/sites/default/files/public/Research/International%20 Law/290512summary.pdf [28 May 2014].

Orakhelashvili, A. (2006) *Peremptory norms in international law*, Oxford: Oxford University Press.

Papain, T. (2011) 'North Korea and cyberwarfare: how North Korea's cyber attacks violate the laws of war', *Journal of Korean Law*, vol. 11, pp. 29–54.

Remus, T. (2013) 'Cyber-attacks and international law of armed conflicts; a *jus ad bellum* perspective', *Journal of International Commercial Law and Technology*, vol. 8, no. 3, pp. 179–89.

Roscini, M. (2010) 'World wide warfare – *Jus ad bellum* and the use of cyber force', *Max Planck Yearbook of United Nations Law*, vol. 14, pp. 85–130.

Roscini, M. (2014) *Cyber operations and the use of force in international law*, Oxford: Oxford University Press.

Schmitt, M.N. (1999) 'Computer network attack and the use of force in international law: thoughts on a normative framework', *Columbia Journal of Transnational Law*, vol. 37, pp. 885–937.

Schmitt, M.N. (2010) 'Cyber operations in international law: the use of force, collective security, self-defense and armed conflicts', Committee on Deterring Cyber Attacks, Nations Research Council: The National Academic Press.

Schmitt, M.N. (2011) 'Cyber operations and the *jus ad bellum* revisited', *Villanova Law Review*, vol. 56, pp. 569–605.

Schmitt, M.N. (2013) 'Cyberspace and international law: the penumbral mist of uncertainty', *Harvard Law Review Forum*, vol. 126, pp. 176–80.

Schmitt, M.N. (2014) 'Legitimacy versus legality redux: arming the Syrian rebels', *Journal of National Security Law and Policy*, vol. 7, pp. 139–59.

Shackelford, S.J. (2009) 'From nuclear war to net war: analogizing cyber attacks in international law', *Berkley Journal of International Law*, vol. 27, pp. 192–251.

Shackelford, S.J. and Andres, R.B. (2011) 'State responsibility for cyber attacks: competing standards for a growing problem', *Georgetown Journal of International Law*, vol. 42, pp. 971–1016.

Sharp, W.G (1999) *Cyberspace and the use of force*, Falls Church: Aegis Research Corp.

Silver, D.B. (2002) 'Computer network attack as a use of force under Article 2(4)', *International Law Studies*, vol. 76, pp. 73–98.

Singer, P.W. and Friedman, A. (2014) *Cybersecurity and cyberwar: What everyone needs to know*, Oxford: Oxford University Press.

Sofaer, A.D., Clark, D. and Whitfield, D. (2010) 'Cyber security and international agreements', *Proceedings of a Workshop on Deterring CyberAttacks: Informing Strategies and Developing Options for US Policy*, National Research Council, The National Academic Press [online], available: www.nap.edu/catalog/12997.html [27 May 2014].

Sudworth, J. (2009) 'New "cyber attacks" hit S. Korea', 9 July, *BBC* News [online], available: http://news.bbc.co.uk/1/hi/world/asia-pacific/8142282.stm [3 July 2014].

Sullivan, S. (2013) 'Networking customary law', *Kansas Law Review*, vol. 61, pp. 659–698.

Tibori Szabó, K. (2011) *Anticipatory action in self-defence: Essence and limits under international law*, The Hague: TMC Asser Press (Springer).

Tsagourias, N. (2012) 'Cyber-attacks, self-defence and the problem of attribution', *Journal of Conflict and Security Law*, vol. 17, no. 2, pp. 229–44.

Tubbs, D., Luzwick, P.G. and Sharp Sr, W.G. (2002) 'Technology and law: the evolution of digital warfare', *International Law Studies*, vol. 76, pp. 7–20.

Waters, C.P.M. and Green, J.A. (2010) 'International law: military force and armed conflict', in Kassimeris, G. and Buckley, J.D. (eds) *Ashgate research companion to modern warfare*, Farnham: Ashgate.

Waxman, M.C. (2011) 'Cyber-attacks and the use of force: back to the future of Article 2(4)', *Yale Journal of International Law*, vol. 36, pp. 421–59.

Waxman, M.C. (2013) 'Self-defensive force against cyber attacks: legal, strategic and political dimensions', *International Legal Studies*, vol. 89, pp. 109–22.

Wu, L. (2000) 'East Asia and the principle of non-intervention: policies and practices', *Maryland Series in Contemporary Asian Studies*, vol. 160, no. 5, pp. 1–39.

6 The regulation of cyber warfare under the *jus in bello*

Heather A. Harrison Dinniss

Introduction

It is clear that many states now view the cyber domain as a zone of potential military operations – whether in support of traditional military war-fighting operations or as an alternative method of achieving strategic results in complex conflict scenarios. A recent report from the United National Institute for Disarmament Research (UNIDIR, 2013) indicated that 41 states, representing all regions of the world, now have cyber security programmes that give some role to the armed forces. Of these, 27 have established specific military cyber warfare entities, 17 of which are actively pursuing offensive cyber capabilities (the data is compiled from publicly available media reports, other states may well be proceeding more covertly) (UNIDIR, 2013: 3). As states step up their military capabilities in cyberspace, national, regional and international discussions have been taking place on the extent to which international law can or should be applied to the cyber domain.

Following on from the examination of the way in which the *jus ad bellum* regulates cyber warfare in Chapter 5, this chapter is dedicated to the legal issues raised by the use of cyber operations during an armed conflict and the specific body of law that regulates the conduct of hostilities. Although this body of law – the *jus in bello* (International Humanitarian Law, or IHL) – does not reference cyber operations explicitly, much of that body of law is framed in general terms that may be applied regardless of technological advances. Thus the chapter explores the way in which those laws may be interpreted, adapted and applied in the cyber context. As with the other contributions to this book, this chapter takes as its starting point an 'interstate' dimension to cyber-attacks and, in particular, the existence of an international armed conflict between two states that involves a cyber element; thus it takes as its point of departure the premise that cyber operations will accompany more traditional kinetic hostilities. The chapter likewise assumes the involvement of the armed forces of a state or other state organs (such as intelligence services or cyber defence units) and will therefore not address the use of proxies or other non-state actors.

The chapter first considers the general applicability of the *jus in bello* to cyber operations. It then turns to the crucial principle of distinction, and assesses how this is to be applied in the cyber context. In particular, this section of the chapter assesses what may be targeted (i.e. what constitutes a 'military objective', the issue of 'dual-use' objects in the cyber context and the prohibition on indiscriminate attacks. The chapter then considers the various ways in which the principle of precaution may be relevant to cyber-attacks. It also provides an examination of a number of *jus in bello* requirements for measures of special protection, and assesses how these rules are relevant to cyber warfare. The final section turns to IHL's restrictions on the 'means and methods' of warfare, including – but not limited to – the law of weaponry.

Application of the *jus in bello*

The *jus in bello* applies to all situations of armed conflict, whether or not war is declared, and regardless of whether the parties involved recognise the state of armed conflict, or indeed the opposing force. As this chapter takes as its starting point the existence of an international armed conflict between two states, many of the issues pertaining to the applicability of that body of law are somewhat moot (for example, the level at which cyber operations occurring *outside* the ambit of traditional hostilities amount to an armed conflict will not be addressed here). Despite the lack of any international law instruments specifically addressing cyber operations, it is indisputable that the law applies to all cyber operations that are taken in the context of and related to an armed conflict. Even those states that seek to prohibit or restrict cyber warfare more generally (for example, China and Russia) have now affirmed the applicability of the law to cyber operations occurring within the context of an armed conflict. That is not to say that all cyber operations that occur during an armed conflict will be governed by IHL. Those cyber operations that do not take place in the context of, nor are related to the ongoing conflict – for example, cyber operations that are merely criminal in nature and have no connection to the hostilities – will continue to be governed by domestic laws regulating cybercrime, corporate espionage, etc.

Once applicable, IHL applies to the whole territory of the warring states, or in the case of what international law refers to as 'non-international armed conflicts', the whole territory under the control of a party to the conflict, whether or not actual combat takes place there (*Tadić* case, 1995: para. 70). This is of particular importance in modern armed conflicts where advanced technologies allow the armed forces of a state to be involved in hostilities taking place in armed conflicts half a world away without ever leaving their state's territory. The use of these technologies – as well as the increasing emergence of conflicts involving transnational terrorism – has led to an intensive debate in recent years regarding the proper extent of the geographical scope of the law. In particular, some states (notably the United States) now argue that the geographical scope should be determined by following the actors taking direct part in the conflict, rather than following state borders or geographical lines of control. However, at the time of writing it appears that the majority of states still adhere to the standard set out in the *Tadić* decision.

Distinction in targeting cyber operations

The principle of distinction raises some of the most interesting issues for the application of the *jus in bello* to cyber operations. The principle is widely accepted as one of the cornerstones of IHL; in the words of the International Court of Justice (ICJ), it is an 'intransgressible principle' of customary international law (*Nuclear Weapons*, 1996: para. 226).

Attacks and operations – the extent of the principle

There is no doubt that the principle of distinction also applies to cyber operations, however the type of acts or operations that are subject to the principle have been the cause of some debate. The discussion stems from the ability of cyber operations to cause significant harm and disruption without causing any physical damage to a targeted system. For example, data may be manipulated, corrupted or deleted to cause massive harm or even complete loss of functionality of a computer system or network without ever causing physical damage to the system, its components or surroundings. The modern restatement of the principle of distinction can be found in Article 48 of Additional Protocol I to the Geneva Conventions (API, 1977):

> In order to ensure respect for and protection of the civilian population and civilian objects, the Parties to the conflict shall at all times distinguish between the civilian population and combatants and between civilian objects and military objectives and accordingly shall *direct their operations* only against military objectives (emphasis added).

The basic rule, thus stated, is general in nature and is set out at the beginning of a series of more specific rules which, *inter alia*, prohibit the targeting of civilians and civilian objects; however, these subsequent rules are phrased in terms of the prohibition or restriction of 'attacks' rather than operations. For example, Article 52 of API (1977) sets out that 'civilian objects shall not be the object of attack' and that 'attacks shall be limited to military objectives'. Likewise, after setting out a general rule with regard to operations, Article 57 provides a list of specific precautions that must be taken 'with respect to attacks'. The term 'attack' is a defined term in IHL: Article 49 of API (1977) defines attacks as 'acts of violence against the adversary, whether in offence or defence'. Given the requirement of 'violence' in the definition, and the general acceptance that this denotes the use of physical force, commentators have been divided over whether cyber operations that do not rise to the level of physical harm are covered by the rules governing the conduct of hostilities. Some commentators (e.g. Schmitt, 2011; *Tallinn manual*, 2013) have argued that the structure and wording of the Additional Protocols is such that the true operationalisation of the principle of distinction occurs only in the articles and paragraphs that follow the basic rule – i.e. those that are phrased in terms of attacks. Thus, according to these commentators, only those operations that meet the definition of attacks are subject to the customary international law principles of distinction, proportionality and precaution in attack.

The present author has argued elsewhere (Harrison Dinniss, 2012) that restricting the application of these principles solely to those cyber operations that constitute attacks effectively renders those provisions of the law that relate to military operations superfluous or redundant. Given that states involved in the drafting of the Additional Protocols to the Geneva Conventions chose to differentiate between the general principles expressed in terms of 'military operations' in API (1977) Article 48 and the first paragraphs of Articles 51 and 57 (each also expressing a general principle followed by specific rules), and the more specific rules expressed in terms of 'attacks' for which they provided a definition, it is hard to imagine that the choice to use different terminology was not deliberate. If that is the case, the specific provisions that relate to attacks set out the way in which the general rule is to be applied in the particular circumstances of an attack, in line with a *lex specialis* approach to harmonising norms (i.e. in this instance, the notion that 'specialised' legal rules may apply or elaborate on more general ones, see Koskenniemi, 2006: 54). Such an approach makes sense given that attacks are clearly the most obvious component of military operations that expose the civilian population and civilian property to the dangers of military operations; however, they are not the only such component (Harrison Dinniss, 2012: 5)

For the difference between attacks and operations to have any meaning, it must then be determined what constitutes a military 'operation' as distinct from an attack. According to the International Committee of the Red Cross (ICRC) commentary to API (1977) Article 48, the term 'operations' should be understood to refer to *military* operations (as opposed to political or other kinds of operations) which 'refers to all movements and acts related to hostilities that are undertaken by the armed forces' (Pilloud *et al.*, 1987: para. 1875). Likewise, the commentary to Article 51 refers to military operations as 'all the movements and activities carried out by the armed forces with a view to combat' (Pilloud *et al.*, 1987: para. 1936); in Article 57 'the term "military operations" should be understood to mean any movements, manoeuvres and other activities whatsoever carried out by the armed forces with a view to combat' (Pilloud *et al.*, 1987: para. 2191). Thus the notion of an 'operation' can be seen as a distinctly broader concept than that of an attack, albeit one that is still closely connected with the conduct of hostilities. To fall within the definition of a military operation and the restriction imposed by the general rules, therefore, a cyber operation must be associated with the use of military force, but does not have to result in violent consequences itself (Harrison Dinniss, 2012: 6). Any assertion that cyber operations that do not amount to attacks (but *do* amount to military operations) may therefore be directed against the civilian population or civilian objects cannot be supported.

As noted above, the part of a military operation most likely to cause harm to civilians and civilian objects is an attack: an act of violence against the adversary, whether in offence or defence. It is important, therefore, to determine which cyber operations will amount to attacks and be subject to the specific rules referred to above. Although the definition of attack refers to 'acts of violence', there is general agreement that it is the violent consequences of an attack that are of significance rather than the means by which damage is inflicted. For example, biological and chemical attacks are universally regarded as attacks, despite not necessarily involving the use of kinetic, physical force, because of their capacity to cause death and injury to human beings. Likewise, the fact that a cyber operation utilises a data stream rather than physical force will not preclude the operation from becoming an 'attack' if it causes the necessary consequences.

So what are the consequences that will fulfil the definition of an attack? It is generally agreed by commentators that cyber operations that result in death or injury to people, or physical damage or destruction to property will constitute attacks under the *jus in bello*. Thus a cyber operation such as the Stuxnet worm, which resulted in physical damage to nearly one thousand centrifuges in Iran's Nantanz uranium enrichment facility in 2010, would constitute an attack had it taken place during an armed conflict. The difficulty comes in determining the status of cyber operations that do *not* result in death, injury, or physical damage or destruction. In the beginning the debate was fairly polarised. Michael Schmitt, offering a restrictive view of the definition of attack, initially argued that the notion of attacks is limited solely to those cyber operations that cause physical damage or destruction to property, or death or injury to people (Schmitt, 2002: 194). Thus, in light of his conclusion regarding attacks and operations (see above; Schmitt, 2011), he determined any cyber operation falling outside that definition may be directed against non-military objectives (i.e. civilian objects). At the other end of the spectrum, Knut Dörmann (2004: 142–3) argued that physical damage was not a requirement of an attack. Based on the idea that neutralisation is amongst the possible outcomes listed within the definition of a military objective, Dörmann argued that the inclusion of this term meant that it was 'irrelevant whether an object was disabled through destruction or in any other way' (Dörmann, 2004: 142–3). Dörmann's approach is attractive in that it includes a wider scope for attacks beyond those which cause physical destruction, some of which may cause a great deal of disruption (for example, switching off an electricity grid for thousands of people). However, Dörmann's understanding would also be broad enough include disruption of any other system, including social media sites such as Facebook, and online shopping sites like Amazon; an outcome that is clearly beyond what the drafters of the law intended to be included in the definition of attacks. There are also some interpretational difficulties with Dörmann's approach (Harrison Dinniss, 2012: 197–8).

Over time the debate has evolved somewhat, and, in 2013, the authors of the *Tallinn manual* defined a cyber-attack as 'a cyber operation, whether offensive or defensive, that is reasonably expected to cause injury or death to persons or damage or destruction to objects' (*Tallinn manual*, 2013: 106). While the commentary in the *Tallinn manual* reveals that there was extensive debate amongst the authors over the requirement of physical damage, it appears there is now at least a broad agreement that where functionality of an object or system is lost without physical damage it may fall within the definition of an attack (*Tallinn manual*, 2013: 108–9; see also Harrison Dinniss, 2011: 4).

However, there does not seem to be agreement as to whether, in order to qualify as an attack, the loss of functionality should require the replacement of a physical component, the reinstallation of the operating system, or some other wider form of data reinstallation. This poses a problem for the classification of data-only cyber operations such as the Shamoon virus launched in 2012 against the Saudi Aramco oil refinery systems and Razgas in Qatar. While neither of these attacks took place in the context of an armed conflict, they provide a useful factual example of a data-only cyber operation. The Shamoon attack (as with the Wiper virus attack against Iranian oil production systems that was its likely inspiration) sabotaged computer systems by corrupting and deleting files on the hard drives of the affected systems rendering them unusable and eventually overwriting the master boot record making the computer itself inoperable (Tarakanov, 2012). The malicious software (or malware) thus destroyed the functionality of the system without causing any physical damage to its component parts. The present author considers that damage to a physical component is not required, and that such data-only attacks, particularly those that necessitate the computer being rebuilt, constitute an attack for the purposes of the *jus in bello*.

Military operations that combine cyber and kinetic means should be assessed on the attack as a whole rather than on its constituent parts. For example, Operation Orchard was a 2007 attack carried out by the Israeli Air Force against an alleged Syrian nuclear site at Dayr al-Zawr. Although very little is known about the details of the attack, it appears to have used both electronic warfare and cyber operations to disable the Syrian air defences during the strike and conventional air strikes to destroy the target (Fulghum *et al.*, 2007). Thus, because the operation contained a kinetic element it undoubtedly qualifies as an attack; a separate assessment of the cyber element is not required.

What may be targeted?

As noted, the principle of distinction requires that parties to an armed conflict distinguish between civilians and combatants on the one hand and civilian objects and military objectives on the other.

Targeting persons

In relation to persons, lawful targets of attack include members of the armed forces, including militias and volunteer corps affiliated with them; members of organised armed groups who perform a continuous combat function; participants in a *levée en masse* (i.e. civilians spontaneously taking up arms to resist invading forces); and civilians who directly participate in hostilities (for a more detailed treatment than is possible in this chapter, see Harrison Dinniss, 2013; *Tallinn manual*, 2013). The ability of cyber operations to target persons directly is currently limited (there is evidence that the possibility of attacks against remotely monitored heart implants such as pacemakers has been developed, however the numbers of targetable people using this type of technology will be low). Nonetheless, it should be recalled that targeting is not restricted to cyber means. Those persons falling within the categories discussed may also be targeted with traditional kinetic means regardless of whether their participation in the conflict is restricted to cyber operations.

IHL sets out a regime of protection for those who do not, or no longer, take part in hostilities, much of which is found in Article 51 of API (1977). Civilians enjoy a general protection against the dangers arising from military operations (Article 51(1)), and more specifically are protected against being made the object of attack (Article 51(2)), or subjected to indiscriminate attacks (Articles 51(4) and (5)), or to acts or threats of violence designed to spread terror amongst the civilian population (Article 51(2)).

Civilians retain these protections unless and for such time as they take a direct part in hostilities (Article 51(3)). However, once civilians directly participate in hostilities, they lose their protection and become directly targetable, whether by cyber or other means. The notion of direct participation in hostilities has been the subject of much legal debate in recent years and is of particular significance for cyber operations given the relative ease with which participants can 'join in' hostilities from anywhere in the world. In 2009 the ICRC issued *Interpretative Guidance* on the matter, offering three cumulative criteria that have been widely accepted by commentators. It should be noted that although the general criteria discussed below were agreed upon by all the experts taking part in the consultation process that resulted in the *Interpretative Guidance*, the exact contours of the three criteria remain the subject of debate.

First, to amount to direct participation in hostilities an act must be likely to adversely affect the military operations or military capacity of a party to an armed conflict or, alternatively, to inflict death, injury, or destruction on persons or objects protected against direct attack (threshold of harm) (ICRC, 2009). For cyber operations, it is significant that the act only needs to adversely affect the military operations or capacity of a party rather than resulting in damage (whether physical or otherwise). Thus the issues discussed above in relation to the definition of attacks, or the question of limitations on military operations, do not arise when discussing direct participation. Second, there must be a direct causal link between the act and the harm likely to result either from that act, or from a coordinated military operation of which that act constitutes an integral part (direct causation) (ICRC, 2009). Although the ICRC guidance calls for 'one-step' causation, this has proved one of the more controversial aspects of the *Interpretative Guidance* and it is by no means clear that states would adopt this standard. This is of particular relevance in the cyber context where second-order effects are of increased importance. Finally, the act must be specifically designed to directly cause the required threshold of harm in support of a party to the conflict and to the detriment of another (belligerent nexus) (ICRC, 2009). Thus cyber operations launched by so-called patriotic hackers in support of state military activities (for example, those launched in support of Russian military operations in Georgia in 2008) would meet this criterion; however, cyber operations that are purely criminal in nature – i.e. operations that merely take advantage of the circumstances of the armed conflict for personal gain – would not.

Targeting objects – what is a military objective?

Of all the issues raised by the advent of cyber operations with respect to the principle of distinction, perhaps the most difficult is the question of what objects may be lawfully attacked. The basic rule is simple: the principle of distinction requires that parties to the armed conflict direct their attacks and operations solely against military objectives. Conversely, civilian objects are protected from attack; they are defined negatively as 'all objects that are not military objectives' (API, 1977: Article 52(1)). This results in a binary distinction between civilian objects and military objectives. The definition of military objectives is provided in Article 52(2) of API (1977) and is reflective of customary international law:

> Attacks shall be limited strictly to military objectives. In so far as objects are concerned, military objectives are limited to those objects which by their nature, location, purpose or use make an effective contribution to military action and whose total or partial destruction, capture or neutralization, in the circumstances ruling at the time, offers a definite military advantage.

As with many of the issues raised by cyber operations the devil is in the detail, or in this case, in the data. The use of the term 'object' in the definition of military objectives has resulted in a debate amongst commentators as to whether data may be targeted in and of itself, or if the object of attack must have some physical form (see e.g. *Tallinn manual*, 2013; Harrison Dinniss, 2015). Based on the intangible nature of data, most of the group involved in drafting the *Tallinn manual* (2013) came to the conclusion that data on its own could not amount to a military objective with the result that legitimate targets of attack are restricted to hardware components. The present author considers that this view is not supported by the context of the provision or the modern interpretation of the term as a matter of law (Harrison Dinniss, 2015). The ability of cyber operations to cause catastrophic damage to the computer systems and networks that underlie our everyday life without causing physical harm or damage is based on their manipulation of data. Thus, while there may be merit in distinguishing between content-level data (for example, the content of web pages, databases or this book) and operational-level data (the operational code that runs computer systems, etc.), a blanket exclusion of data per se as a legitimate military objective does not fit with modern interpretations of the law (Harrison Dinniss, 2015).

Questions of data aside, to qualify as a legitimate military objective an object must by its nature, location, purpose or use make an effective contribution to military action. Objects that are inherently military in nature and of relevance to cyber operations include military communication systems and networks, command

Regulation under the jus in bello 133

and control systems, weapons, weapons systems and other *materiel*. It also includes objects directly used by the armed forces such as equipment, transports, fortifications, depots, buildings occupied by armed forces, staff headquarters and communications centres (Pilloud *et al.*, 1987: paras 2007–8) many of which contain military systems and infrastructure that may be directly affected by cyber operations.

Objects that qualify as military objectives through the criterion of location are generally considered to be geographic areas, although the criterion was introduced to the definition of military objectives without explanation. Traditional examples include geographical features such as mountain passes, ice bridges or trails through marshland or swamps. Such an area might qualify where it is a site that must be seized, which must be denied to the enemy or from which the enemy must be forced to retreat (Pilloud *et al.*, 1987: paras 2020–4). The drafters of the *Tallinn manual* (2013: 128) argue that where a cyber operation can be used to deny or neutralise such an area the characterisation of the geographical feature justifies a cyber-attack on surrounding targets to achieve that effect. Although direct examples in the cyber context are difficult to find, where a system or network makes an effective contribution to military action through its physical location (for example a civilian WiFi network located in an area in which an enemy is operating may enable the enemy to piggy-back communications on the signal, and denying the enemy use of that network may give a direct and concrete advantage to the attacking forces), it will qualify as a military objective through the location criterion (Harrison Dinniss, 2012: 185–6; 2015).

A more interesting question is whether an object may qualify as a military objective through its network location rather than its location in physical space (Harrison Dinniss, 2012: 185–6). Cyber infrastructural equivalents of relevant geographical features might include Internet kill switches, undersea cable landing points or primary nodes of the state's internal telecommunications networks, each of which would make an effective contribution to military action. Further, denying particular data routes to military traffic by neutralising particular network nodes (thus forcing the traffic over less secure or monitored switches) would provide a definite military advantage to an attacking force. Subject always to the principle of proportionality, there is no reason why a particular node's network location should not form the basis for attacks on such targets by analogy, although in practice it is likely that such strategic objects would also qualify through purpose or use.

Qualification of a military objective through its purpose is notoriously difficult as such a determination must be based on an established intention rather than speculation or guesswork. However, where it becomes known that a party to an armed conflict is trying to acquire a particular system or a piece of software, it will become a military objective as soon as the intention is established, rather than upon acquisition (assuming fulfilment of the remainder of the definition). Thus a party to a conflict could legitimately 'spike' the desired software with malicious code prior to the enemy ever getting their hands on it.

Where a civilian object is used by a party to the armed conflict for military purposes, it will become a military objective through its use. Classic examples include civilian airfields, transport and buildings which are used by the military; however it also includes the use of civilian networks, computer systems and other infrastructure. The object will continue to be a military objective until such time as the military use ends and regardless of whether the object continues to be used by civilians while being used by the military (see the discussion of dual-use objects in the next section). When the military use of the object is discontinued, the object will revert back to its civilian status. As even a small amount of military use of a network or system is sufficient to qualify it as a military objective, care must be taken in determining the appropriate level of specificity at which to define the qualifying objective when targeting (i.e. network, system, component, etc.) (Harrison Dinniss, 2015). An entire computer network does not qualify as a military objective based on the mere fact that an individual router so qualifies (*Tallinn manual*, 2013: 128).

In order to qualify as a military objective through one of the four criteria, an object must also make an 'effective contribution to military action'. This criterion will almost always be met in relation to objects that are of a military nature, however a determination must be made in every case. While all states accept the requirement of an effective contribution as being reflective of customary international law, there remains an enduring disagreement regarding the nature of the contribution required. The United States interprets the clause more broadly, maintaining that targets that make an 'effective contribution to the enemy's war-fighting or war-sustaining capability' qualify (*Commander's handbook on the law of naval operations*, 2007: para. 8.2). While 'war-fighting' equates to military action, the inclusion of 'war-sustaining' means that 'economic objects of the enemy that indirectly but effectively support and sustain the enemy's war-fighting capability may also be attacked' (*Commander's handbook on the law of naval operations*, 2007: para. 8.2.5). With regard to cyber-attacks, this interpretation opens a large swathe of targets during an armed conflict; for example, it would justify attacks such as those conducted against the Iranian or Saudi oil industries where they are the state's primary source of budgetary income for the (hypothetical) war effort. The majority of states do not subscribe to this view. It moves the target of the operations away from the military effort of the parties to the armed conflict and onto the political command and control and its resource base; thus giving up the requirement of a close nexus between the target and ongoing military operations (see Oeter, 2007: 56). Most of the *Tallinn manual* (2013: 131) authors also considered that customary international law:

> limits the notion of military objectives to those objects that are war-fighting (used in combat) or war-supporting (otherwise make an effective contribution to military action, as with factories making hardware or software for use by the military) and otherwise fulfil the criteria of a military objective.

War-*sustaining* objects are too far removed.

The second limb of the definition of military objectives requires that the destruction, capture or neutralisation of the object in question offers a 'definite military advantage'. The military advantage to be gained must be concrete rather than hypothetical: thus any cyber operation in which the anticipated results are indeterminate or purely speculative will be prohibited. Likewise, the advantage gained by the attack must be military in nature; operations which produce an economic or political advantage do not qualify (although such advantages may well be desirable second-order effects, as long as the attack produces a military advantage as well). As noted earlier, the advantage to be gained is assessed from the attack as a whole, rather than on its isolated or particular parts (ICRC, 2005: 31 and associated state practice). This is of particular relevance to cyber operations that support a traditional kinetic operation, such as the Israeli attack against a suspected nuclear site in Syria, or cyber operations that require the disabling of multiple nodes to achieve their effect. In all cases an assessment of the military advantage to be gained from the attack must be carried out with regard to the 'circumstances ruling at the time'. As noted above with regard to the 'use' criterion, objects that qualify as a military objective at one point in time may no longer qualify at a later date, either because the military use has discontinued or because a military advantage no longer accrues from attacking it, and vice versa.

Dual-use objects

Although it is certainly not a problem unique to cyber operations, the vast number of computers, computer systems, networks and other elements of cyber infrastructure that are shared by both military and civilian traffic make the issue of dual-use objects particularly problematic in any conflict involving a cyber element. 'Dual-use' objects are those objects that have both a military and a civilian use; however the term, while useful to describe the function of certain objects, is not one found anywhere in the *jus in bello*. As noted, IHL defines civilian objects negatively, in that they are defined as any object that is *not* a military objective (API, 1977: Article 52). This results in a binary distinction insofar as it relates to objects: objects are either military objectives or they are civilian objects. This means that where an object that is used for both military and civilian purposes meets the definition of a military objective either through its nature, location, purpose or use (see above section), the object becomes a legitimate military target in its entirety. Any effects on civilian function are considered through the operation of the proportionality principle. As Droege (2012: 563) notes, the dangers in cyberspace are evident: virtually the entirety of the international cyber infrastructure – that is, computers, servers, routers, cables and satellites – is used for both civilian and military communications. The fact that all of cyberspace is used for military operations means that in any armed conflict it will be of important strategic interest to degrade the adversary's communication networks and access to cyberspace; 'this will mean denying the adversary access to critical routes in cyberspace, degrading its main routers or access to major communication nodes, not just targeting specific computer systems of the military infrastructure' (Droege, 2012: 563). The present author has argued elsewhere that parties to an armed conflict may have an obligation to define military objectives as narrowly and specifically as possible in order to avoid this problem (Harrison Dinniss, 2015).

Indiscriminate attacks

The *jus in bello* prohibits indiscriminate attacks. This prohibition is established as customary international law in both international and non-international armed conflicts, and is codified in Article 51(4) of API (1977). Indiscriminate attacks may result either from the use of a means or method of warfare in an indiscriminate manner, or by the use of a means or method of warfare that is indiscriminate by its very nature. As it relates to the latter, this means that the weapon concerned either cannot be directed at a specific military objective or that the effects of the weapon cannot be limited as required by the *jus in bello*, so that it will strike both military objectives and civilian objects without distinction. The sophistication of the coding in the Stuxnet attack offers proof that malware may be programmed with a great deal of precision both in targeting the attack and in limiting its effects. In that case, initial versions of the malware were designed to spread only to a set number of computers within a local network from the infection point (an infected USB drive). However, when these failed to achieve the desired results, the malware's designers widened the propagation window (Keizer, 2010), first to a 21-day window (i.e. the virus would stop spreading after the set number of days), and eventually to spread fairly indiscriminately. In all cases the malware was programmed to deploy its payload component only once the specific conditions were fulfilled that would indicate that it was on the targeted system (Falliere *et al.*, 2011; Zetter, 2011). Thus although the later versions of the malware appeared to propagate and spread fairly indiscriminately, the portion of the code that would constitute an attack was deployed in a very discriminate manner. It was this very sophisticated and discriminating coding that tipped virus researchers off to the fact that Stuxnet was probably an attack launched by a state. Of course, most common forms of malware designed purely for criminal purposes spread widely in order to maximise the returns; highly targeted approaches tend to be reserved for cyber espionage, whether corporate or state, and for specific directed threats (on the precision of cyber-attacks, see Chapter 2 of this volume). Having said this, it should be noted that the number of targeted attacks has increased in recent years (*Symantec Corporation*, 2014).

Stuxnet also illustrates the ability to limit the effects of an attack. The code was designed to deploy its payload only on systems where the parameters entered by the coders existed: the system needed to be running a particular type of software, have certain components installed, and have those components set to a certain frequency (Falliere *et al.*, 2011; Zetter, 2011). All of these measures were designed to ensure that one particular system was targeted, and the effects of the malware were limited to the Nantanz nuclear facility in Iran (this chapter will not address the question of whether the nuclear facility would constitute a legitimate military objective had the attack taken place during an armed conflict). The fact that the code also caused problems outside the targeted system (for example, security researchers were alerted to the existence of the malware by a client whose computer system was stuck in a reboot loop) does not detract from the discriminate nature of the code involved.

TARGET AREA BOMBING

One of the examples of indiscriminate attacks prohibited by the *jus in bello* is set out in Article 51(5) of API (1977). Commonly known as target area bombing, it prohibits 'an attack by bombardment by any methods or means which treats as a single military objective a number of clearly separated and distinct military objectives located in a city, town, village or other area containing a similar concentration of civilians or civilian objects'. The prohibition is considered customary international law and is applicable in international and non-international armed conflicts (ICRC, 2005). In respect of cyber operations the issue is also related to the definition of military objectives and the level of specificity at which such definition occurs (i.e. network, system, component or even code). This is of particular significance in an era of extensive dual-use systems and increasing virtualisation of both data storage and services (in which civilian and military services or data may be provided from the same hardware platforms). Where it is possible to define the military objective narrowly to a particular piece of code or a component of a system, states should attempt to do so (Harrison Dinniss, 2015). The law requires that where the targets are 'clearly separated' they must be attacked separately – 'clearly separated' has been interpreted by states to mean that the distance 'be at least sufficiently large to permit the individual military objectives to be attacked separately' (ICRC, 2005). In the cyber realm this will be dependent on the type of system or network that is the intended target.

PROPORTIONALITY

The second type of indiscriminate attacks that are prohibited by API are attacks that breach the principle of proportionality. The principle is reflective of customary international law in both international and non-international armed conflicts and is expressed in Article 51(5)(b) of API (1977) thus:

> an attack which may be expected to cause incidental loss of civilian life, injury to civilians, damage to civilian objects, or a combination thereof, which would be excessive in relation to the concrete and direct military advantage anticipated.

The same formulation is found in Article 57(2)(iii) in relation to precautions in attack (see below); any intentional violation of the principle is considered a grave breach of the Protocol and a war crime. The dual-use nature of much of the cyber infrastructure and the increased impact of indirect or knock-on effects due to the high degree of interconnectivity makes the principle of proportionality of particular relevance to cyber operations. Proportionality deals with the effects of cyber-attacks that are not intentionally directed at civilians, but which nevertheless cause damage to civilian objects, or death or injury to civilians despite being directed at a legitimate military objective. The standard is one of 'excessiveness' in relation to the military advantage, a measure that is not defined in international law. As with the discussion of damage in relation to military objectives above, only certain types of effects of cyber operations will be included in the calculation. Where physical damage occurs, or operational data is destroyed such that the functionality of a computer, system, or network is impaired or destroyed, the damage will be included in the proportionality assessment; mere inconvenience will not.

Both the expected civilian losses (commonly referred to as 'collateral damage') and the military advantage anticipated must, of necessity, be calculated *ex ante;* that is, as the operation is being planned rather than being determined after the fact. This requires that commanders and others planning an operation use all information reasonably available to them at the time of the decision, and that all decisions are carried out with due diligence and in good faith. With regard to cyber operations, this may necessitate network analysis being carried out by technical specialists, rather than reliance on the ordinary expertise of the military commander on the ground. However the standard required in the proportionality assessment is ultimately one of reasonableness. In the *Galić Case* (2003), the Trial Chamber of the International Criminal Tribunal for the Former Yugoslavia (ICTY) held that:

> in determining whether an attack was proportionate, it is necessary to examine whether a reasonably well-informed person in the circumstances of the actual perpetrator, making reasonable use of the information available to him or her, could have expected excessive civilian casualties to result from the attack.

As with any non-cyber applications of the principle of proportionality, the military advantage anticipated and weighed must be 'concrete and direct'; that is, it may not be speculative. The ICRC commentary to the Additional Protocols (Pilloud *et al.*, 1987: para. 2209) notes that the expression 'concrete and direct' was used to indicate that the 'advantage concerned should be substantial and relatively close, and that advantages which are hardly perceptible and those which would only appear in the long term should be disregarded'. As noted, several states have stated that the military advantage to be calculated should be that of the military attack regarded as a whole and not only from isolated or particular parts of it (ICRC, 2005: 49). This is of particular relevance when cyber-attacks are used to enable (or accompany) more traditional kinetic attacks. For example, in 2007, Israeli air force fighters crossed into Syrian airspace and launched air strikes on a suspected Syrian nuclear site at Dayr al-Zawr. The remarkable feature of the raid (other than the almost complete silence from both Israeli and Syrian officials regarding the strikes: see Green, 2007) was the apparent ability of the Israeli aircraft to carry out their mission without being engaged or even detected by Syrian air defences. It appears that a combination of electronic warfare techniques (such as jamming) and cyber methods allowed specialists to hack into the Syria's networked air defence system, blinding it to the fighters, and ensuring the success of the mission (Fulghum *et al.*, 2007). In such a case the military advantage to be considered results from the entire attack, including the kinetic strikes rather than just the cyber element directed against the air defence network. Likewise, any collateral damage caused by a series of coordinated cyber-attacks against multiple components or nodes of a network or system would need to be assessed against the attack taken as a whole rather than by viewing each component of the attack in isolation.

One of the other questions raised by cyber operations in relation to proportionality relates to the expected 'knock-on' or indirect effects on civilians and civilian objects. There is now general agreement that such effects should be taken into account in the proportionality calculation, however the extent to which such second-, third- or even higher-order effects must be taken into account is not clear. It seems reasonable to assume, however, that the words 'may be expected' in the article include any indirect effects that are reasonably foreseeable, and thus should be factored into the proportionality equation (Droege, 2012: 573; *Tallinn manual*, 2013: 160). Given the high levels of interconnectivity between civilian and military systems, particular care will need to be exercised when performing network reconnaissance to take this into account.

The drafters of the *Tallinn manual* have also noted that cyber-attacks on military objectives are sometimes launched via civilian infrastructure, cables, satellites etc. which may result in damage (2013: 160). In other words, a cyber-attack can cause collateral damage both during transit and because of the attack itself: both forms of damage are to be considered in the application of proportionality. While agreeing in principle that the damage must be calculated, the present author has argued elsewhere that the damage to these so-called 'gateway targets' requires a slightly more complex assessment than is suggested by the *Tallinn manual* approach, which will be highly dependent on the attack vector and malware design chosen by the attackers (Harrison Dinniss, 2011). However, it is sufficient to note here that in some cases, the transitory damage may in fact amount to a prohibited attack directed at that civilian infrastructure.

The principle of precaution

The *jus in bello* requires that parties to an armed conflict take certain precautionary measures both in carrying out military operations and attacks, and against the effects of attacks. Both sets of obligations are reflective of customary international law in both international and non-international armed conflicts, and have been recognised as such by the Appeals Chamber of the ICTY in both the *Tadić* (1995) and *Kupreškić* (2000) cases.

Precautions in attack

Article 57 of API (1977) requires that attackers take precautionary measures when carrying out military operations and attacks. Article 57(1) sets out the general rule, expressed in terms of military operations: in the conduct of military operations, constant care shall be taken to spare the civilian population, civilians and civilian objects. However as with the rules relating to targeting, the majority of the specific rules are limited to those operations that constitute attacks. The precautions required include doing everything feasible to verify the targets of the attack, choosing means and methods of attack to avoid or minimise collateral damage, choosing targets that will cause the least collateral damage for similar advantage when possible, and providing warnings of attacks where possible; each of these will be addressed in the following sections. Further, in addition to attacks that are prohibited through the operation of the principle of proportionality, the principle of precaution also requires those who plan or decide on an attack to cancel or suspend an attack where it becomes apparent that it would cause excessive collateral damage (API, 1977: Articles 57(2)(a)(iii) and 57(3)). The issues associated with the principle of proportionality are addressed in the above section and are not repeated here.

In most cases the *jus in bello* requires those who plan and decide on attacks to take 'feasible' measures. Feasibility has been interpreted by many states to mean 'those precautions that are practicable or practically possible, taking into account all the circumstances ruling at the time, including humanitarian and other considerations' (ICRC, 2005: 54). It should be noted that the standard of feasibility applies to all attacks against targets on land (from whatever platform they are launched); attacks against targets in the air or at sea are subject to 'all reasonable' precautions, which may be interpreted as 'a little less far-reaching' than the feasibility standard (Pilloud *et al.*, 1987: para. 2230).

Verification of objectives

Those who plan or decide on an attack are required to do everything feasible to verify that the target or targets of the attack are military objectives and that it is not prohibited to attack them (API, 1977: Article 57(2)(a)(i)). In cases of a predetermined cyber-attack against a specified target, this obligation is unlikely to be problematic. Extensive system surveillance and scanning to establish entry points and efficient outcomes will be required in order to make the attack a success, thus determining the nature of the target will be easy to ascertain. Targets of opportunity or automated 'hack-backs' will pose more of an issue because of the danger of hacking back against a target computer that has been spoofed, where the source of the attack has not been accurately attributed (i.e. the source appears to be the attacking computer when in actuality it is not). The fact that the majority of cyber-attacks conceal their origins does not make them unlawful per se (see below on perfidy and ruses), however it does mean that those deciding on attacks will need to be particularly vigilant regarding the verification of targets.

Military commanders must make their decisions on the basis of information from all sources that are available to them at the time and many military manuals stress that the commander must obtain the best possible intelligence including information on concentrations of civilians, important civilian objects, specifically protected objects, the natural environment and the civilian environment of military objectives (ICRC, 2005: 54–5 and associated state practice). In its *Final Report to the Prosecutor* (2000: para. 29) the committee established to review the NATO bombing campaign against the Federal Republic of Yugoslavia noted that this obligation included setting up an 'effective intelligence gathering system to collect and evaluate targets' and the obligation to direct his or her forces to 'use available technical means to properly identify targets'. When gathering intelligence for cyber operations this may include both active and passive methods of network or system reconnaissance, mapping, and ensuring that personnel with the appropriate technical skills or qualifications are involved in both the reconnaissance and targeting processes.

The *jus in bello* also requires that those who plan or decide on attacks, cancel or suspend an attack if it becomes apparent that the target is not a military objective or that it is subject to special protection (API, 1977: Article 57(2)(b)); (likewise, an attack must also be cancelled or suspended if it is determined that it will breach the principle of proportionality). This obligation will extend to those who carry out or monitor the attack and results in an obligation to ensure that the planners and decision-makers are kept informed of updated intelligence regarding the targeted system and its environment.

Choice of means and methods

Attackers are required to take all feasible precautions in the choice of means and methods of attack with a view to avoiding, and in any event to minimising, incidental loss of civilian life, injury to civilians and damage to civilian objects (API, 1977: Article 57(2)(a)(ii)). The provision is accepted as customary international law applicable in international and non-international armed conflicts (ICRC, 2005: 57).

In the cyber domain, the ability of cyber operations to achieve their desired effects without causing physical harm to surrounding civilian objects may mean that states with the ability to launch an attack by cyber means should utilise those options in preference to more traditional kinetic means. However this will not necessarily always be the case; the interconnectedness of the cyber environment also increases the potential for knock-on effects to cause more collateral damage than might result from a more conventional attack. Thus the assessment will necessarily be highly fact-dependant on both the operation planned and the type of cyber-attack anticipated. For example, the Stuxnet virus was specifically crafted to deploy its payload only when it reached a particular system containing a set combination of software and hardware operating at particular frequencies. This allowed the attackers to minimise the collateral damage to surrounding systems, despite deliberately utilising civilian gateway targets as their attack vector. Conversely, the United States decided not to attack the Iraqi Tiger-song air defence network using cyber means, due to its cross-wiring with the oil pipeline communications system (Smith, 2003), opting instead for more traditional air attacks and carbon filament munitions, in order to limit effects solely to military objectives located within Iraq.

It should also be noted that the rule that all feasible precautions must be taken in the choice of means and methods of attack applies independently of the principle of proportionality. That is, the choice of means and methods of attack must be taken even where neither of the methods under consideration would result in excessive damage to civilians or civilian objects such that it would breach the proportionality principle. It is an additional measure designed to minimise the effects of hostilities on the civilian population.

Choice of targets

Article 57(3) of API (1977) provides that:

> when a choice is possible between several military objectives for obtaining a similar military advantage, the objective to be selected shall be that the attack on which may be expected to cause the least danger to civilian lives and to civilian objects.

The obligation is recognised as customary international law in international armed conflicts and, arguably, in non-international armed conflicts (ICRC, 2005: 65).

This obligation is particularly important given the large amount of interconnectedness and the high incidence of dual-use systems in the cyber environment. As the obligation requires a choice between military objectives, it is also impacted by the definition of military objectives (discussed above) and in particular the level of specificity at which the objective is defined. Cyber warfare offers unique opportunities in this regard, because of the ability to break down targeted networks and systems into ever smaller components in order to locate and affect precisely the exact military objective required to achieve the desired result. For example, a targeted system may be neutralised either by disabling an essential component of the system so that it is unable to function, by attacking the system as a whole, by attacking the network on which that system resides, or by shutting off the electrical supply to the site containing the targeted system. All would achieve the same or similar military advantage (i.e. denying the targeted system to the adversary). However, in many cases attacking the network as a whole or shutting off the electrical supply, unless they are isolated systems, will also have an impact on civilian portions of the network or other civilian infrastructure. The rule requires attackers to select the military objective that will achieve a similar advantage while causing the least danger to civilian lives and property (it should be noted that the advantage does not have to be identical). Thus, in that situation, states have an obligation to choose the most specific target possible.

A final point worth noting in relation to the obligation is that it is not an absolute requirement but is limited to situation where 'a choice is possible'. Whether alternative targets are possibilities will depend on facts such as the ability to access the required portions of the network, the ability to determine the effects of neutralising a particular component, and whether the appropriate systems can be accessed and assessed in time for the purposes of the operation or mission.

Warnings

The *jus in bello* requires that parties to an armed conflict must give effective advance warning of that which may affect the civilian population, unless circumstances do not permit (API, 1977: Article 57(2)(c)). As noted in the ICRC study, *Customary International Humanitarian Law* (ICRC, 2005: 62), this is a long-standing rule of customary international law already recognised as such by the Lieber Code of 1863 and codified in Article 26 of the Hague Regulations of 1907. While the rule undoubtedly applies to cyber operations, the majority of the drafters of the *Tallinn manual* have argued that the obligation does not apply to situations in which civilian objects will be damaged or destroyed without the civilian population being placed at risk (2013: 174). This is particularly relevant in the cyber context given that cyber-attacks will often damage civilian cyber infrastructure without risking harm to persons, and may well be carried out while the population remains in situ. Although the primary purpose of warnings is to protect the civilian population from death or injury, denying the applicability of the precaution to attacks that will affect civilians through damage to civilian property appears to be an innovation on the part of the *Tallinn manual* drafters. Thus cyber-attacks that will affect the civilian population by damaging civilian objects should also be preceded by effective warnings where possible, in order to enable civilians to take appropriate measures to protect themselves and their property. Warnings may be general in nature, however they must be effective. A warning of impending cyber-attacks does not necessarily need to be given by cyber means, it will be sufficient that the method used can be expected to be understood by the population, in sufficient time that they can take appropriate precautions.

As with other precautions in attack, the obligation to give effective warnings is not an absolute obligation. The attacker may dispense with the warning in cases where 'circumstances do not permit', reflecting the principle of military necessity that undergirds the *jus in bello*. Examples of such circumstances include situations where the element of surprise is necessary for the success of the mission, or where the casualties that the attacking forces are likely to sustain would be significantly increased by issuing a warning.

Precautions against the effects of attacks (precautions in defence)

IHL also places obligations on defenders in respect of the civilian population, individual civilians and civilian objects. Article 58 of API (1977) requires parties to a conflict, to the maximum extent feasible, to (1) endeavour to remove the civilian population, individual civilians and civilian objects under their control from the vicinity of military objectives; (2) avoid locating military objectives within or near densely populated areas; (3) take the other necessary precautions to protect the civilian population, individual civilians and civilian objects under their control against the dangers resulting from military operations. The obligation is recognised as customary international law applicable in international armed conflicts, although some debate over its customary status in non-international armed conflicts still exists.

Like many other precautionary measures, precautions in defence are limited to what is feasible: in this case the wording is to the 'maximum extent feasible' by the party. In the cyber environment, precautions in defence are particularly problematic. The feasibility or practicality of completely separating military objectives and civilian cyber infrastructure is simply not possible at this stage. Far from meeting the obligations required by the *jus in bello*, states have thus far failed to extricate the majority of their military cyber infrastructure from civilian systems. While there are certainly military systems and networks that are separated from civilian infrastructure, a 2010 estimate placed 98 per cent of US government communications as still travelling over civilian networks (Jensen, 2010: 1533). Likewise, as defence budgets decrease and the military increasingly use off-the-shelf systems and civilian personnel and support mechanisms, the trend is in the reverse direction.

The *Tallinn manual* (2013: 176) usefully lists several examples of so-called 'passive precautions' including separating military from civilian infrastructure; segregating computer systems on which critical civilian infrastructure depends on the Internet; backing up important civilian data; making arrangements to ensure the timely repair of important communications systems; digitally recording important cultural or spiritual objects to facilitate reconstruction in the wake of their destruction; and using anti-virus (AV) measures to protect civilian systems that might suffer damage or destruction during an attack on military cyber infrastructure.

A question also remains regarding the wording 'under their control' and what that might mean in the cyber environment. The ICRC commentary makes clear that at the time of drafting, this was aimed at measures that a defending party must take with respect to territory under its control (either its own or that which it occupies) (Pilloud *et al.*, 1987: para. 2239). However in the cyber environment, territory is not a reliable indicator of control, and most critical infrastructure and networks that are likely to be exposed to the effects of cyber-attack are under the control of the private sector. The measures that may be feasible for states to take may be limited to having critical infrastructure planning and coordination processes in place (including any supporting legislation), rather than taking concrete steps to provide protection measures themselves. Certainly any publicly controlled information and systems, or systems in which the party can dictate its operation (*Tallinn manual*, 2013: 178), whether through legislative or other means, will fall within the obligation of the state.

Measures of special protection

IHL provides certain persons and objects with special protection. While the state of technology is not yet at the point where cyber operations can be advantageously used directly against personnel (although those wearing digitally controlled devices such as pacemakers and other implants may be vulnerable), other objects such as hospitals and medical units, dams, dykes and nuclear power-generating stations, water sanitation and irrigation systems as well as other objects considered indispensable to the civilian population are all vulnerable to attack via cyber means and are offered special protection under the law. This section addresses the issues that arise in applying IHL to cyber operations against certain of these persons and objects with protected status. Other objects that benefit from special protection under IHL such as the natural environment, cultural property and demilitarised zones are addressed elsewhere (see Harrison Dinniss, 2012).

Specially protected persons

As noted above, at the current state of technology, there are very limited situations where cyber operations targeted directly against personnel will be of military use. However where the technology does exist, persons with special protection under the *jus in bello* retain the same protection against cyber operations as with any other means or method of warfare. Personnel benefiting from specific protection under the law include medical and religious personnel, United Nations personnel, prisoners of war and other detained persons, and children. The duties of humanitarian relief personnel and journalists also benefit from specific protection under the law; however, the persons carrying out such duties do not receive additional protection over and above their protected civilian status.

Aside from direct attacks against persons offered special protection by the *jus in bello*, certain other protections must be taken into account when conducting cyber operations that may impact these categories of persons. To take one of the examples above, detainees and particularly prisoners of war must be respected and protected from humiliating or degrading treatment, outrages to human dignity, and must not be exposed to public abuse and curiosity (GC III, 1949: Articles 13 and 14). Any cyber operations that contribute to, or result in, such treatment are likewise prohibited (for additional details see *Tallinn manual*, 2013: 214–15). For example, publishing personal or defamatory data (whether information or images) about detainees on the Internet, or publicly exposing demeaning information of a personal nature to social media and other sources would be prohibited. Likewise, precautions must be taken to prevent unauthorised access to such material by any other actor and ensuring that detainee records (an obligation under the relevant treaties for all detainees, whether prisoners of war, civilian internees or other detainees) are kept separately from data and systems that may constitute a military objective (*Tallinn manual*, 2013: 214–15). Detainees also have a customary right to personal correspondence with family members and other private persons that must not be interfered with by a party to the conflict (ICRC, 2005: 445), including by cyber operations, subject to reasonable conditions as to frequency and censorship by the detaining authorities. These, and other restrictions like them (for example, on the recruitment of child soldiers), must be carefully assessed by the parties to the armed conflict and applied with equal rigor in conflicts involving cyber operations, as they would be during more traditional armed conflicts.

Medical units, medical transports and hospitals

Hospitals, medical units and medical transport (including hospital ships and aircraft) all receive special protection under the IHL, both as a matter of customary international law and through specific treaty protections. In respect of international armed conflicts, the obligation to respect and protect medical units (GC I, 1949: Articles 19 and 33; API, 1977: Article 12) requires a party to the armed conflict to refrain from attacking medical units but also from unnecessarily hindering them in carrying out their duties and where necessary, defending them from attack. Such protections remain in force in respect of cyber operations as well as more traditional military operations. Thus where databases, computer systems and networks are used for the delivery of these protected medical services they undoubtedly form part of the material and supplies of those services and share in their protection. However that requirement to respect and protect the resources of medical units, etc. is not absolute – protection may cease where the unit (including its resources) is used to commit, outside of their humanitarian function, acts harmful to the enemy (the customary rule in respect of international armed conflicts is reflected in GC I, 1949: Article 21; GC IV, 1949: Article 19; API, 1977: Article 13). However, even in such cases a warning must be given prior to any attack against medical units, setting a reasonable time limit whenever appropriate; the attack can only take place after such a warning has remained unheeded. In relation to cyber operations the obligation to respect and protect medical units and the circumstances in which such protection may be lost will require the parties to separate the computer systems and data used for the provision of medical services from systems and data that may comprise a legitimate military objective; under no circumstances should they be used to attempt to immunise a military objective from attack (API, 1977: Article 12(4)). As noted, medical systems and datasets should not be used for any acts that may be construed as harmful against the enemy – not only does this prohibit the use of such systems to launch cyber operations, for intelligence gathering or military communications, but arguably also use of the datasets for weapons development research or other such uses outside the humanitarian function of medical units and transports. As the ICRC commentary notes, the concept of 'acts harmful to the enemy' includes not only direct attack, but also acts that deliberately hinder the enemy's military operation in any way whatsoever (Pilloud *et al.*, 1987: paras 550–2).

It is clear that in order to ensure that these protective rules can be complied with by an adversary, parties to the conflict should take all feasible measures to identify the computer systems, networks and data of medical units and transport. Rules regarding the marking of medical units and their stores are found in Geneva Conventions I, II and IV as well as the Additional Protocols and are reflective of customary international law. Specifically designated electronic marking and file tagging will provide an easy technological answer to these requirements and can be easily communicated to the enemy to ensure their ability to comply with the protections with regard to cyber operations. However, it should be noted that failure to identify or notify the enemy of such markings, or of the location of medical units, transport or their resources does not deprive them of their protected status.

Installations containing dangerous forces

The *jus in bello* conflict grants special protection to certain installations containing dangerous forces, namely dams, dykes and nuclear electrical generating stations, in circumstances where attacking them risks the release of the dangerous forces they contain. Where these installations constitute civilian objects, they are protected from attack by their civilian status, however where the installation would otherwise qualify as a military objective, Article 56(1) of API (1977) requires that the attacker take particular care in order to avoid releasing the dangerous forces contained therein, and the consequent severe losses amongst the civilian population. This obligation, which was innovative at the time the protocol was drafted, is now recognised as customary international law applicable in both international and non-international armed conflicts (ICRC, 2005: 139). A similar provision exists in Additional Protocol II (APII, 1977). In addition, other military objectives that are located at or in the vicinity of such installations may also not be attacked if the attack could cause the release of the dangerous forces and the consequent severe losses amongst the civilian population. Cyber operations increase the risk for these installations through network proximity, but also provide the ability to target sites that otherwise have been prohibited due to the risk of releasing dangerous forces. For example, a hydroelectric dam and its associated power-generating capacity that provides power to an adversary may be targeted through cyber operations where traditional means such as air strikes would risk breaching the dam and causing catastrophic damage downstream should the water be released. A cyber operation on the other hand may simply disconnect the power station or turbines from the dam's sluice gates, thus denying the electricity to the adversary without risking the downstream collateral damage that would occur should the water contained in the dam be released.

It should be noted that the list of protected installations is exhaustive. The ICRC commentary notes that although a wider list was proposed during the drafting process, agreement on the text was only reached once the special protection granted by the article was limited to dams, dykes and nuclear electrical generating systems (Pilloud *et al.*, 1987: paras 2147–50). This means that had the 2010 Stuxnet attack against the Nantanz uranium enrichment facility been conducted during an armed conflict, it would not have fallen foul of this provision; however any attacks that were directed against the Bushehr nuclear power plant would have done so.

Objects indispensable to the civilian population

Article 54(2) of API (1977) prohibits attacking, destroying, removing or rendering useless objects that are essential to the survival of the civilian population for the specific purpose of denying their sustenance value to that population. This is a rule of customary international law and applies in both international and non-international armed conflicts (APII, 1977: Article 14 also contains equivalent wording).

In terms of cyber operations, any operation conducted against targets such as water treatment plants, irrigation works, or food processing systems that result in the above-mentioned harm is prohibited. There have been multiple peacetime incidences of such installations being breached, indicating their susceptibility to cyber-attack. While these peacetime attacks have generally occurred for personal reasons of the attacker (such as employment disputes), it should be noted that during an armed conflict, the purpose of the attack must be to deny the object's sustenance value to the civilian population or to the adverse party, regardless of the motive – whether it is in order to starve out civilians, make them move away, or for any other reason. The prohibition does not extend to collateral damage against objects in an attack against a legitimate military objective, nor in circumstances in which the object attacked has become a military objective (for example through its use by the armed forces). The purpose is to provide additional protection to a narrow category of civilian objects (which are already protected by virtue of their civilian status), that are required for subsistence. The authors of the *Tallinn manual* (2013: 227) also state that the Internet (or other communications networks) would not, in and of itself, qualify as an object indispensable for the survival of the civilian population.

The protection set out in the Additional Protocol prohibits 'attacking, destroying, removing or rendering useless objects'. This phrasing is far broader than the prohibition against attacks, and makes any discussions regarding the type of cyber operation which is prohibited moot (see above) in respect of this category of object.

Means and methods of warfare

The law of weaponry

'The right of belligerents to adopt means of injuring the enemy is not unlimited': this well-established principle of customary international law is codified in Article 22 of the Hague Regulations (1907), Article 35(1) of API (1977), and the Preamble to the Convention on Certain Conventional Weapons (CCW). It reflects the principle of limited warfare and forms the basis of the legal regulation of means and methods of conflict (Oeter, 2008: 126). Known as the 'law of weaponry', it reflects the same balance between humanitarian considerations and military necessity as the rest of the *jus in bello*, and consists of both general principles and specific rules prohibiting or limiting the use of particular weapons or methods of warfare. While there are no specific rules directly regulating cyber operations, a few of the specific provisions are nevertheless relevant to the cyber domain. Further, as noted previously the general principles apply regardless of the technology of the weapon employed.

The first general principle, the prohibition of means and methods of warfare that are of a nature to cause superfluous injury or unnecessary suffering, is reflected in both treaty and customary international law and is considered one of the cardinal principles of IHL (*Nuclear Weapons*, 1996: para. 238). It applies equally to cyber operations; thus, where a cyber operation is 'of a nature to cause harm greater than that unavoidable to achieve legitimate military objectives' (*Nuclear Weapons*, 1996: para. 238) it will be prohibited. The terms 'superfluous' and 'unnecessary' are comparative terms, thus the test necessarily involves a balance between the military effectiveness and likely advantage gained by the cyber operation on the one hand, and the likely injury and suffering caused to combatants on the other. If an operation is likely to needlessly aggravate the suffering or injury of combatants it will be prohibited.

The principle of distinction is also considered one of the cardinal principles of the *jus in bello*. In respect of the law of weaponry, it is expressed in the prohibition of means and methods of warfare that are incapable of distinguishing between civilian and military targets (as opposed to means and methods that are merely used in that manner). The principle was discussed above in relation to indiscriminate attacks. Other principles that form part of the law of weaponry are also discussed elsewhere in this text. For example, the rules relating to perfidy will be discussed in the following section.

The final general principle to be discussed here, the Martens Clause, was first included in the Preamble to the Hague Convention of 1899, and finds its modern formulation in Article 1(2) of API (1977):

> In cases not covered by this Protocol or by other international agreements, civilians and combatants remain under the protection and authority of the principles of international law derived from established custom, from the principles of humanity and from the dictates of public conscience.

As the ICJ has noted in relation to nuclear weapons, the clause has proved to be an effective means of addressing the rapid evolution of military technology (*Nuclear Weapons*, 1996: para. 78). Thus, in the cyber context, the clause confirms that despite the lack of any rule or agreement in the law that specifically bans or restricts the use of cyber operations during armed conflicts, where those operations would have results that violate the principles of humanity and the dictates of public conscience per se, general principles still apply and it cannot be assumed to be lawful.

In addition to the general principles, the law of weaponry also contains specific rules that either prohibit or limit the use of certain weapons. While none of these address cyber operations directly, a few are relevant to the cyber context. For example, the use of booby-traps in warfare is limited by Protocol II (1980) and Amended Protocol II (1996) of the CCW, both in terms of prohibitions of certain types of booby-traps and restrictions on others. The provisions reflect customary international law insofar as a booby-trap is attached to, or associated with, objects or persons entitled to special protection or objects likely to attract civilians (ICRC, 2005: 278). The definition contained in those instruments is broad enough to apply to those cyber-attacks that are 'designed, constructed or adapted to kill or injure and which function unexpectedly when a person disturbs or approaches an apparently harmless object or performs an apparently safe act' (CCW, Protocol II, 1996 as amended: Article 2(2)). Thus a piece of malware will be prohibited where it is designed and intended to cause death or injury (for example, by causing a physical component to explode or causing a contaminant to leak into water supplies), and is triggered by a person disturbing a harmless object (for instance opening a laptop) or performing an apparently safe act (for example, opening an email from the Red Cross). It is important to note, however, that the law only applies to booby-traps designed to kill or injure; malware designed to wipe information from a system or render it unusable (common in domestic computer crime) would not be covered by the provisions.

The *jus in bello* also requires that states conduct a review to ensure that any cyber means of warfare they acquire or use complies with the rules of IHL that bind that state (*Tallinn manual*, 2013: 153). For those states party to API (1977) this obligation is codified more broadly in Article 36, which requires that:

> In the study, development, acquisition or adoption of a new weapon, means or method of warfare, a High Contracting Party is under an obligation to determine whether its employment would, in some or all circumstances, be prohibited by this Protocol or by any other rule of international law applicable to the High Contracting Party.

This provision undoubtedly includes cyber operations; the ICRC commentary specifically notes that 'methods and means' include weapons in the widest sense, as well as the way in which they are used (Pilloud *et al.*, 1987: para. 1402). The determination must be made based on the normal or expected use of the malware – it does not have to take into account all possible uses, or misuses, of the code. As malware is often adjusted and tweaked to ensure its effectiveness while a cyber operation is underway, a question arises as to when the amended code will constitute a 'new' method or means, requiring a fresh legal review. A common sense approach would dictate that any change that adjusts the operational effects of the malware would necessitate a new review, whereas simple bug fixes or adjustments would not.

Perfidy and ruses of war

Cyber operations provide ample opportunity in modern armed conflicts for parties to engage in tactics designed to deceive and mislead the enemy or induce them to act recklessly. While deception and other ruses of war are entirely permissible and have a long and renowned history in warfare, where the deception invites the confidence of the enemy as to the existence of protected status under international law in order to attack them, the act crosses the line into perfidy (or treachery) and is prohibited under the *jus in bello*. Both the permissibility of ruses and the prohibition against perfidy are reflective of customary international law.

Ruses are defined in Article 37(2) of API (1977) as:

> acts which are intended to mislead an adversary or induce him to act recklessly but which infringe no rule of international law applicable in armed conflict and which are not perfidious because they do not invite the confidence of an adversary with respect to protection under that law.

Traditional examples of permissible ruses are the use of camouflage, decoys, mock operations and misinformation. The *Tallinn manual* (2013: 184) provides the following list of examples of permissible ruses in the cyber context:

a creation of a 'dummy' computer system simulating non-existent forces;
b transmission of false information causing an opponent erroneously to believe operations are about to occur or are underway;
c use of false computer identifiers, computer networks (e.g. honeynets or honeypots), or computer transmissions;
d feigned cyber attacks that do not [spread terror amongst the civilian population];
e bogus orders purported to have been issued by the enemy commander;
f psychological warfare activities;
g transmitting false intelligence information intended for interception; and
h use of enemy codes signals and passwords.

Perfidy, which is also prohibited as treacherous killing in Article 23(b) of the Hague Regulations (1907), is defined in Article 37(1) of API (1977) as acts 'inviting the confidence of an adversary to lead him to believe that he is entitled to, or obliged to accord, protection under the rules of international law applicable in armed conflict, with intent to betray that confidence'. The key difference between deceptions that amount to lawful ruses and those that constitute prohibited perfidy is the exploitation of a deliberately induced trust on the part of an adversary in order to kill, injure or capture (Oeter, 2008: 228). Manipulating information systems to mislead the enemy into thinking that troops are surrendering in order to ambush them at the designated surrender point would constitute perfidy, as would changing enemy systems so that attacking combat vehicles appear to be medical transports. It should be noted, however, that the act of deception or betrayal of confidence itself is not sufficient – it must be in order to kill, injure or capture the adversary. In respect of cyber operations it is of particular note that the prohibition against perfidy does not include damage to property. Thus an email purporting to come from the ICRC that includes malware designed to damage or render enemy computer systems useless would not amount to perfidy (although it would constitute misuse of the Red Cross symbol, which is also prohibited).

In the cyber domain one of the key difficulties in determining the threshold between legitimate ruses and prohibited perfidy is caused by the civilian nature of much of the cyber infrastructure. Feigning civilian status in order to mount an attack is a classic example of perfidious behaviour; however in cyber operations one of the most common tactics is the routing of an attack through multiple 'stepping-stone' hosts (routers, servers and computers, etc.) in order to disguise the origin of the attack. While there is no prohibition on concealing the origin of the attack per se, as most of the hosts will be civilian in nature, there is a risk that the victim of the attack may conclude that one of civilian stepping-stone hosts is the originator of the attack. Where this technique is carried out in such a manner as to invite that conclusion (or the conclusion that it originates from any other host with protected status) and the operation results in the death, injury or capture of the adversary it will amount to perfidy.

Espionage and sabotage

IHL does not prohibit espionage or acts of sabotage directed at a legitimate military objective; however the clandestine nature of both acts results in a saboteur or spy belonging to the armed forces losing their combatant immunity and consequently their entitlement to prisoner-of-war status (civilian saboteurs and spies are not entitled to such status in any event).

Espionage is, however, prohibited in the domestic jurisdictions of most states and peacetime cyber espionage in particular has been increasing exponentially in recent years. Conversely, during an armed conflict, the gathering of intelligence about the enemy is an accepted and necessary part of any military campaign, particularly when it comes to the fulfilment of the parties' obligation to take precautions in attack. Thus it is specifically noted in Article 24 of the Hague Regulations (1907) that 'the employment of measures necessary for obtaining information about the enemy are considered permissible'. Where, then, lies the threshold between lawful and anticipated intelligence gathering and espionage resulting in the loss of combatant status? Article 29 of the Regulations defines espionage by stating that a person may only be considered a spy when 'acting clandestinely or on false pretences, he obtains or endeavours to obtain information in the zone of operations of a belligerent, with the intention of communicating it to the hostile party'. Similar wording is found in the paragraphs of Article 46 of API (1977). Thus it is the clandestine nature of the information gathering that results in the loss of status. Whether clandestinely accessing a computer system (for example, through an unauthorised back door), or through false pretences (for example, by utilising a legitimate user's credentials), the covert nature of the act moves it into the realm of espionage (and sabotage if the result of the act is damage rather than merely information gathering).

Given the ability of cyber operations to be carried out from anywhere, one of the issues is where the act must take place. Under the Hague Regulations (1907), a key factor in the definition of espionage is the attempt to gain information in the 'zone of operations of a belligerent'; API (1977) extends that area to all territory controlled by the enemy. A question remains whether this requires that the spy is physically present in the territory, or if it is sufficient that proactive penetration of a system and that the act of collecting the information takes place in the territory. There is no doubt that clandestine intelligence-gathering operations that are conducted within that territory – for example by insertion of a USB drive into a closed system or other close-access operations – would amount to espionage. Conversely, intelligence gathering from data traffic crossing routers or cables situated outside the territory would not constitute espionage. The present author has argued that a grey area falls on the proactive accessing of networks, systems and computers situated in enemy-controlled territory by an actor situated outside that territory (Harrison Dinniss, 2012: 158), and that such behaviour would amount to espionage. This position is not adopted by the *Tallinn manual*, which insists on the physical presence of the actor in the territory (2013: 194). In many cases the question will be moot, as combatants who are engaged in espionage are excused for any liability for their acts as soon as they rejoin the armed forces to which they belong (Hague Regulations, 1907: Article 31; API, 1977: Article 46(4)). Thus, if a member of the armed forces does not leave their lines to engage in the espionage, they will never be exposed to capture before regaining their combatant privileges. The rule is explicitly limited to combatants; civilian spies, including contractors involved in cyber espionage for a party to the armed conflict, may be captured and punished as spies at any time during the armed conflict and remain liable for their actions long after the conflict is over.

A similar approach could be taken in relation to sabotage, which also traditionally results in loss of combatant immunity and prisoner-of-war status for the perpetrator (Harrison Dinniss, 2012: 152–5). However, the nature of cyber operations is such that most cyber operations causing damage will fall within this category. It therefore appears unlikely, based on the emerging approach of states to cyber-attacks generally, that states will treat such cyber-attackers any differently upon capture.

The protection of property

The basic principle regarding an adversary's property in armed conflict is set out in Article 46 of the Hague Regulations (1907), which provides that private property must be respected and cannot be confiscated. Article 23(g) also provides that it is forbidden to destroy or seize the enemy's property, unless 'imperatively demanded by the necessities of war'. Pillage is absolutely prohibited. These provisions are all reflective of customary international law; failure to comply is recognised as a war crime, codified in Article 8(2)(b)(v) and (xiii) of the Rome Statute of the International Criminal Court (1998). These provisions, and their exceptions, raise interesting issues in regard to cyber operations.

The fact that the property in question may be intangible is not unique to cyber operations and is no bar to the application of the *jus in bello* or liability for offences committed under it. The Nuremburg war crimes tribunal in the *Krupp Trial* (1948: 164) was in no doubt that:

> Property offences recognised by modern international law are not, however, limited to physical tangible possessions or to open robbery in the old sense of pillage, but include the acquisition of intangible property and the securing of ownership, use or control of all kinds of property by many ways other than open violence.

The approach was confirmed in the *I.G. Farben Trial* (1948: 46) which held that there was no 'distinction between "plunder" in the restricted sense of acquisition of physical properties ... and the plunder of spoliation resulting from the acquisition of intangible property such as involved in the acquisition of stock ownership or control through any other means'. These rulings indicate that both the intangible nature of property and the concept of seizure may be readily adapted to apply to cyber operations.

While destruction of property is fairly straightforward in relation to the targets of cyber operations, the concept of seizure is more complicated. The tangible aspects of a system or network may be physically seized; however, it is possible to assume control of such objects without doing so. Although seizure is not defined in any international instruments, Downey (1950: 492) has argued that the property must be in the 'firm possession' of the capturing state and placed under guard; firm possession requires some manifestation of intention to seize and retain the property involved, and some affirmative act or declaration of a possessory or custodial nature. This same approach has been applied by the Israeli Supreme Court in *Al Nawar v. Minister of Defence et al.* (1985: 326), in which the Court also noted the practical impossibility of seizing all property at once, and stated that in order to effect seizure, it would suffice to arrange for a general guarding or patrolling of the area where the property was located. In respect of cyber operations, seizure may be said to occur where a party accesses a system or network and prevents the lawful owner from accessing and controlling that system or network (Harrison Dinniss, 2012: 266–8). The act of changing the access codes to exclude the original owner both reflects the intent to retain control of the network or system and is a guard on the property. Ensuring that the AV protection is up to date and all software patches and updates are installed would also equate to general guarding of the seized system.

The *jus in bello* contains a number of exceptions to the prohibition on destroying or seizing enemy property. First, all movable state property (with the exception of cultural property) captured on the battlefield may be appropriated by a party to an armed conflict as booty of war. Title to the property passes automatically on seizure to the belligerent state whose armed forces have seized it, irrespective of the military character of the property (that is, not only weapons and ammunition, but also money, food and stores) (Dinstein, 2010: 247). While private property is generally immune from seizure, the Court in *Al Nawar* (1985) held that any private property that is actually used for hostile purposes may be appropriated by the belligerent state. If this line of reasoning is followed with regard to the cyber realm, any commercial network, system or computer that is utilised by a state in the course of their military operations may also be seized by an opponent as booty. Given the dual-use nature of much of the cyber infrastructure and the large amount of military communications that travel over civilian networks, this is a matter of significant concern for states. Further all weapons, ammunition, military equipment, military papers and the like may also be seized regardless of whether they are private property, or whether they may be used for military operations or not. While one could make the argument that this could apply to almost all networks operating in the battlespace, including practically every home computer, laptop or smartphone with an Internet connection, such an interpretation would be overly broad (Harrison Dinniss, 2012: 271–2). The exception appears to be intended to cover things that are inherently military in nature (of course, as discussed above, where the computer or other equipment is actually *used* for hostile purposes it becomes lawful to seize it).

The second exception to the destruction and seizure of an adversary's property relates to occupied territory. Article 53 of the Hague Regulations (1907) allows parties to take possession of any movable property belonging to the state that may be used for military operations and, *inter alia*, communications equipment in occupied territory (even if it is private property). The *jus in bello* thus recognises the right of the occupying state to requisition private property, confiscate any movable property belonging to the occupied state that may be used for military operations and the right to administer and enjoy the use of any real property belonging to the occupied state (Hague Regulations, 1907: Articles 52, 53 and 55). Unlike the acquisition of booty, title to property requisitioned or confiscated under these rules does not transfer to the occupying state; the property must be restored and compensation fixed when peace is made. Most computer networks and other cyber infrastructure undoubtedly fall with in this exception, either as movable property where it belongs to the state, or as objects 'adapted for the transmission of news', where it is either state or private property. Where cyber infrastructure is immovable or fixed (for example, as part of a fibre optic network embedded in a building or bridge), the occupying state will have the right to use the infrastructure but may not damage its capital value (Hague Regulations, 1907: Article 55). Specific rules exist for submarine cables (including those used for cyber operations); such cables connecting occupied territory with neutral territory may only be seized or destroyed in cases of absolute military necessity and must be restored and compensation fixed when peace is made (Hague Regulations, 1907: Article 54).

The absolute prohibition against pillage is firmly rooted in both customary and treaty law where it is also recognised as a war crime. Traditionally pillage consisted of looting or plundering enemy property (whether public or private) for private ends, and generally required an element of violence in the acquisition of the property concerned (Harrison Dinniss, 2012: 274). However recently, a series of cases involving property offences (including offences of spoliation in many judgments immediately following the Second World War) have seemingly widened its ambit. First, as noted above in relation to seizure, the fact that property is intangible is no barrier. Second, the requirement of violence may no longer be necessary. Given that cyber operations designed to appropriate property are likely to be nonviolent in nature, it is worth noting that some courts have been happy to consider property seized by enemy forces as pillage even when violence is not used, for example the seizure of bonds and shares abandoned by an owner in occupied territory (*Mazzoni v. Minister of Finance*, 1927–1928; *Re Otto Wallemar*, 1948). Third, the trial chamber of the Special Court for Sierra Leone has concluded that the requirement that pillaged property be appropriated for personal use was an unnecessary component of the offence (*Prosecutor v. Fofana and Kondewa*, 2004). Although it is worth noting that the Court conflated the terms pillage, plunder and spoliation, which other courts have declined to do (see e.g. the judgment of the international war crimes tribunal in the *Flick Trial*, 1947; and of the ICTY in *Celebici Case*, 1998). With regard to cyber operations a further question must be asked as to whether the owner of the property must be dispossessed of it entirely, or whether it is sufficient that certain of the owner's property rights are infringed, namely the right to exclude others, the right to control the use made of the property, and the right to profit from it (Harrison Dinniss, 2012: 275). If the former is the case then individual criminal liability for pillage (or similar property offences) will not attach in situations of digital theft through copying of files and even their subsequent deletion in any cases where back-up copies exist.

Conclusion

Cyber operations raise unique challenges for the application of the *jus in bello*. While a great many of these issues are outlined in this chapter, a work of this size cannot hope to address them all. For those who are involved in issues concerning the legal regulation of cyber operations, a number of final points are worth recalling. First, although none of the laws governing the conduct of hostilities deal with cyber operations explicitly, the laws are framed in general terms that may be interpreted to incorporate technological advances such as cyber. General principles such as the principle of distinction, proportionality and the requirement to take appropriate precautions in attack remain at the core of the commitment to the law regardless of the technology involved. For those tasked with applying the law to cyber operations, it is essential to maintain not only a thorough knowledge of the specific provisions of IHL and the reasons for which they were adopted, but also a basic understanding of the way in which cyber operations and the affected technology work. It is in the application of the law that the effects of modern technology and the changing values and concepts brought about by the information revolution (for example, in relation to property) will be seen and reflected.

References

Documents, treaties and cases

'Hague Regulations, 1907': Convention Respecting the Laws and Customs of War on Land and its annex: Regulations concerning the Laws and Customs of War on Land, 36 Stat. 2277, TS no. 539, 18 October.

Mazzoni v. Minister of Finance (1927–1928) AD Case no 348.

'*Flick Trial*, 1947': *The Trial of Friedrich Flick and Five Others*, Law Reports of Trials of War Criminals, United States Military Tribunal, Nuremburg, IX, 1, 20 April–22 December.

'*Krupp Trial*, 1948': *Trial of Alfied Felix Alwyn Krupp Von Bohlen Und Halbach and Eleven Others*, Law Reports of Trials of War Criminals, United States Military Tribunal, Nuremburg, X, 69, 31 July.

'*I.G. Farben Trial*, 1948': *Trial of Carl Krauch and Twenty-Two Others*, Law Reports of Trials of War Criminals, United States Military Tribunal, Nuremburg. X, 1, 14 August 1947–29 July.

Re Otto Wallemar [1948] ADIL 619.

'GC I, 1949': Geneva Convention for the Amelioration of the Condition of the Wounded and Sick in Armed Forces in the Field, 75 UNTS 31, 12 August.

'GC III, 1949': Geneva Convention relative to the treatment of prisoners of war, 75 UNTS 13, 12 August.

'GC IV, 1949': Geneva Convention relative to the Protection of Civilian Persons in Time of War, 75 UNTS 287, 12 August.

'API, 1977': Protocol Additional to the Geneva Conventions of 12 August 1949, and Relating to the Protection of Victims of International Armed Conflicts, 1125 UNTS 3, 8 June 1977 (Additional Protocol I).

APII, 1977': Protocol Additional to the Geneva Conventions of 12 August 1949, and relating to the Protection of Victims of Non-International Armed Conflicts, 1125 UNTS 609, 8 June 1977 (Additional Protocol II).

'CCW, 1980': Convention on Prohibitions or Restrictions on the Use of Certain Conventional Weapons which may be deemed to be Excessively Injurious or to have Indiscriminate Effects (with Protocols I, II and III), 1342 UNTS 137, 10 October.

Al Nawar v. Minister of Defence et al. [1985] Israel Supreme Court. 39(3) PD: 449.

'*Tadić* case, 1995': *Prosecutor v. Dusko Tadić*, interlocutory appeal on jurisdiction, IT-94–1-AR, International Criminal Tribunal for the Former Yugoslavia (ICTY), Appeals Chamber, 2 October.

'CCW, Protocol II, 1996 as amended': Protocol on Prohibitions or Restrictions on the Use of Mines, Booby-Traps and Other Devices, 1342 UNTS 168, as amended 3 May.

'*Nuclear Weapons*, 1996': *Legality of the Threat or Use of Nuclear Weapons*, advisory opinion, ICJ Reports 226, 8 July.

'*Celebici Case*, 1998': *Prosecutor v. Zejnil Delalic et al.*, judgment, IT-96–21-T, International Criminal Tribunal for the Former Yugoslavia (ICTY), Trial Chamber, 19 November.

Rome Statute of the International Criminal Court (1998) 2187 UNTS 3, 17 July.

'*Kupreškić*, 2000': *Prosecutor v. Kupreškić et al.*, judgment, IT-95-16-T, International Criminal Tribunal for the Former Yugoslavia (ICTY), Trial Chamber, 14 January.

Final Report to the Prosecutor of the Committee Established to Review the NATO Bombing Campaign Against the Federal Republic of Yugoslavia (2000), The Hague, ICTY [online], available: www.icty.org/x/file/Press/nato061300.pdf [9 October 2014].

'*Galić Case*, 2003': *Prosecutor v. Stanislav Galić*, judgment and opinion, IT-98-29-T, International Criminal Tribunal for the Former Yugoslavia (ICTY), Trial Chamber, 5 December.

Prosecutor v. Moinina Fofana and Allieu Kondewa (2004) decision on preliminary motion based on lack of jurisdiction (child recruitment), SCSL-04-14-T, Special Court for Sierra Leone, 3 March.

ICRC (2005), *Customary International Humanitarian Law* (editors: Henckaerts, J.-M. and Doswald-Beck, L.) Cambridge, Cambridge University Press.

US Navy, US Marine Corps and US Coast Guard (2007) *The commander's handbook on the law of naval operations*, NWP 1–14M/MCWP 5–121/COMDTPUB P58007A.

ICRC (2009) *Interpretive Guidance on the Notion of Direct Participation in Hostilities*. Geneva: International Committee of the Red Cross.

Tallinn manual on the international law applicable to cyber warfare (2013) Prepared by the International Group of Experts at the Invitation of the NATO Cooperative Cyber Defence Centre of Excellence (general editor: Schmitt, M.N.), Cambridge: Cambridge University Press.

'UNIDIR, 2013': United National Institute for Disarmament Research (2013) *The Cyber Index: International Security Trends and Realities*, Geneva, UNIDIR.

Academic works and media reports

Dinstein, Y. (2010) *The Conduct of Hostilities under the Law of International Armed Conflict*, 2nd edition, Cambridge: Cambridge University Press.

Downey, Jr, W.G. (1950) 'Captured enemy property: Booty of war and seized enemy property', *American Journal of International Law*, vol. 44, pp. 488–504.

Droege, C. (2012) 'Get off my cloud: Cyber warfare, international humanitarian law, and the protection of civilians', *International Review of the Red Cross* vol. 94, article no. 886), pp. 533–78.

Dörmann, K. (2004) *Applicability of the Additional Protocols to computer network attacks*, International Expert Conference on Computer Network Attacks and the Applicability of International Humanitarian Law, Stockholm, Swedish National Defence College.

Falliere, N., O Murchu, L. and Chien, E. (2011) 'W32.Stuxnet dossier', 11 February, *Symantec* [online], available: www.symantec.com/content/en/us/enterprise/media/security_response/whitepapers/w32_stuxnet_dossier.pdf [9 October 2014].

Fulghum, D.A., Wall, R. and Butler, A. (2007) 'Israel shows electronic prowess', 25 November, *Aviation Week and Space Technology* [online], available: http://seclists.org/isn/2007/Nov/100 [14 October 2014].

Green, J.A. (2007) 'An unusual silence', *New Law Journal*, vol. 157. pp. 1478–9.

Harrison Dinniss, H.A. (2011) 'Attacks and operations: the debate over computer network "attacks"', paper for *New Technologies, Old Law: Applying International Humanitarian Law in a New Technological Age*, Minerva Center for Human Rights, Hebrew University,

Jerusalem, Israel [online], available: http://law.huji.ac.il/upload/5_HarrisonDinniss.pdf [9 October 2014].
Harrison Dinniss, H. (2012) *Cyber warfare and the laws of war*, Cambridge: Cambridge University Press.
Harrison Dinniss, H. (2013) 'Participants in conflict – cyber warriors, patriotic hackers and the laws of war', in Saxon, D. (ed.) *International humanitarian law and the changing technology of war*, Leiden: Martinus Nijhoff.
Harrison Dinniss, H.A. (2015) 'The nature of objects: targeting networks and the challenge of defining cyber military objectives', *Israel Law Review*, vol. 48, no. 1, forthcoming.
Jensen, E. (2010) 'Cyber warfare and precautions against the effects of attacks', *Texas Law Review*, vol. 88, pp. 1533–69.
Keizer, G. (2010) 'Secrets of the Stuxnet worm's travels', 3 October, *Computerworld* [online], available: www.pcworld.com/article/206822/secrets_of_the_stuxnet_worms_travels.html [9 October 2014].
Koskenniemi, M. (2006) *Fragmentation of international law: Difficulties arising from the diversification and expansion of international law*, Report of the Study Group of the International Law Commission, 13 April 2006, UN Doc A/CN.4/L.682.
'Lieber Code, 1863': Instructions for the Government of Armies of the United States in the Field, 24 April 1863, available in Schindler, D. and Toman, J. (eds, 1988) The law of armed conflicts, Leiden: Martinus Nijhoff.
Oeter, S. (2007) 'Comment: is the principle of distinction outdated?', in Heinegg, W.H.v. and Epping, V. (eds) *International humanitarian law facing new challenges*, Berlin/New York: Springer.
Oeter, S. (2008) 'Methods and means of combat', in Fleck, D. (ed.) *The handbook of humanitarian law in armed conflicts*, Oxford: Oxford University Press.
Pilloud, C., De Preux, J., Sandoz, Y. and Zimmermann, B. (1987) *Commentary on the Additional Protocols of 8 June 1977*, Geneva: Martinus Nijhoff.
Schmitt, M.N. (2002) 'Wired warfare: computer network attack and international law', *International Law Studies*, vol. 76, pp. 187–218.
Schmitt, M.N. (2011) 'Cyber operations and the *jus in bello:* key issues', *International Law Studies*, vol. 87, pp. 89–110.
Smith, C. R. (2003) 'US information warriors wrestle with new weapons', 13 March 2003, *NewsMax.com* [online], available: www.newsmax.com/archives/articles/2003/3/12/134712.shtml [7 July 2011].
Symantec Corporation (2014) 'Internet Security Threat Report 2014', vol. 19 [online], available: www.symantec.com/content/en/us/enterprise/other_resources/b-istr_main_report_v19_21291018.en-us.pdf [3 October 2014].
Tarakanov, E. (2012) 'Shamoon The Wiper: further details (Part II)', 11 September, *Securelist* [online], available: www.securelist.com/en/blog/208193834/Shamoon_The_Wiper_further_details_Part_II [19 June 2014].
Zetter, K. (2011) 'How digital detectives deciphered Stuxnet, the most menacing malware in history', 11 July 2001, *Wired* [online], available: www.wired.com/2011/07/how-digital-detectives-deciphered-stuxnet/all/ [9 October 2014].

7 The relevance of the Just War Tradition to cyber warfare

David Whetham and George R. Lucas, Jr

Introduction

Representing a set of principles that have emerged over time, in part, through a dialogue between deontological and consequentialist reasoning, the Just War Tradition has provided a useful framework for balancing ethical considerations in times of conflict for over two millennia. It represents a 'fund of practical moral wisdom' (Johnson, 1984: 15) that has evolved over time to reflect the changing character of war, and because it contains prudential calculations that acknowledge that context must be taken into account when determining a correct course of action.

The peculiar challenges posed by attacks in the cyber realm have led some to conclude that it is simply inappropriate to apply existing Just War Tradition principles to this new area of conflict. Its principles were developed to cope with conventional war, rather than this new phenomenon, which although it can still be seen as 'war', demands a new, more relevant framework by which to judge its normative dimension (see e.g. Dipert, 2010). Others, like Rid (2012, 2013), agree that it should be judged by a more appropriate set of ethical standards, but argue that this is because it should not even be considered warfare at all, but rather something akin to espionage or sabotage, or even that it should remain squarely in the realm of criminal activity.

Does cyber conflict represent an entirely new form of warfare that requires a bespoke normative framework for us to make sense of it? This is not merely an academic debate: as Neal-Hopes (2011: 4) points out, without an appropriate ethical framework to support the planning and prosecution of cyber operations, there is a very real risk that the cyber equivalent of Dresden may occur with the true implications of the action not being recognised until after the terrible event. This chapter will explore whether the Just War Tradition can continue to respond to this new context, and – if it can remain relevant as a framework – whether the current Just War principles themselves are appropriate as they are, or whether some may need adapting, interpreting differently or replacing entirely for the Tradition to remain relevant. In particular, we argue in this chapter that the negative and dismissive judgements concerning the relevance of the Just War Tradition for the moral evaluation of cyber conflict *rest upon a widespread but fundamental misconception of the nature of the Tradition itself.* The misconception is grounded in a simple historical fallacy, one that confuses the origins and historical development of the Just War Tradition with the normative substance and applicability of the *kind of moral reasoning* that applying the principles of the Tradition entails.

The Just War Tradition

The origins of the Just War Tradition, in the West at least, lie in a synthesis of classical Greco–Roman and later Christian values (Johnson, 1981). However, it also broadly resonates with ideas, cultures and religious principles to be found all over the world, so should certainly not be regarded as a peculiarly Western body of thought (see e.g. Sorabji and Rodin, 2007: 5). It is hardly surprising that all cultures have found the need to restrain the wars they fight in some way, as 'military victory makes no sense unless it can be transformed into political success and that can only be hampered by ignoring the normative dimension of conflict' (Whetham, 2010: 68). The ubiquitous nature of the Just War Tradition therefore provides 'a common language for discussing and debating the rights and wrongs of conflict' (Whetham, 2010: 65). As will be discussed below, the Tradition today underpins and informs the international legal structures that govern the use of force in international affairs.

The Just War Tradition has developed around two related but distinct ideas, which today are also reflected in the two branches of international law relating to the use of force and the conduct of armed conflict. As has already been discussed in the legal context, in Chapters 5 and 6 of this volume, these are *jus ad bellum* – what is required to justify going to war – and *jus in bello* – the limits on the use of force within war. This separation allows us to draw a line of responsibility between the decision to go to war and the actual conduct of that war. Soldiers are not responsible for the decision to go to war, but they are responsible for its conduct. Very senior military officers may straddle the line, but, as Walzer (1992: 39) points out, this means that we can be fairly confident about where that line should be drawn. The two levels of responsibility do remain connected in some respects. For example, while one cannot make an unjust cause morally acceptable by fighting it well, one can certainly undermine an otherwise just cause by conducting it badly.

Jus ad bellum

Jus ad bellum criteria help to establish the conditions under which, or context in which, it is permissible to do something that is otherwise considered wrong – i.e. use force against another actor. While the Just War criteria have evolved over time and, in their current form, may vary slightly between different authorities (see e.g. Whetham, 2009), their nature (if not character) is broadly consistent and covers the following issues. While the Just War criteria do not represent a 'check list' of legitimacy, they do collectively present questions that require genuine and robust answers. The less convincing those answers are when taken overall, or if one particular area poses profound problems, the harder it is to claim legitimacy for one's actions.

If one's war is to be considered just, be it waged employing cyber or conventional means, it must have a *just cause*. The clearest example of a just cause in the twenty-first century is self-defence in response to an attack such as an invasion of one's territory. This is accepted in Article 51 of the UN Charter, which states that '[n]othing in the present Charter shall impair the inherent right of individual or collective self-defence if an armed attack occurs' (the question as to whether or not this would include a cyber-attack is addressed below). Just causes could also include coming to the defence of a friend or ally (for example, the Kuwaiti government asking for assistance from the international community in 1991) or, increasingly, it is becoming argued in legal terms that acting in defence of those in peril who cannot defend themselves is also a just cause (this is the so-called right of 'humanitarian intervention'). If a state proves itself to be unable or perhaps even unwilling to carry out its responsibilities to protect its population from human rights abuses, some argue that responsibility can in some situations be transferred to the international community so that it can act instead, using peaceful means where possible and military force only as a last resort. Such arguments remain highly controversial, legally speaking, but – for those that adopt them – their invocation clearly relates the emerging 'Responsibility to Protect' idea back to those ethical arguments about protecting the innocent put forward by Ambrose and later Augustine in the fourth and fifth centuries AD. This basic ethical position is that sacrifice on behalf of the innocent can be consistent with the common good, and one should not turn away from those in need if one is able to do something about it: '[a]nyone who does not prevent an injury to a companion, if he can do so, is as much at fault as he who inflicts it' (Ambrose, Book 1, Chapter XXXVI: 179 – see Swift translation, 1983).

Does that mean that one can respond justly only once an attack has taken place? Sometimes a threat must be anticipated if it is to be successfully defended against, and this is something that has long been understood. As far back as the thirteenth century, Raymond of Peñafort argued that killing an ambusher before they strike, 'if there is no other way to counter the threat', was considered lawful. The contemporary security environment with the existential threat posed by weapons of mass destruction (WMDs) make such concerns even more pressing, but how far can pre-emption legitimately be taken? Domestic law in the United Kingdom interprets this idea so that an act of self-defence requires the person carrying out the defensive act to have 'an honest belief' that the action is required, but it is not absolutely necessary that the defendant be attacked first. As Lord Griffith said (*Beckford v. R*, 1988), '[a] man about to be attacked does not have to wait for his assailant to strike the first blow or fire the first shot; circumstances may justify a pre-emptive strike'. However, whether acting as an individual or on behalf of a state, if you just decide that somebody, at some unspecified time in the future, just might become a threat, attacking them 'cannot be considered self-defence, either legally or morally. The key to legitimacy is getting the balance right' (Whetham, 2010: 77). Otherwise, 'preventive self-defence' may amount to little more than felonious assault (Chatterjee, 2013).

While acting in self-defence does not require any additional permission to sanction it, anything that does not fall within this category requires that the action is carried out with *legitimate authority*. On the face of it, this should be straightforward – if a state is acting in self-defence then no further authority is required. However, in the absence of an attack (or imminent threat of attack) in response to which a state may lawfully defend itself, prior approval of the UN is required for any other type of military action directed against another actor. As was discussed in detail by James A. Green in Chapter 5 of this volume, Article 2(4) of the UN Charter prohibits the use of military force between states. As such, the UN Security Council needs to agree that a special situation exists and therefore to authorise an exception to this general prohibition (under Articles 39–42 of the Charter). In part, this explains why states are often keen to characterise the defensive nature of their activities.

Most people would accept that the motivation for an act has an effect on whether it is considered morally good or bad, so the Just War Tradition requires that actors have the *right intention*. 'Creating, restoring or keeping a just peace, righting wrongs and protecting the innocent would all clearly qualify as right intentions, while seeking to expand one's territory, enslave or convert others to one's religion, hatred or revenge would not' (Whetham, 2010: 78). If one's intention is correct, then it will shape one's conduct. As long as one were trying to do the 'right thing', then one would naturally make a distinction between those who were at fault for the harm that initiated the conflict, and those who were not, saving those who are blameless from being harmed (Whetham, 2010: 72).

Having the right intention will also help ensure that the goal pursued will be *proportionate* to the offence that prompted the war. Not all wrongs can legitimise war – one must ask if the overall harm likely to be caused will be less than that 'caused by the wrong that is being righted' (Bellamy, 2006: 123). How many combatant and civilian deaths, how much damage and destruction are likely to result on both sides and what can really be justified? This is a particularly difficult calculation to make in advance of military action; however, the Just War Tradition requires that actors make a credible attempt to answer this question before resorting to the use of force.

Considered one of the more prudential rather than a core criterion, one is supposed to ensure that there is a *reasonable prospect of success* before embarking on a military course of action. This requires asking what one is actually trying to do and whether it can be achieved (note that it is 'success' rather than 'victory' that is required – a subtle but important distinction). Clausewitz (2007: 223) made clear that 'no-one starts a war – or rather, no-one in his senses ought to do so – without being clear in his mind what he intends to achieve by that war and how he intends to conduct it'. Professional soldiers need to understand and ask the right questions from their political masters about what exactly it is that they are being asked to do before this question can be answered.

Finally, is the resort to force a genuine *last resort*? Has every rational nonviolent alternative that might also work in the specific situation, from diplomacy to sanctions, been attempted before armed force is employed?

Jus in bello

Regardless of who 'started it', both sides are required to conduct their conflict within limits and must apply both *proportionality* in their use of force and *discrimination* against whom it is applied. Just as the war itself must be a proportional response to the injury suffered, the principle of proportionality at the *in bello* level requires that the damage, losses or injury resulting from any military action should not be excessive in relation to the expected military advantage. So, for example, destroying an entire town to neutralise one enemy sniper is likely to be considered disproportionate (Whetham, 2008a: 54). In accordance with this principle, certain types of weapons or methods of war have always been considered too inhumane due to the suffering inflicted when compared to the military advantage achieved by their use. Such examples include the use of poisoned weapons – banned to Hindus in the Laws of Manu and also prohibited in the warfare of the Ancient Greeks and Romans (Roberts and Guelff, 1995: 29). A more modern example would be the ban on chemical or biological weapons today (see, for example, the 1997 Chemical Weapons Convention).

Discrimination relates to who may be legitimately targeted in the conduct of hostilities. Plato (1989: 710) put forward the idea that only those who are actually responsible for the dispute are to be treated as enemies. Contemporary law remains consistent with this line, making a clear separation between two types of people:

> Only combatants are permitted to take a direct part in hostilities. It follows that they may be attacked. Civilians may not take a direct part in hostilities and, for so long as they refrain from doing so, are protected from attack.
> (UK Manual, 2004: 24)

In practice, this means that members of the military forces, members of an organised guerrilla force, whether or not they are in uniform, and anyone who takes up arms in a conflict other than in direct self-defence, can all be legitimately targeted. However, once someone is no longer capable of taking a direct part in hostilities because they are *hors de combat* – they are wounded or have surrendered – they cease to be a legitimate target. If there is any doubt as to what category someone (or, indeed, something) belongs, they are to be considered to be civilians and therefore cannot be attacked (see e.g. API, 1977: Article 50(1)).

Double effect

The Just War Tradition, or rather the way that its principles are applied, is informed by the Doctrine of 'Double Effect'. This was clarified by Aquinas in the thirteenth century and represents the idea that individuals are not necessarily morally responsible for the foreseeable, yet *unintended* side effects of an otherwise legitimate action. This might mean that a mission to destroy an enemy bridge, essential for communications and movement of tanks, can still go ahead even though it is predicted that due to civilian traffic, a single civilian might also be killed. This does not mean that *anything* can be justified just because it was not intended, however. Double effect can only justify military activities that harm the innocent up to a point. In practice, this means that any non-combatant casualties are to be avoided as far as is possible and still require special justification, however they might be caused. The foreseeable side-effects of any hostile action must still be proportionate to the expected military utility of the target, so that, in the case above, one would need a very good reason why that bridge could not be destroyed at night when there was little or no civilian traffic. If the decision is taken to strike it just as the bridge is filled with market traffic, then one would need a very powerful argument indeed.

The preceding sections have set out the conventional understanding of the Just War Tradition and its key principles. The analysis will now turn to how these principles relate to the emerging phenomenon of cyber warfare.

Is cyber war really warfare and does it matter?

In their seminal article, 'Cyberwar is coming!', John Arquilla and David Ronfeldt (1993: 147) predicted that cyber war would be 'to the twenty-first century what blitzkrieg was to the twentieth century'. As one can imagine, such claims prompted much debate, with one of the most influential responses coming from Thomas Rid, in 2012, with the view that not only had cyber war failed to take place in the intervening years, it was also highly unlikely ever to do so in the future. According to Rid (2012: 8), a true act of war must be *violent* (or at least potentially violent); *instrumental*, in the sense that it is directed towards achieving some political purpose; and *attributed*, as 'history does not know acts of war without eventual attribution'. Rid argued (2012: 6) that due to the lack of these essential features defining 'war', political (as opposed to merely criminal) cyber offences should be considered 'neither crime nor war, but rather in the same category as subversion, spying or sabotage, existing somewhere on the spectrum between apolitical crime at one end and genuine war at the other'.

We believe (see e.g. Lucas, 2013b; Whetham, 2015) that to deliberately exclude all cyber-attacks from the definition of an 'act of war' in this way goes too far, making the resulting classification decidedly unhelpful as a result. For example, insisting that physical violence is a definitional requirement of an act of war appears straightforward enough, but in a practical sense, what government in the world is not going to consider a cyber-attack an act of war if an enemy grounded all of its air defence assets, sealed its hardened silos preventing a nuclear launch or crippled its stock market to the tune of $1Trn? As was noted in this volume's Introduction, one can accept that attacks of such severity have not yet taken place without also having to concede that it is inconceivable that they ever will:

> Violence will indeed normally involve bloodshed, but violence, in some contexts, need not equate to *physical* harm – violence can still involve hurt, and injury without physical harm in the real world.
>
> (Whetham, 2015)

If a cyber-attack is directed towards achieving a specific political goal, then it would appear to satisfy the instrumental criteria. Similarly, as has been discussed in previous chapters of this volume (especially by Neil C. Rowe in Chapter 3), attribution is not a problem unique to the cyber realm (see also Dinstein, 2013: 281); however, the inability to satisfactorily attribute an attack does not stop it from potentially being considered an act of war in the meantime. One might, for example, consider submarine warfare as an example of this: if one's ships are being sunk by submarines, but it is unclear which state is responsible, or an as yet unidentified party has mined your harbours, this does not stop the attack from constituting an act of war. Why should that be any different in the cyber realm?

However, putting aside these objections to Rid's position for the moment, if we were – for argument's sake – to accept that cyber war is not really 'war' at all, then, on the face of it, trying to use the Just War Tradition as a framework for normative judgements in this area would appear to be flawed. This objection parallels similar criticisms raised in trying to apply the Just War Tradition to other forms of conflict that are also not, strictly speaking, 'war', such as humanitarian intervention (e.g. Rodin, 2014). These critiques, in turn, parallel those raised in international law, concerning whether International Humanitarian Law (IHL) can be applied to a conflict confined within the cyber domain, which does not, strictly speaking, constitute a 'use of force' or an 'armed conflict' in any conventional sense (for discussions of these debates, see Chapters 5 and 6 of this volume, respectively).

The case of whether or not international law can be applied to instances of cyber warfare has been extensively addressed by international lawyers, particularly in the aftermath of the cyber-attacks against Estonia in 2007. An especially notable recent collaborative legal project on the subject resulted in the *Tallinn manual on the international law applicable to cyber warfare* (2013), which purports to demonstrate the interpretation and application of existing international legal regimes (governing the use of force and conventional armed conflict) to the cyber domain. This collection of legal opinions builds upon and collates much of the existing legal literature on cyber warfare. With varying degrees of success, the *Tallinn manual* proposes to bridge the divide between the straightforward commission of crimes in the cyber domain, as addressed within the 2001 Budapest Convention on Cybercrime, and forms of conflict such as industrial and state espionage, sabotage, and outright acts of war in that realm that result in effects similar to those of a conventional armed attack. An example of this might be the Stuxnet worm of 2010, which worked by introducing random changes to the speed of the centrifuges used to enrich uranium. The Stuxnet attack permanently damaged critical machinery and set back Iran's nuclear enrichment programme by approximately five years (*The Telegraph*, 2011).

In contrast to the extensive legal analysis of the subject, the case is less clear, and certainly less carefully explored, with respect to ethics and moral philosophy. With few exceptions, the prevailing opinion in the ethics literature seems to be that cyber conflict is sufficiently distinctive in ontological perspective (e.g. lacking geographical boundaries, concrete and attributable agency or agent-identity, as well as the doing of genuine physical harm) as to defy the normal canons of moral reasoning concerning the declaration and conduct of conventional warfare (Dipert, 2013). If, as the revisionist Just War theorist David Rodin objects, the Just War Tradition 'ought not to be applied to Humanitarian Intervention, simply because Humanitarian Intervention itself is not war' (Rodin, 2014), then this seems an even more pertinent objection to lodge with respect to cyber conflict (as Dipert and others have argued).

It is, of course, true that malevolent cyber activities come in many varieties, and that most of these do not rise to the level of a use of force or an armed conflict, even when carried out by agents of one state against the citizens of another. Industrial espionage and the theft of confidential corporate secrets, patents or designs, for example, are generally all considered to be criminal acts falling within the domestic jurisdiction of the state in which they occur. It was the intention of the Budapest Convention on Cybercrime, moreover, to clarify the extent to which international and interstate cooperation amongst affected domestic jurisdictions (both those victimised, and those in which the criminal activities were perpetrated) would be required in combating and rectifying such injustices.

Espionage, even in its more familiar, conventional forms, has long been a form of low-intensity and ongoing interstate activity in which the international community has been loath to intervene. From the perspective of international law, espionage is largely an ungoverned activity. The specific acts of espionage, however, always constitute a crime within the domestic jurisdiction within which they occur, and the perpetrators are always operating under the threat of apprehension by domestic authorities of the regime within which they operate, and consequent serious criminal penalties (including capital punishment in many jurisdictions) for their involvement in these activities.

Malevolent cyber activities beyond crime and vandalism appear to constitute a new wave of sophisticated and highly effective espionage. Since this is likewise not war, and not heretofore covered under international law, the case has been advanced (for example by Rid and Dipert) that neither IHL nor the Just War Tradition apply to these activities. The magnification of the reach of covert activities instead seems to constitute an argument in favour of a new legal or moral regime within which to understand, interpret and constrain such activities.

Sabotage, by contrast, has long been considered an 'act of war', inasmuch as physical harm to persons and vital civil or military infrastructure can result from a use of physical force. It is up to the aggrieved or victimised nation whether or not to respond to acts of sabotage directed against its government, military or citizens. There has never been serious consideration, however, of whether such acts would constitute a legitimate *causus belli*. That 'just cause' for the declaration of, or resort to, war would then also need to be balanced against the other criteria set out above to determine if an armed response would, amongst other considerations, prove to be appropriate and justified.

In both legal and moral discourse, in particular, a so-called 'effects-based' assessment of the damage done (e.g. to the state's financial system, or civil infrastructure) would determine the degree to which the harm inflicted by an act of cyber sabotage rose to the equivalent level of a conventional armed attack (see e.g. Graham, 2010; for detailed discussion in the legal context, see Chapter 5 of this volume). If the consequent destruction of property or harm to life and limb were judged to be equivalent to that which might have been inflicted by a conventional attack, this line of reasoning goes, then the cyber-attack is equivalent to a conventional attack and therefore constitutes a legitimate *causus belli*.

Famously, in the case of Estonia in 2007, that state's allies within NATO argued that the massive and wholesale Distributed Denial of Service attack on Estonia's cyber infrastructure did *not* meet that burden of proof. However, other subsequent attacks (such as in the case of Stuxnet against Iran) may have done so, had they been recognised and properly attributed to known perpetrators at the time (see e.g. Jenkins, 2013; Lucas, 2013c, 2014). According to the *Tallinn manual* (2013: 48), while specifically excluding acts that merely generate inconvenience or irritation, 'acts that kill or injure persons or destroy or damage objects are unambiguously uses of force'. While the international group of researchers who wrote the *Tallinn manual* do not speak for the UN or even NATO, they do represent a broad international consensus, and they were unanimous in their view that Stuxnet did constitute an 'armed attack', meaning that Iran would have been entitled to respond in self-defence (Waterman, 2013).

What is unarguably the case is that the meteoric rise of the frequency of such malevolent events in the cyber realm has blurred the distinction between low- and higher-intensity interstate conflict and, at the same time, has blurred the distinction between espionage, sabotage and outright warfare in particular. Either one must be led (like Thomas Rid) to enforce the traditional boundaries and distinctions and refuse to acknowledge that any of these malevolent acts constitutes 'war' in the usual sense, or one must acknowledge that this traditional distinction has been so eroded as to be unsupportable (thus lowering the threshold for resorting to 'warfare' of any sort in the resolution of interstate conflict). If we follow the lead of Rid and Dipert in the cyber case (or of Rodin in the instance of humanitarian intervention), it seems abundantly clear that these varieties of conflict do not constitute 'war' in any conventional sense, save perhaps on rare exceptions (through the infliction of massive real harm, rather than virtual harm). On the basis of these restrictive understandings of 'war', it appears to be true analytically, or tautologically, that the Just War Tradition provides little guidance in relation to cyber-attacks, notwithstanding the fact that international lawyers stubbornly persist in interpreting the law on the use of force and IHL as applying to such instances as well as conventional attacks.

We believe, however, that this is a mistaken inference, grounded in a concatenation of erroneous judgements about both the Just War Tradition and the proper reach of the law. If anything, we hold that the opposite conclusion should be reached. On one hand, the law, which has defined jurisdictional authority very well, should not be misapplied or extrapolated to areas where it has no authority whatsoever (e.g. to espionage, or to the majority of activities within the cyber domain in general). Whether a new legal regime could or should be constructed to address the foregoing lacuna regarding the erosion of distinctions between espionage and war is another matter that we do not address any further here. The desirability of such a regime is debatable; and, in any case, the political prospects for supporting any further extension of black-letter international law into these areas seems utterly absent at the present moment.

In its 'classical' formulation, the Just War Tradition was not tied to any specific international arrangement or political paradigm. Admittedly, the same cannot be said of Michael Walzer's otherwise magisterial and revisionary account of Just War concepts in the late twentieth century. The Walzerian conception of justified war, grounded in what he terms the 'legalist paradigm' and the 'War Convention' (1992: 61, 44), rather clearly presupposes conflict within the modern nation-state system, bound together loosely within the framework of current international law. Still it remains the case that, in the main, the Just War Tradition more broadly arose prior to, and was itself largely the source of the most fundamental ideals and humanitarian content of much of what we now understand as IHL.

While historically the moral reasoning invoked was applied casuistically to war (hence resulting in the Just War Tradition), that reasoning itself could be (and often was) applied in a variety of other non-martial contexts as well. Thomas Aquinas, for example, rather unsystematically applied moral reasoning, in passing, to a variety of practical moral conundrums in the *Summa Theologica* (see Fathers of the English Dominican Province translation, 1948), ranging from obedience to legal authority, to self-defence, and to war (in which the famous questions about whether it is always sinful to wage war occur in the context of a broader discussion of Christian charity).

This historical fact provides a clue to the underlying nature of the reasoning itself – one that should prove illuminating to the present debate about whether the Just War Tradition could apply to situations that are not, strictly speaking, 'war' at all. Consider Aquinas' case of legal jurisdiction and obedience to the rule of law. He, and other political philosophers from Socrates and Plato to Rawls, Oakeshott, and Nozick, agree that the default position of the citizen ought to be towards the authority, legitimacy, and hence obedience to the rule of law in their community. However, on some rare occasions, some of these political philosophers admit that there may be exceptions to this 'rule' or default position. If a particular legal regime is patently unjust or immoral (as in the case of apartheid in the United States and South Africa in different historical periods, for example), or if that regime is enforced unjustly by illegitimate authority, then the case may be made for principled disobedience and resistance. In short, any claim for non-compliance must be based upon a grave and serious breach of moral propriety within the administration of the law itself: what we might usefully call a 'just cause' for civil disobedience.

More recently, the Just War Tradition has frequently been employed as a useful decision-making framework for meeting the practical ethical challenges faced by a military commander in a coalition environment when their coalition partner does not appear to share the same ethical values (Whetham, 2008b). Adopting the role of such a commander, you might question whether you should intervene or avoid a diplomatic incident and allow injustice to take place? Because of the way that it has evolved, the Just War Tradition represents a set of principles that have emerged, in part, through a long-running dialogue between deontological (acts-based) and consequentialist (ends-based) reasoning. It has survived and evolved precisely because it also contains prudential calculations that acknowledge that context must be taken into account when determining a correct course of action. So, for example, is there really a just cause for intervening? Does the context within which the offensive act is taking place give it some legitimacy despite your reservations, or is it an act that is simply wrong no matter where it takes place and there is no possible way that it could be justified? Is the act sufficiently serious to constitute an attack on core values that therefore require defending, thus providing sufficient authority for action? Would you be motivated by the right intention, or are selfish concerns clouding your judgement? Will your action ultimately cause more harm than good – specifically, is the likely fallout from your actions (a fractured alliance, loss of coalition harmony and trust, subsequent loss of the campaign, etc.) justified by the harm caused by the action you are trying to prevent? Does it matter if you intervene, or will the situation continue anyway – is there a chance of success? Finally, are there any alternatives – have you tried everything else that might make a difference before directly intervening?

One way of approaching this problem (as the foregoing illustration suggests) is thus to recognise that although the Just War Tradition does not itself provide the answers, it can still provide a structured approach to decision-making even when considering matters that are not directly related to the use of deadly force. One could just as easily look at the necessary conditions that might be collectively sufficient to permit (or even require) whistle-blowing or deception in some situations. The type of reasoning, and the criteria informing that reasoning, are going to be very similar to those required for a justified declaration of war: just cause, legitimate authority/publicity, right intention, last resort, and proportionality of harm suffered to harm done through the exception. Likewise, there are principles, similar to those regarding the just conduct of war, that apply to these other contexts: for example, those who choose to be disobedient to the civil authority must accept the legal consequences of that disobedience, and refrain from the use of violence when possible, and surely not deliberately or recklessly do or bring about harm to innocent third parties.

All of these kinds of reasoning are concerned to some extent with 'exceptions' to what is normally permitted – i.e. when a normally established rule or moral principle may justifiably be set aside or violated (Lucas, 1987, 2012, 2013a). Whatever their distinct and individual historical origins, the Just War Tradition shares with them a common pattern. Each is the species of a genus of practical moral reasoning about setting aside, or making occasional exceptions to, fundamental and widely held universal moral principles (such as not killing, not lying, not disobeying or being disloyal, for example).

Conclusion

So how does this apply to the cyber domain – what normative framework should one apply to cyber war? Our answer is that even in light of claims of Internet anarchy, the cyber realm does not appear to be altogether free of broad and widely accepted principles of governance. Instead, injunctions not to lie, cheat, steal, harm or deceive others have as much purchase there as anywhere, even if the prospects for escaping accountability for perpetrating such actions is greatly enhanced in this domain. It is merely as though Gyges' famous 'ring' had been widely manufactured and distributed. The unscrupulous make use of their lack of accountability, and in so doing, do great harm to others. States are, unfortunately, not an exception. But, otherwise, nothing has fundamentally changed.

In particular, amongst scrupulous actors in the cyber domain, it must still be important to know when, if ever, it would be morally (and legally?) justifiable to commit acts of deception or engage in strategies that might inadvertently or deliberately result in the doing of harm to others. Presumably, the problems of obedience to law are less stringent in this allegedly 'lawless frontier'. But loyalty still looms large, perhaps larger. Even if espionage is not 'war' in the conventional sense, it is a strategy that involves disobedience, lying, deception and sometimes the doing of harm. The Just War Tradition and its cognate species of moral reasoning demand that such actions be undertaken only if there is a compelling, morally justifiable reason, that the doing is undertaken with the right intentions, authorised by those who have the legitimacy to sanction the suspension of the normal principles, that the harms that the action may produce in both the short and long term are proportionate to what is at stake, has some prospect for success, and that there are not alternative options that may do less harm and still produce results.

It is vital to recognise that, even were we to dispense with the Just War Tradition in its historical manifestations, from Augustine, Socrates and Sun Tzu to Walzer, and proceed to reason *a priori* about this new realm of agency, we would predictably end by producing a very similar list of necessary conditions for justification: just cause, right intention, legitimate authority, last resort and proportionality, at the very least. Likewise, we would need to appeal to certain principles to guide the conduct of the exception: such as discrimination to ensure that any harm brought about really is necessary, that harm to the innocent is nevertheless limited and proportionate to what we are trying to achieve.

Hence, while we are not smelling or naming roses in this instance, it still appears the case that an exception to accepted practice by any other name is still an exception, and hence not to be entered into without grave and serious justification. The conditions defining that gravity, again by whatever name, will apply and will constrain and evaluate the behaviour of agents in the cyber domain every bit as much as they do in the remaining, more familiar domains of human agency and action.

References

Documents, treaties and cases

'API, 1977': Protocol Additional to the Geneva Conventions of 12 August 1949, and Relating to the Protection of Victims of International Armed Conflicts (Protocol I), Geneva, Switzerland, 75 UNTS 17512, 8 June.

Beckford v. R [1988] AC 130, Privy Council.

'Chemical Weapons Convention' (1997): Convention on the Prohibition of the Development, Production, Stockpiling and Use of Chemical Weapons and on their Destruction, Geneva, Switzerland, 1974 UNTS 317, 29 April.

Convention on Cybercrime (2001), Budapest, Hungary, 2296 UNTS 167, 23 November.

'UK manual, 2004': UK Ministry of Defence (2004) *The manual of the law of armed Conflict*, Oxford: Oxford University Press.

Tallinn manual on the international law applicable to cyber warfare (2013) Prepared by the International Group of Experts at the Invitation of the NATO Cooperative Cyber Defence Centre of Excellence (general editor: Schmitt, M.N.) Cambridge: Cambridge University Press.

Academic works and media reports

Ambrose (1983 edition) 'On the duties of the clergy', in Swift, L.J. (ed. and trans.) *The early fathers on war and military service*, Wilmington: Michael Glazie.

Aquinas, T. (1948) *Summa theological*, Fathers of the English Dominican Province trans., 5 volumes, Westminster: Christian Classics.

Arquilla, J. and Ronfeldt, D. (1993) 'Cyberwar is coming!', *Comparative Strategy*, vol. 12, no. 2, pp. 141–65.

Bellamy, A.J. (2006) *Just wars: From Cicero to Iraq*, Cambridge: Polity Press.

Clausewitz, C. von (2007) *On war*, Oxford: Oxford University Press.

Chatterjee, D.K. (ed.) (2013) *The ethics of preventive warfare*, Cambridge: Cambridge University Press.

Dinstein, Y. (2013) 'Cyber war and international law', *International Law Studies*, vol. 89, pp. 276–87.

Dipert, R.R. (2010) 'The ethics of cyber warfare', *Journal of Military Ethics*, vol. 9, no. 4, pp. 384–410.

Dipert, R.R. (2013) 'The essential features for an ontology for cyberwarfare', in Yannakogeorgos, P.A and Lowther, A.B (eds) *Conflict and cooperation in cyberspace*, Boca Raton: CRC Press/Taylor and Francis.

Graham, D.E. (2010) 'Cyber threats and the law of war', *National Security Law and Policy*, vol. 4, no. 1, pp. 87–102.

Jenkins, R. (2013) 'Is Stuxnet physical? Does it matter?', *Journal of Military Ethics*, vol. 12, no. 1, pp. 68–79.

Johnson, J.T. (1981) *The just war tradition and the restraint of war*, Princeton: Princeton University Press.

Johnson, J.T. (1984) *Can modern war be just?*, New Haven: Yale University Press.

Lucas, G.R. Jr (1987) 'Moral order and the constraints of agency: toward a new metaphysics of morals', in Neville, R.C. (ed.) *New essays in metaphysics*, Albany: State University of New York Press.

Lucas, G.R. Jr (2012) '*Jus ante* and *post bellum*: Completing the circle, breaking the cycle', in Patterson, E. (ed.) *Ethics beyond war's end*, Washington, DC: Georgetown University Press.

Lucas, G.R. Jr (2013a) 'The argument for preventive war', in Chatterjee, D.K. (ed.) *The gathering threat: Essays on preventive and pre-emptive war*, Cambridge: Cambridge University Press.

Lucas, G.R. Jr (2013b) '*Jus in silico*: moral restrictions on the use of cyber warfare', in Allhoff, F., Evans, N.G. and Henschke A. (eds) *The Routledge handbook of war and ethics*, Oxford: Routledge.

Lucas, G.R. Jr (2013c) 'Can there be an ethical cyberwar?', in Yannakogeorgos, P.A and Lowther, A.B (eds) *Conflict and cooperation in cyberspace*, Boca Raton: CRC Press/ Taylor and Francis.

Lucas, G.R. Jr (2014) 'Permissible preventive cyber warfare', in Floridi L. and Taddeo, M. (eds) *Ethics and information warfare*, Amsterdam: Springer.

Neal-Hopes, T. (2011) *Preventing a cyber Dresden: How the evolution of air power can guide the evolution of cyber power*, School of Advanced Air and Space Studies, Montgomery: BiblioScholar.

Plato (1989) *Republic V.*, in Hamilton, E. and Cairns, H. (eds) *Plato: The collected dialogues*, Princeton: Princeton University Press.

Rid, T. (2012) 'Cyber war will not take place', *Journal of Strategic Studies*, vol. 35, no. 1, pp. 5–32.

Rid, T. (2013) *Cyber war will not take place*, Oxford: Oxford University Press.

Roberts, A. and Guelff, R. (eds) (1995) *Documents of the laws of war*, 2nd edition, Oxford: Oxford University Press.

Rodin, D. (2014) 'Rethinking the responsibility to protect: the case for human sovereignty', in Scheid, D.E. (ed.) *The ethics of armed humanitarian intervention*, Cambridge: Cambridge University Press.

Sorabji, R. and Rodin, D. (eds) (2007) *The ethics of war: Shared problems in different traditions*, Aldershot: Ashgate.

Telegraph, The (2011) 'How Stuxnet works', 21 January [online], available: www.telegraph.co.uk/technology/8274488/How-Stuxnet-works-what-the-forensic-evidence-reveals.html [June 2014]

Walzer, M. (1992) *Just and unjust wars: A moral argument with historical illustrations*, 2nd edition, New York: Basic Books.

Waterman, S. (2013) 'US–Israeli cyber attack on Iran was "act of force", NATO study found', 24 March, *Washington Times* [online], available: www.washingtontimes.com/news/2013/mar/24/us-israeli-cyberattack-on-iran-was-act-of-force-na/?page=all [7 June 2014].

Whetham, D. (2008a) 'Ethics, war and human rights', *Defence & Strategy*, vol. 8, no. 1, pp. 49–58.

Whetham, D. (2008b) 'The challenge of ethical relativism in coalition operations', *Journal of Military Ethics*, vol. 7, no. 4, pp. 302–16.

Whetham, D. (2009) *Just wars and moral victories: Surprise, deception and the normative framework of European war in the later Middle Ages*, Leiden: Brill.

Whetham, D. (2010) 'The just war tradition: a pragmatic compromise', in Whetham, D. (ed.) *Ethics, law and military operations*, Basingstoke: Palgrave Macmillan.

Whetham, D. (2015) 'Cyber chevauchées: cyber war can happen', in Allhoff, F., Henschke A. and Strawser, B.J. (eds) *Binary bullets: The ethics of cyberwarfare*, Oxford: Oxford University Press.

Index

Page numbers in **bold** denote figures.

9/11 *see* September 11 terrorist attacks

AbdAllah Internet 19
Abkhazia 18
Additional Protocols to the Geneva Conventions: dangerous forces, installations containing 147; defenders, obligations on 143–4; Martens Clause, modern formation 149; objects indispensable to the civilian population 148; perfidy, definition 151; principle of distinction, modern restatement 127–8 (*see also* principle of distinction); principle of precaution 140 (*see also* principle of precaution); principle of proportionality 137 (*see also* principle of proportionality); prohibition on indiscriminate attacks 136; ruses, definition 151; target selection 142; weaponry, law of 148–9
Aegis ballistic-missile defence system 13
Afghanistan 75
Agent.btz worm 21, 23
'air-gap' (no connection to another network) 82, 87–8
Al Nawar v. Minister of Defence et al. 154–5
Al Qaeda 75
Alexander, Keith 14, 24
Amazon 129
Ambrose 162
Andress, J. 73
ANO (Advance Networks Operations) 23
anonymisers 63
API (Additional Protocol I to the Geneva Conventions) *see* Additional Protocols to the Geneva Conventions

APII (Additional Protocol II to the Geneva Conventions) 148; *see also* Additional Protocols to the Geneva Conventions
APT1 report 12, 57
Aquinas, T. 164, 169
armed attack: force and intervention, relationship between the concepts **111**; ICJ ruling 110
'armed force', the meaning of *see* meaning of 'armed force'
Armin, Jart 19
Arquilla, J. 74–6, 165
assets at risk during a cyber mission 57
attack steps, simplified model **39**
attacks: API definition 127; indiscriminate, and the principle of distinction 136–9; polymorphic 43, 65; taxonomy of characteristics 43–53; *see also* cyber-attacks
attribution: backtracing 64–5; correlation of information between attacks 65; countermeasures 67; and establishing standards of control 113; and evidentiary standards 114; explicit attributability 69–70; factors contributing to the difficulty of 61–2; files 62–3; illegal methods 69; *jus ad bellum* regulation and the issue of 113–15; national responsibility, levels of 68; network traffic 63–7; *Nicaragua* 'effective control' test 113; planting beacons 66–7; proving to the international community 68–9; semantic analysis 67; to a state 67–70; *Tadić* 'overall control' test 113; technical issues 114–15; voluntary attributability, desirability of 69–70
Augustine 162

backtracing 64–5, 67–8
Banks, W. 109
Barkham, J. 108
Benatar, M. 107
Betz, D. 76
BGP routing attacks 46, 54, 56
bitcoin 37
BitTorrent 36
Blitzkrieg (Arquilla/Ronfeldt) 76
blowback 76, 92
'blue screen of death' 49
Bonner, E.L. III 80
booty 155
botnets 11, 18–19, 52, 64, 68, 78–80, 99
Brazil 101
Brenner, S. 78
Brownlie, I. 103–4
Bryansk.ru 19
Buchan, R. 107–9
'Buckshot Yankee' 23–4
Budapest Convention on Cybercrime 64, 96, 166–7

CAPEC (Common Attack Pattern Enumeration and Classification) 39
Carpenter, Shawn 9, 13–14
Carr, J. 73
causus belli 167–8
CCDCOE (Cooperative Cyber Defence Centre of Excellence) (NATO) 26, 85–6, 96
Cebrowski, Arthur 16
Celebici Case 156
characteristics of cyber-attacks: controllability 46; covertness 50–1; effect 48–50; mitigatability 51–3; persistence 46–8; targetability 45–6
China: cyber arming history 27; cyber espionage attack on RSA 13–14; Defence Industrial Base attack 13; growth of cyber espionage attacks and the role of 9–14; instances of cyber espionage 11–14
civil disobedience, just cause 169
civilian objects, definition 132
civilian populations, special protection for objects indispensable to 148
Clark, D. 69
Clarke, R.A. 23, 74–5
Clausewitz, C. von 2, 163
closed network, infiltration requirements 82
cloud technology 36, 52
coercive economic action: as breach of non-intervention principle 108; and the prohibition of the use of force 100
Cold War analogies, preference for in American literature 77
collateral damage: assessing 139; cyber-attacks' potential for 141; definition 138; minimising 141; and special protection on civilian objects 148
combatants, distinguishing between civilians and 130–2 (*see also* principle of distinction)
communication protocol 37
Confront and conceal (Sanger) 81
connectivity, and vulnerability to cyber-attack 77
control, attributability and establishing standards of 113
controllability, as characteristic of cyber-attacks 46
conventional military operations, synchronisation of cyber-attacks with 80
cookies 66
Cornish, P. 76
counterattack, difficulty of in cyber warfare context 61
counterinsurgency, as focus of strategic thinking post-9/11 75
countermeasures, restrictions on 119
covertness, as characteristic of cyber-attacks 50–1
Crimea: and cyber-attacks on Ukraine 3; Russian invasion 61
CrowdStrike 27
cryptographic hashing 62, 65
Cuckoo's Egg (Stoll) 9
Customary International Humanitarian Law 143
'cyber 9/11' 75
cyber arms race, the law's responsibility for escalation 115
cyber-attacks: assets 57; as breaches of principle of non-intervention 108; characteristics 43–53 (*see also* characteristics of cyber-attacks); interstate *see* interstate cyber-attacks; stages 39–43 (*see also* stages of cyber-attack); stages *see* stages of cyber-attack
cybercrime, Budapest Convention on 64, 96, 166–7
cyber defence, US budget 3
cyber espionage: growth of attacks and the role of China 9–14; instances of Chinese 11–14
cyber infrastructure, dual use 135

Index

Cyber Kill Chain 9–10, 39; methodology 14
cyber operations, governing in the criminal context 126
'cyber Pearl Harbor' 75
cyber power, pervasiveness 89
cyber sabotage, effects-based assessment 168
cyber security programmes, number of states with 125
Cyber war (Clarke/Knake) 74–5
Cyber war will not take place (Rid) 75
Cyber warfare (Andress/Winterfield) 73
cyber warfare: the concept of 1–2; definition 8; as tool of 'mass disruption' 91
cyber warfare treaty 116–17
CyberCommand, rise of 24–5
cyberspace: definition 36; *jus ad bellum* regulation and the militarisation of 115–16; three layers 87
'Cyberwar is coming!' (Arquilla/Ronfeldt) 74, 76

Dalai Lama 11–12
dangerous forces, special protection for installations containing 147–8
DDoS (Distributed Denial of Service) attacks: backtracing 64; ease of launching 79; on South Korea and the United States 99; *see also* DDoS attacks against Estonia; DDoS attacks against Georgia
DDoS attacks against Estonia: and applicability of international law 166 (*see also Tallin manual*); available knowledge 78–9; effects-based assessment of damage 168; impact 79, 83; and the meaning of force 104; origins 78; phases of response and recovery 18; political consequences 83; and the Schmitt criteria 106–7; strategic implications 7, 77–9; targets 78
DDoS attacks against Georgia: culprit 67; establishing sources 63; Estonia's provision of assistance 20; impact 80–1, 83; international reaction 20; and the meaning of force 104; political consequences 83; strategic implications 79–81; synchronisation with Russian conventional military operations 80; targets 80; two-tier approach 79–80
Decoding the Virtual Dragon (Thomas) 10
defence, precautions in 143–4

Defence Industrial Base (DIB) 13
Denning, D.E. 81
Dinstein, Y. 104
Dipert, R.R. 168
distinction, principle of *see* principle of distinction
DNS (Domain Name System), function 49
'DNS poisoning' 49
DoD (Department of Defense) 14, 23–4
'doomsday' scenarios: examples of 104; and self-defence 111, 119
Dörmann, K. 129
Double Effect Doctrine, Just War Tradition and 164–5
Douhet, G. 76
Downey, W.G. Jr 154
Dresden, risk of the cyber equivalent of 160
drive-by downloads 53–4, 66
Droege, C. 135
DropBox 36
Drummond, David 12
due diligence, duty of 118–20, 138
Dunn Cavelty, M. 3, 75–6
duty to prevent: applicability to cyber warfare 117; problems 118–19; shift of focus towards 116–20; *Tallin manual* reference 117–18

economic harm, and the use of force 104, 108
Ecuador 101
effect, as characteristic of cyber-attacks 48–50
'effective control' test of attribution 113
electronic warfare, acts of 28
espionage: API definition 152–3; constituent of the new wave 167; erosional distinctions between war and 169; as interstate activity 167; *jus in bello* regulation and 152–3; notable instances of Chinese cyber espionage 11–14; role of China in the growth of cyber espionage attacks 9–14
Estonia: connectivity and vulnerability to cyber warfare 77; cyber arming history 26; cyber-attacks against *see* DDoS attacks against Estonia; scale of internet connectivity 77
Evron, Gadi 17
exploit delivery stage of cyber-attacks 41–2
exploit stage of cyber-attacks, characteristics taxonomy 43–53

F-35 Joint Strike Fighter 13
Facebook 129
file-hosting and -sharing services 36
Flame 43
Flick Trial 156
Foltz, A.C. 85
food processing systems, prohibition of harm 148
force: relationship between the concept of intervention, armed attack and **111**; *see also* meaning of 'armed force'; use of force
Friedman, A. 79
F-Secure 23

Galić Case 138
Gartzke, E. 75, 90–1
GCHQ (Government Communications Headquarters) 26, 88
Geneva Conventions, Additional Protocols *see* Additional Protocols to the Geneva Conventions
Georgia, vulnerability to cyber-attack 88 (*see also* DDoS attacks against Georgia)
Germany, cyber arming history 26
Global Information Grid (GIG) 24
Global Operations and Security Control Centre (GOSCC) 25
Goodman, W. 80
Google 12, 80
Graham, D.E. 117
Gray, C.S. 73
Gulf War 76

hacking back 140
Haddick, R. 79–80
Hague, William 85
Hague Convention (1899) 149
Hague Regulations (1907) 143, 148, 151, 153, 155; on espionage 152; on private property 153
Harrison Dinniss, H. A. 100, 112
hash values 62, 65
hashing, cryptographic 62, 65
Hayden, Michael 3
Healey, J. 68
Herzog, S. 79
historical perspectives: attacks against US military 22–4; Chinese cyber espionage, instances of 11–14; Chinese thinking on cyber warfare 10; cyber arming in other states 25–7; cyber warfare 'proper' 16–22; DDoS attacks on Estonia 17–18 (*see also* DDoS attacks on Estonia); DDoS attacks on Georgia 18–20 (*see also* DDoS attacks on Georgia); Defence Industrial Base attack 13; GhostNet 11–12; growth of cyber espionage attacks and the role of China 9–14; Operation Aurora 12; revolution in military affairs 14–16; the rise of cyber commands 22–7; Stuxnet 20–2 (*see also* Stuxnet worm); Titan Rain 9–10; US CyberCommand, rise of 24–5
hospitals, special protection 146–7
Hughes, R. 85
humanitarian intervention 162, 166–7; as just cause 162; Just War Tradition and 162, 166–7

I.G. Farben Trial 154
ICJ (International Court of Justice) 107, 110, 117, 127; on the Martens Clause 149; on the principle of distinction 127
IHL (International Humanitarian Law), and the applicability of to cyber operations during armed conflict 126 (*see also jus in bello* regulation)
Ilves, Toomas Hendrik 17
importance of cyber warfare, hyperbolic versus sceptical schools of thinking 74–5
India, cyber arming history 26
indiscriminate attacks: and the principle of distinction 136–9; and the principle of proportionality 137–9; prohibition on in *jus in bello* regulation 136–9; target area bombing 137
Inside cyber warfare (Carr) 73
installations containing dangerous forces, special protection for 147–8
international cooperation, on tracing criminal activity in cyberspace 64, 68
international law, scholarly writings as source of 106
Internet, layers **37**
Internet activity, proposals for increasing attributability 69
Internet Explorer, vulnerabilities 19
interstate cyber-attacks: downplaying of threat posed by 2; investigation procedures 69
intervention: humanitarian (*see* humanitarian intervention); relationship between the concept of armed attack, force and **111**
IP address(es) 9, 11–12, 38, 40, 49, 53, 63
IPv4 protocol 63

Iran, Natanz nuclear facility 7, 20–1, 81–2, 84, 129; *see also* Stuxnet worm
Iraq 75, 142
irrigation works, prohibition of harm 148
Israel: attack against a suspected nuclear site in Syria 135, 138–9; cyber arming history 27; cyber-attacks against 27; and Stuxnet 20, 82, 84
Israeli–Palestinian conflict, third-party involvement 67
Israeli Supreme Court 154
iteration stage of cyber-attack 43

Joint Forces Command 26
jus ad bellum: criteria 161–4; definition 85
jus ad bellum regulation: the 'Article 2(4) debate' 98–107 (*see also* prohibition of the use of force); and the attribution issue 113–15; duty to prevent, refocusing the debate towards 116–20; main approach in existing scholarship 97; the meaning of 'armed force' 102–7 (*see also* meaning of 'armed force'); the meaning of 'force' 100–2; the militarisation of cyberspace 115–16; principle of non-intervention 107–12 (*see also* principle of non-intervention); problems with existing approaches 112–16; prohibition of the use of force 98–9 (*see also* prohibition of the use of force); the 'qualifying terms' in Article 2(4) 99
jus cogens 98, 105, 110
jus in bello: criteria 164; definition 85
jus in bello regulation: application 126; espionage and sabotage 152–3; geographical scope, determining 126; indiscriminate attacks, prohibition on 136–9; legitimate targets 164; perfidy and ruses of war 151–2; principle of distinction 127–39 (*see also* principle of distinction); principle of precaution 139–44 (*see also* principle of precaution); property 153–6; proscribed weaponry 164; special protection 145–8 (*see also* special protection); warfare, methods and means 148–56; weaponry, the law of 148–50
just cause: examples of 162; humanitarian intervention as 162; sabotage as 167; self-defence as 162
Just War Tradition: applicability to cyber war 165–71; appropriateness of applying the principles to the cyber realm 160; and Double Effect Doctrine 164–5; ethical perspective 167; guidance in relation to cyber-attacks 168; and humanitarian intervention 162, 166–7; *jus ad bellum* criteria 161–4 (*see also jus ad bellum* regulation); *jus in bello* criteria 164 (*see also jus in bello* regulation); legal context 161; legitimacy of pre-emption 162–3; misconceptions about 161; moral and ethical perspectives 169–71; origins in Western thought 161; right intentions 163; self-defence as just cause 162

Kanuck, S.P. 117
Kastenberg, J.E. 80
Kello, L. 74
kernel panics 49
Khrushchev, Nikita 17
Knake, R.K. 74–5
Korns, S.W. 80
Kupreškić case 139

Laasme, H. 77
Landau, S. 69
Lawrence Berkeley National Laboratory 9
layers of the Internet **37**
legal perspectives: consensus on strategic understanding of cyber warfare 85–6; interaction between cyberspace and 'the law' 96; International Court of Justice *see* ICJ; lawful targets of attack 130–9; the law's responsibility for escalation of the cyber arms race 115; rule of law, exceptions to 169; scholarly writings, as source of international law 106; *see also jus ad bellum*; *jus in bello*; *Tallinn manual*
levée en masse 16
Lieber Code 143
Lindsay, J.R. 82
Lockheed Martin 9, 14
Lynn, W.J. III 23–4

Machbot software 80
'Machete' attack campaign 58
malware libraries 62
Mandiant 12, 27, 57
Manning, Bradley 21
Margulies, P. 113
Marshall, Andrew 14–16
Martens Clause 149
meaning of 'armed force': effects-based approach 102–5; kinetic nature-based approach 102; the 'Schmitt criteria' 105–7

medical facilities, special protection 146–7
Meyer, P. 85
Microsoft 21, 24, 35
Milevski, L. 82
militarisation of cyberspace, and *jus ad bellum* regulation 115–16
military objectives: definition of 132–4, 137, 142; distinguishing between civilian objects and 132–5 (*see also* principle of distinction); qualifying objects 133; when civilian objects become 133–4
Military–Technical Revolution 8, 15
mitigatability, as characteristic of cyber-attacks 51–3
Morris, Robert Tappan 21

Natanz nuclear facility, Iran 7, 20–1, 81–2, 84, 129; *see also* Stuxnet worm
national security: and the challenges of multilateral treaties 116; 'cyber Pearl Harbour' analogy 75; cyber war as next great threat to 74–5; implications of attack on RSA for 13–14
NATO (North Atlantic Treaty Organisation) 18, 26, 56, 64, 85–6, 141, 168
NATO CCDCOE (Cooperative Cyber Defence Centre of Excellence) 26, 85–6, 96
Neal-Hopes, T. 160
Netherlands, the, cyber arming history 26
NetOps Strategic Vision (DoD) 24
Netwitness 13
Network-centric Warfare (NCW) 15–16, 24
network location, as legitimate target of attack 133
network traffic, attribution 63–7
New York Times 12, 20
Nguyen, R. 106–7
Nicaragua 'effective control' test of attribution 113
non-intervention, principle of *see* principle of non-intervention
North Korea, alleged responsibility for DDoS attacks on South Korea and the United States 99

Obama, Barack 20
Obama administration, and the 'cyber budget' 3
O'Connell, M.E. 115
Open Malware site 62

Operation 'Olympic Games' 7, 20, 27, 81
outsourcing, of cyber warfare 80–1
OWASP (Open Web Application Security Project) 39

pacemakers, vulnerability to cyber-attack 145
packets 37–8, 42, 63–6, 69
Paet, Urmas 78
'passive precautions' 144
Patriot missile 13
payload injection stage of cyber-attack 42–3
Pearl Harbour 75
peer-to-peer communication (P2P) 36–7
perfidy: API definition 151; examples of 151, 152; exceptions from prohibition rules 152; *jus in bello* regulation 151–2
persistence, as characteristic of cyber-attacks 46–8
pervasiveness of cyber power 89
phishing attacks 19, 51
pillage: *jus in bello* regulation 153–4, 156; traditional meaning 156
PLA Unit 61398 27
Plato 164
plunder 154, 156
Poison Ivy Trojan 58
Poland 20
polymorphic attacks 43, 65
precaution, principle of *see* principle of precaution
pre-emption, legitimacy of 162–3
prevention, duty of 116–20
principle of distinction: applicability to cyber operations 127; attacks and operations 127–30; as cardinal principle of *jus in bello* 149; dual-use objects 135–6; extent 127–30; indiscriminate attacks 136–9; *jus in bello* regulation 127–39; lawful targets of attack 130–9; modern restatement 127; objects 132–5; persons 130–2
principle of non-intervention 107–10, 112, 114, 117; and coercive economic or political pressure 108; cyber-attacks as breaches of 108; legal status 110; nature and applicability of 107–8; omission from the debate, reasons for 108–9; regular breaching of by states 109; and the right to self-defence 110–12; source of 107–8; weakness of and special 'weight' of Article 2(4) 109–10

principle of precaution: defence, precautions in 143–4; means and methods, choice of 141–2; precautions in attack 140–4; targets, choice of 142–3; verification of objectives 140–1; warnings 143

principle of proportionality: API formulation 137; and the calculation of military advantage 138; and effects on civilian function 135; and precautionary measures 142; requirements 164; violation of as war crime 137

prohibition of the use of force: arguments for exclusion of cyber warfare from 102; assumptions regarding cyber warfare 99; and coercive economic action 100; comprehensiveness of intent 99; legal status 110; non-intervention principle vs Article 2(4) 'weighting' 109–10; as peremptory norm 98; qualifying terms 99; self-defence as exception to 110; and the *travaux préparatoires* of the Charter 101

property, *jus in bello* regulation 153–6

proportionality, principle of *see* principle of proportionality

proscribed weaponry, *jus in bello* regulation 164

protection of property, exceptions 154–5

'Rampart Yankee' 23
Ranum, M. 69
Raymond of Peñafort 162
reconnaissance stage of cyber-attack 39–41
'red lines' 84
resources, balancing 58
responsibility to protect 162
Rid, T. 75, 78, 79, 80, 81, 82, 91, 160, 165, 168
RMA (Revolution in Military Affairs): Gulf War origins 14–15; and Network-centric Warfare 15–16
Rodin, D. 167–8
Roki Tunnel 19
Ronfeldt, D. 74, 76, 165
Roscini, M. 113
rule of law, exceptions to 169
Rumsfeld, Donald 16
ruses: API definition 151; examples of permissible 151; *jus in bello* regulation 151–2
Russia: confrontation between Georgia and 79–81; draft treaty on cyber warfare 116; invasion of Crimea 61; invasion of Georgia 19; likely source of cyber-attacks 3; and the Military–Technical Revolution 8–9, 15; as originator of DDoS attacks against Estonia 78 (*see also* DDoS attacks against Estonia); routing of Georgian Internet traffic through 88

Russian Business Network (RBN) 19

Saakashvili, Mikheil 18, 20, 80
sabotage: as act of war 167; *jus in bello* regulation and 152–3; and loss of combatant immunity 153; and loss of combatant immunity and prisoner-of-war status 153; risks for perpetrators 87; Stuxnet as act of 22
Sandia Labs 14
Sanger, D. 20, 81
Saudi Aramco 48
Schmitt, M.N. 86, 105, 107, 110, 129
Schmitt criteria: criticisms 106; legal status 106; listed 105; for the meaning of 'armed force' 105–7
script kiddies 49, 53
SCSM (System Center Service Manager) 24
Second World War 156
self-defence: as just cause 162; and the legitimacy of pre-emption 162–3; and the potential for military escalation 115–16; the principle of non-intervention and the right to 110–12; right to use force in 98; in UK law 162
September 11 terrorist attacks 75
services vulnerable to attack 36
ShadowServer Foundation 18
Shakarian, P. 2
Sheldon, J.B. 86, 89, 92
Shen Weiguang 10
Siemens equipment, and the Stuxnet worm 21, 82
SillyFDC 23
Singer, P.W. 23, 79
SIPRNet (Secret Internet Protocol Routing Network) 21, 23; vulnerability 21
Skype 36
'Snake' virus 90
Snowden, Edward 20–1, 88
social engineering attacks 40, 56
Social Engineering Toolkit 35, 58
social media 36, 40, 129, 145
social network exploitation attacks, characteristics 56–7

Sorenson, Jeffrey 23
South Africa 169
South Korea: attacks on broadcasters and banking institutes 48; DDoS attacks 99
South Ossetia 18–19, 79, 83
sovereignty, *Tallinn manual* ruling 86
Special Court for Sierra Leone 156
special protection: installations containing dangerous forces 147–8; medical units, transports and hospitals 146–7; objects indispensable to civilian populations 148
spoofing 14, 63–4, 66, 68, 140; detection methods 64
SQL (Structured Query Language) injection attacks 46
SQL Slammer worm 21
stages of cyber-attack: exploit delivery 41–2; exploit stage, characteristics taxonomy 43–53; iteration 43; payload injection 42–3; reconnaissance 39–41
Stavridis, James 56
stealth, as one of cyber power's attributes 86
stealth technology 28
steganography, and voluntary attributability 70
Step 7 Software, Siemens' 21
Stevens, T. 76
Stoll, C. 9
StopGeorgia.com 19
strategic implications: for geography 87–9; infancy of cyber warfare 89; permanence of cyber warfare 90; of the practical application of cyber warfare 77–83; strategic significance of cyber warfare 91
strategic understandings of cyber warfare: ambiguity of cyber warfare 92; current state of scholarly thinking 74–6; impediments 3; and the lack of empirical evidence 76–7; legal consensus 85–6; as peacetime resort 86–7; political consequences 83–5; preference for Cold War analogies 77; weakness 73–4
Stuxnet worm: and the 'air-gap' 21, 87; alleged creators 7, 20, 81; delivery method 20, 38; discriminatory ability 82; effectiveness 82–3; as example of sabotage 166; exploit stage 43; geographical implications 88; goal 21, 48; impact 2, 7, 20, 22, 82, 104, 129, 166; intent behind 81; intention 87; and

jus in bello 147–8; in the media 20; minimisation of collateral damage 141; modus operandi 20–2, 82; origins 20–2; political consequences 83–4; Snowden on 20; sophistication of the coding 136; steps involved in the attack 21; strategic implications 16, 20–1, 81–3, 84, 136; success 20; Symantec report on 57; *Tallinn manual* writers view as armed attack 168; target 20, 81–2; targeting precision 136, 141; throttling of 21; and the utilisation of stealth 87
submarine cables 87, 155
subversion 75, 165
Syria, Israeli attack against a suspected nuclear site in 135, 138–9 (*see also* Dayr al-Zawr)

Tadić case 113, 126, 139
Tadić 'overall control' test 113
Tallinn manual on the international law applicable to cyber warfare 86; on collateral damage 139; on defining military objectives 133–4; definition of cyber-attack 129–30; on the duty to prevent 117–18; on espionage 153; first rule regarding sovereignty 86; function 166; on the Internet's qualification as indispensable object 148; on passive precautions 144; permissible ruses, examples of 151; on protections 145; publication 85; on the Schmitt criteria 105; status 86, 96, 106, 168; on the targeting of data 132; on the use of force 99, 106, 168; on warning obligations 143
targetability, as characteristic of cyber-attacks 45–6
targeted attacks, countermeasure requirements 22
TCP/IP (Transmission Control Protocol/Internet Protocol) 37
Tempora surveillance program 88
Terminal High Altitude Area Defense 13
territorial integrity 98–9, 101
terrorism 75, 126
Thomas, T. L. 10
Titan Rain 9–10, 14
Tor 63
tradecraft 43, 57; examples of collected data 57
treacherous killing, prohibition of 151
treaty on cyber warfare 116–17
Tsagourias, N. 112

TTnet 19
Turkey 19
'Turla' virus 90

Ukraine 3, 19, 90
UN General Assembly's Declaration on Friendly Relations 101
UN General Assembly's Definition of Aggression 102
understanding cyber-attacks: examples of attack characteristics 53–7; influences on attack tool choices 57–8; stages of attack 39–43 (*see also* stages of cyber-attack); taxonomy of attack characteristics 43–53; the technical environment 36–9
UNIDIR (United National Institute for Disarmament Research) 125
United Kingdom: cyber arming history 25–6; pre-emption, legitimacy of 162
United States: cyber-attacks against the military 22–4; 'cyber budget' under the Obama administration 3; DDoS attacks on 99; indictment of Chinese hackers 61; rise of CyberCommand 24–5; the RMA and Network-centric Warfare 15–16
USB devices, and security risks 20–1, 23–4, 38, 153
USCYBERCOM 14, 23–5
use of force: the meaning of 'armed force' 102–7 (*see also* meaning of 'armed force'); the meaning of 'force' 100–2; prohibition of *see* prohibition of the use of force; *Tallin manual* definition 168

voluntary attributability, desirability of 69–70
vulnerability to cyber-attack, connectivity and 77

Walzer, M. 161, 169
war crimes 67, 137, 154, 156
warnings, *jus in bello* regulation 143
Washington Post 13, 20
water treatment plants, prohibition of harm 148
weaponry, proscribed 164
website request, broken down into the four layers of the Internet **37**
Windows software 21, 24, 49
Winterfield, S. 73
WMDs (weapons of mass destruction), and the legitimacy of pre-emption 162
worms 21, 23, 81
write blocker software 69

Xu Xiaoyan 10

Yugoslavian Republic: NATO bombing campaign against 141; *see also Galić Case*

Zeus crimeware 58